BRUCE CROWTHER
MIKE PINFOLD
Picture Editor
FRANKLIN S. DRIGGS

Facts On File Publications
New York • Oxford

The Count Basie band

First published in the United States of America by Facts On File, Inc.
460 Park Avenue South, New York, New York 10016.

Library of Congress Catalog Card Number 88-081981

First published in Great Britain by
David & Charles Publishers plc Newton Abbot Devon

Printed in Great Britain

10 9 8 7 6 5 4 3 2 1

CONTENTS

TEDDY
STEWART

TUNING UP

There was none of the expectant hush which usually falls upon a theatre audience just before curtain-up. Certainly, there was expectancy, but instead of silence an eager buzz filled the crowded auditorium on this Spring morning in 1937, drowning out the words of Claudette Colbert up there on the neglected screen. It wasn't Claudette's fault, although *Maid of Salem* was not one of her best movies. Responsibility for the excitement lay at the highly polished toe-caps of the leader of a band gathering in the theatre's basement.

The thousands up above, rumbling impatiently now, were not at New York's Paramount Theatre for the movie—not this movie, not any movie. The crowd was here to confirm a truth which had first registered with the bandleader and his musicians eighteen months earlier at a dance hall in California.

That truth, which exploded in a shattering roar of applause as the movie ended and the band rose upwards on the hydraulically-operated stage, was that a new age in American popular music had dawned. The young man, immaculately dressed and smiling tentatively as he clutched his clarinet and gave the downbeat, was the hero of this new age. He was Benny Goodman, and he was the King of Swing.

There had never been a popular music phenomenon like the swing era. It was impossible to listen to the radio, or leaf through a newspaper or magazine, or enter a record store, or a dance hall, or see a movie, without being confronted by swing music.

For many fans, the dozen or so years the era lasted constitute the big band years. But there was so much more besides.

The big band years involved countless musicians in thousands of bands and spread over a period that begins in the 1920s and shows no signs of ending as this century draws to a close.

Yet even the 1920s are not the place to begin for the ingredients which went to make big band music an identifiable form had even then been present in American popular music for more than a quarter of a century...

Dizzy Gillespie

CHAPTER ONE

THE EARLY YEARS

'JAZZ CONVULSIONS'

'It's all there, in the past.'

Nat Pierce

In 1910 a number of New York's leading black musicians, including James Tim Brymn, Professor Walter F. Craig, Will Marion Cook, Joe Jordan, Dan Kildare and Hughie Woolford met and formed the Clef Club, a musicians' union. Elected president was 22-year-old James Reese Europe, an alert and commercially aware young man. Through the application of Europe's business acumen the Clef Club developed from being simply a loosely affiliated group of cabaret musicians into a hugely successful musical organisation.

All kinds of bands flourished throughout the United States in the turn-of-the-century years. Every city and major town had its quota. These bands played popular music of the day, a mix of sentimental ballads, marches, dance music and light classics, which would have been instantly recognised by audiences in Victorian London or Paris or Vienna. But there was also a whiff of exhilarating new musical forms in the air. Uniquely American, from this tentative beginning these new forms eventually changed the voice and face of American popular music.

These indigenous musical forms were three in number; all different in their construction, importance, influence and endurance. The fact that to some extent they fed off one another and were all primarily associated with black Americans, and were a product of their musical imagination, led casual observers to lump them carelessly together as if ragtime, the blues, and jazz were one and the same thing.

The development of this new American music was taking place all across the country with the greatest strides occurring in the more densely populated regions.

In New Orleans, as in other urban centres, music was played by orchestras in dance halls and saloons, at picnics and society affairs, and by brass bands which played at parades and for numerous social occasions.

Among the many brass bands which became a feature of New Orleans street parades, celebrations and funerals were the loftily named Eagle, Excelsior, Imperial, Olympia, Onward, Superior and Tuxedo Brass Bands. Noted figures of early jazz played in these bands: Buddy Bolden, Bunk Johnson, Freddie Keppard, Joe Oliver, Kid Ory, Manuel Perez, Alphonse Picou, Lorenzo and Louis Tio. Of even greater long-term importance were the youngsters, some of whom marched informally alongside street parades thus forming the famed New Orleans tradition of the 'second line'. Among these kids were such luminaries of the early jazz scene as Sidney Bechet, Barney Bigard, Johnny St Cyr and Zutty Singleton but foremost among these budding musicians was Louis Armstrong.

Even today a New Orleans parade, be it for Mardi Gras, a funeral, or just to captivate tourists, still has its marching band.

The venues at which big bands have played across the years varied from the palatial splendour of Catalina Island's magnificent Casino Ballroom to buildings as basically functional, but still grandly named, as the New Casino Pavilion at Walled Lake, Michigan.

NEW CASINO
DANCING
NEW CASINO PAVILION
NEW CASINO PAVILION
DANCE TONIGHT
BROADWAY COLEGIANS

The Sam Wooding band spreading the jazz word to audiences at the UFA Palast Theatre, Berlin, Germany, in 1928. (L to R) Gene Sedric, Willie Lewis, Johnny Mitchell, King Edwards, Freddie Johnson, Wooding, Ted Fields, Billy Burns, Tommy Ladnier, Bobby Martin.

Although New Orleans attained an inviolate if legendary status as the birthplace of jazz, popular music was undergoing near-simultaneous change all across America. In the industrial north, in the more remote towns of the mid-West and Southwest, on the west coast, dance bands were offering much the same mixture of music with, perhaps, local colouring depending upon the national origins of the immediate population.

Ragtime and early jazz were only two forms of popular band music. Brass bands with more orthodox repertoires enjoyed widespread popularity. One of the most famous of the mid-nineteenth-century touring bands had been that led by Patrick S. Gilmore, an Irishman who led military-style bands out of Boston and New York and, in 1878, even toured Europe. In 1880 Gilmore's star was eclipsed by a young man named John Philip Sousa.

When only 26 years old, Sousa became director of the United States Marine Band. Already a composer of some popular marches, in a dozen years this young man's reputation was such that he resigned from the service and, in 1892, became the leader of his own civilian band. In his hey-day, Sousa helped popularise the new music, and alongside the other usual repertoire he played rags and cakewalks, popular Negro dances of the day, even if, when arranged in his own distinctive manner, they bore little true resemblance to their original forms.

Arthur Pryor, a trombone player of phenomenal ability, worked in Sousa's band. Rising quickly to the post of assistant conductor, Pryor's popularity led to his becoming a bandleader in his own right. Phil Wilson, trombone star with Woody Herman in the 1960s, still considers Pryor's technique and mastery of his instrument to be second to none. 'You listen to those old records and you can hear between the scratches that Arthur Pryor can still hold his head high with the wizards of today...'

At the turn of the century, in common with blacks elsewhere, New York's well-established Negro community sought social equality and upliftment with music as close as possible to that enjoyed by whites. Brass band leader Egbert Thompson was even billed as 'The Black Sousa'. Such musical notables as Professors Walter Craig and J. Thomas Bailey purveyed much the same repertoire of light classics, marches and Viennese waltzes as their white contemporaries.

Out of the wealth of Negro music available in the city there evolved the first syncopated orchestras. Established musicians, particularly of the older generation, disapproved of this innovatory music. They believed that the way for the black man to get ahead was to adhere to white standards in all things, even in his taste in music. Despite this disapproval, syncopated orchestras soon overtook the formal black orchestras of Harlem and eventually even the overall popularity of the so-called 'gypsy' orchestras in downtown hotels and restaurants.

The black syncopated bands were show bands, often engaging in spectacular displays which did not always have much to do with music. Enhancing many of these show bands were the drummers. Surrounded by a vast array of equipment, they performed noisily and flashily and performers such as Buddy Gilmore and Louis Mitchell became individually famous for their flamboyance although only rarely troubling to keep time.

A catalytic figure, deeply involved in the changes taking place in popular music was that young man at New York's Clef Club, Jim Europe.

Boat to nowhere:
A pioneer of big band jazz in his American homeland, Sam Wooding was among the first black bandleaders to take the new music to Europe. In 1924 he took an eleven piece band through several northern European countries, Scandanavia, Spain, Turkey and Russia and played an engagement at London's Holborn Empire. For two years in Germany, Wooding's band played the 'Chocolate Kiddies' show which included some of Duke Ellington's early music. Unfortunately for Wooding, he stayed away too long and by his return his music was out of date and he was quickly forgotten. However, in 1976, as part of America's Bicentennial celebrations, Wooding, then in his eighties, led a ten piece band at concerts and for a recording session.

Musicians' reminiscences are filled with accounts of playing in marble-halled hotels or in tobacco warehouses during swings through the Deep South. When playing dance dates at colleges or army bases the most suitable hall might well be the gymnasium, which is where Charlie Barnet and his band with singer Hazel Bruce found themselves when visiting Fort Evtis, Virginia, in 1951.

James in Europe. Jim Europe's 'Hellfighters' band entertaining American Doughboys in France in 1919.

JAMES REESE EUROPE

> With the brass instruments we put in mutes and make a whirling motion with the tongue, at the same time blowing full pressure. With wind instruments we pinch the mouthpiece and blow hard. This produces the peculiar sound which you all know. To us it is not discordant ... we accent strongly in this manner the notes which originally would be without accent. It is natural for us to do this; it is, indeed, a racial musical characteristic. I have to call a daily rehearsal of my band to prevent the musicians from adding to their music more than I wish them to. Whenever possible they all embroider their parts in order to produce new, peculiar sounds.

These words were used by Jim Europe to describe the sound of his music and his attitude towards it.

For the public, Europe's music was new and vitally exciting. In 1913 4,000 people crowded into the Manhattan Casino to listen to Europe's syncopated music. Audiences were content to have 'a James Reese Europe Orchestra' whether or not he was present in person. Europe bands played for New York society's top 400 and he was hired for swanky private functions thrown or attended by the Astors and the Vanderbilts. In 1914 Europe achieved a signal breakthrough when he presented the Clef Club orchestra at Carnegie Hall. The instrumentation of his 125-piece band was quite extraordinary: 47 mandolins and bandores, 27 harp-guitars, 11 banjos, 8 violins, 13 cellos, a saxophone, a tuba, a pair each of clarinets and baritone horns, 8 trombones, 7 cornets, a tympanist, 5 trap drummers and a couple of string bass players. If all this were not enough, 30 pianists took turns playing 10 pianos. This unusual line-up was partly due to circumstances; these were all the men available on the day but sensing the importance of this concert Europe determined to make as big a splash as possible and was able to convey to the press and public that his selection was a result of shrewd planning.

A critical view by Jim Europe: 'Our people are not naturally painstaking; they want, as they put it, "to knock a piece cold" at the first reading. It takes a lot of training to develop a sense of time and delicate harmony.'

James Reese Europe
(New York *Evening Post* 13 March 1914)

Writing of his programming for the concert, Europe commented upon the extravagant use of ten pianos, 'That in itself is sufficient to amuse the average white musician who attends one of our concerts... The result, however, is a background of chords which are essentially typical of Negro harmony.' Additionally, he observed that the use of mandolins and banjos, with their 'peculiar steady strumming accompaniment' gave the music distinctiveness.

The music Europe's aggregation performed at Carnegie Hall included popular marches, tangos, waltzes and 'plantation' songs.

Although Europe's success was a significant breakthrough for black artists, not everyone approved of the material and one black musician wrote in the musical press, 'all races try to develop their art from examples set by masters of other periods; and if we expect to do anything that is lasting from an artistic standpoint, we, too, must study the classics as a foundation for our work.' For his part, Europe had no doubts that the contrary was where the future lay for black music: 'We must strike out for ourselves, we must develop our own ideas, and conceive an orchestration adapted to our own abilities and instincts... The great task ahead of us, as I see it, is to teach the Negro to be careful, to make him understand the importance of painstaking effort in playing and especially to develop his sense of orchestral unity.'

Europe's popularity was enormous but led to dissension at the Clef Club with fellow bandleaders becoming jealous of his success. Shortly after the Carnegie triumph he quit and formed a rival organisation, the Tempo Club. Although the Clef Club continued for many years, and

A critical view of Jim Europe: 'Unaided, [James Reese Europe]has been able to accomplish what white musicians said was impossible: the adaptation of Negro music and musicians to symphonic purposes.' New York *Evening Post* 13 March 1914

Lt. James Reese Europe and his 369th Infantry Regiment band playing for the Allied top brass in France in 1919.

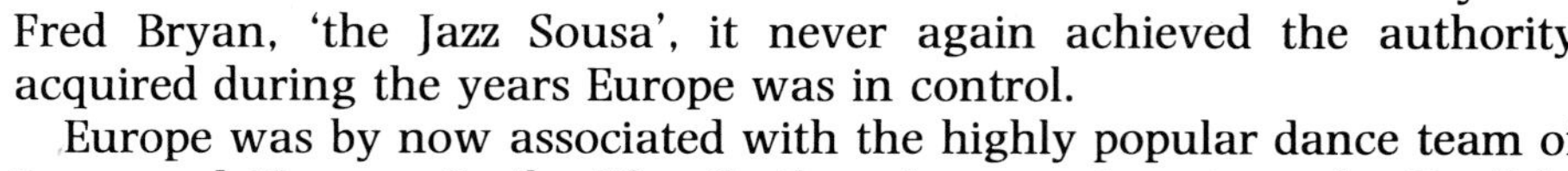

included such noted musicians as 'Father of the Blues' W. C. Handy and Fred Bryan, 'the Jazz Sousa', it never again achieved the authority acquired during the years Europe was in control.

Europe was by now associated with the highly popular dance team of Irene and Vernon Castle. The Castles, she was American, he English, brought about a revolution in ballroom dancing, introducing such new dances as the turkey trot, the one-step and the fox-trot.

Improvisation *v.* arrangements—1: Speaking in 1921, bandleader J. Tim Brymn urged that, 'bands should follow their orchestrations more closely and not try so much of their "ad-lib" stuff'. He added that if they wished to supply 'novelty music' they should allow it to be done by the publisher's arranging staff and, if they felt obliged to improve upon stock arrangements, they should 'have it done on paper so that the improved way of playing will be uniform and always the same'. Jazz musicians might strongly disagree with Brymn's sentiments and certainly few would want to rely solely upon stock arrangements but, nevertheless, many big band enthusiasts do still prefer solos to be played exactly the same in concert as they are on a favourite recording. All would surely agree, however, that no matter how much space is allotted for solo excursions the need to closely follow the arranger's charts is a crucial requirement for a good big band.

When, in 1917, America became embroiled in World War I, Europe enlisted, was commissioned, and quickly set about forming an army band. As part of the 369th Infantry regiment, the Hellfighters, Europe and his orchestra sailed to France. Playing to army and civilian audiences, Europe and his army band repeated the huge success he had enjoyed with his civilian orchestra. Apart from playing for the troops, both black and white, Europe played for civilians including a concert at the Théâtre des Champs-Elysées in Paris after which he remarked, 'Before we had played two numbers the audience went wild. We had conquered Paris.'

Europe returned to New York after the war to great acclaim, determined to advance the cause of black Americans through music. In *Literary Digest*, 26 April 1919, he wrote, 'I have come back from France more firmly convinced than ever that Negroes should write Negro music. We have our own racial feeling and if we try to copy whites we will make bad copies ... if we are to develop in America we must develop along our own lines...' His plans for Negro music were drastically cut short when, on 9 May 1919, before he could capitalise upon his success, which was unparalleled among black American musicians, he was murdered by one of the members of his band. A snare drummer named Herbert Wright became mentally disturbed and while being reprimanded by Europe for some minor infringement stabbed him in the neck, severing the jugular vein.

On the evidence of the handful of recordings made by Europe prior to World War I and those made by the Hellfighters' band, his was a somewhat stately musical style. Caught somewhere between the orthodoxy of the brass bands of Sousa and the formality of ragtime on the one hand, and the informality of the newly-emerging jazz band sounds on the other, Europe's music offers interesting hints of the way at least one black bandleader was thinking at a time of great change in the popular music scene.

It was partly out of this form that the big band sound of the 1920s emerged.

Prominent in New York in the late teens were some of Europe's former associates. James Tim Brymn, Will Marion Cook, Ford Dabney, and others, like Wilbur Sweatman and Will Vodery, all featured in later success stories of black American music.

Tim Brymn was a graduate of Shaw University, North Carolina and of the National Conservatory of Music, New York. Like Europe, Brymn led a military band during World War I and was publicised as playing jazz.

Will Cook took an orchestra to England in 1919, following which he toured Europe until 1922. Once again there was jazz of sorts to be heard, especially from young New Orleans-born clarinetist Sidney Bechet. But Cook's band was more in the nature of a show band blending music from the light classics through ragtime to popular songs of the day lightly touched with jazz and blues inflections.

Many dance halls and theatres become legendary, their names evoking nostalgic memories of music and dancing, of carefree nights on the town in New York or Los Angeles, Chicago and Atlantic City.

Downtown in New York City stands the Roseland Ballroom. In 1988, there is still a Roseland open for business on Broadway with sedate tea dances catering for clients who bear their years lightly even if they cling to their partners less tightly than they hold on to their memories.

In 1927 the original Roseland was where the Fletcher Henderson band established its reputation and throughout the 1930s the hall saw a steady succession of the best in dance bands.

Ford Dabney, who had been Jim Europe's assistant director, took over Europe's mantle after the murder. He was another black musician to enjoy the benefits of an early recording career and such important New York engagements as the flamboyant Broadway shows staged by Florenz Ziegfeld. His band accompanied the 'Midnight Follies' at the Amsterdam Roof and made a number of vertical-cut recordings which have yet to be reissued. Among the personnel Dabney used was cornetist Cricket Smith, who worked with W. C. Handy's band, Jim Europe and also with Louis Mitchell in Europe.

Muted testimony:
In addition to owning Chicago's Dreamland Ballroom during the 1920s, Paddy Harmon was a manufacturer of musical instruments. Today, most trumpeters carry a small but lasting tribute to Paddy's enterprise—the Harmon mute.

Although Wilbur Sweatman was himself an undistinguished musician, he had an ear for talent. In the decade which followed his arrival in New York in 1913 he employed several men who were later to become important jazz and big band musicians, among them Duke Ellington.

Will Vodery had led a successful military band in the war years. A brilliant musical arranger, working extensively in the theatre in the post-war years, Vodery, along with Will Marion Cook, is reputed to have been an important influence upon the young Duke Ellington. Vodery's later career found him working in the movies, one of few black men to gain an important and responsible position in Hollywood.

While New York and the eastern seaboard, and also New Orleans, may have seen intensified development, other cities and towns were musically active during this same period. Chicago became an important entertainment centre in the early years of the twentieth century, attracting first-rate talent from both New Orleans and New York. Black musicians who built a substantial base in the Windy City included the bandleaders Doc Cooke, Charles Elgar, Dave Peyton, Erskine Tate and Joe Oliver.

Charles 'Doc' Cooke's band played the Dreamland Ballroom for six years from 1922 and included in his band such noted jazz stars as cornetist Freddie Keppard and clarinetist Jimmie Noone. Cooke's band played in a manner reflecting dance hall and theatrical conventions of the day and only rarely did a spark of jazz spirit break through.

A very young, slim, unmoustached Paul Whiteman at the Alexandria Hotel, Los Angeles, in 1919. (L to R) Henry Busse, Harold McDonald, Buster Johnson, J. K. Wallace, Whiteman, Charles Caldwell, Les Canfield, Charles Domberger, Mike Pingitore.

Charles Elgar's band played several of Chicago's leading ballrooms and nightspots. Like Cooke, Elgar played very much in the popular, showbiz tradition of the day although its tiny recorded output suggests a band of some technical accomplishment capable of playing complex arrangements with great aplomb.

In addition to leading his own band, Dave Peyton worked as a contractor, forming several bands to take advantage of the available work. Peyton had a band in the pit of the Grand Theatre on State Street during the mid-1920s and at the Regal Theatre in the early 1930s.

Of all the Chicago bandleaders of the early years, black or white, a leading figure, if measured only by the galaxy of musical talent which passed through his band, was Erskine Tate. As his band's title suggests, Erskine Tate and his Vendome Symphony Orchestra was resident at the Vendome Theatre across State Street from the Grand Theatre. During 1926 and 1927 Louis Armstrong worked in Tate's pit band, doubling at various nightclubs. Despite the strong jazz orientation of its personnel, Tate's band played a wide variety of music including show tunes and pieces from the classical repertoire.

By far the hottest band in Chicago was led by Joe 'King' Oliver. His Creole Jazz Band had the whole town listening, especially when he brought in young Louis Armstrong as second cornet. Their two-cornet breaks became legendary. By 1926 Oliver and his Dixie Syncopaters featured a saxophone section which, if a little muddy, still allowed Oliver great scope. Oliver's influence, via the horn of Louis Armstrong and the later arranging innovations of Don Redman proved to be extremely important not only in jazz terms but also to big band music in general.

Among the leading white bands in Chicago in the early years was one led by Charlie Straight, and several working out of the Benson contracting agency's office.

Charlie Straight was highly popular in Chicago but, despite records and broadcasts, never attained a huge national following. Among the sidemen in his band Straight employed drummer-xylophonist-vibraphonist Bob Conselman (who, in 1927, played on the first record Benny Goodman made under his own name). Most noted sideman of all was the wayward cornetist Bix Beiderbecke who worked briefly with the band.

In common with many other bands in Chicago, and elsewhere in the early 1920s, the Benson Orchestra was modelled upon the Paul Whiteman band, then enjoying huge acclaim in New York. Formed by Edgar Benson, a band agent, the Benson Orchestra was soon one of many bearing that name and working extensively in and around the city.

Of all the Chicago-based white bands of the 1920s, the most popular was that led jointly by drummer-vocalist Carleton Coon and pianist-vocalist Joe Sanders. Formed in 1918, radio shows spread the popularity of the Coon-Sanders Nighthawks and in 1924 they opened in Chicago which remained their base for the rest of the band's existence. Nightly broadcasts from the Blackhawk Hotel built upon their popularity and they enjoyed excellent record sales. Musically, their efforts have suffered from the passage of time but records show them to have been a relaxed musical outfit.

For all their popularity, none of these bandleaders, white or black, achieved anything remotely like the accolades and popular appeal of Paul Whiteman. The contrast between Whiteman's music and that of,

Many American bands visited Britain in the 1920s to great acclaim. However, not all lived up to expectation.

Drummer/bandleader, Abe Lyman, brought his band to the London Palladium in 1929. Opening night was marred by Abe's own inability to catch the sticks which he spectacularly tossed in the air during his drum feature. Undeterred Abe continued until the stage was littered with drumsticks.

A crescendo of jeers and catcalls greeted him as he tried to announce the next tune. Asking for requests Abe was visibly shaken when one wag in the audience called for 'Rhapsody In Blue'. The audience was further incensed when Abe quickly gave the downbeat for an obviously pre-arranged current hit tune and they took up the chant, 'RHAPSODY-IN-BLUE, RHAPSODY-IN-BLUE', gleefully accentuating each word with a slow handclap.

Abe, by now livid, hollered to the Palladium audience that if any, or all of them, cared to meet his boys and himself outside after the performance he would be only too pleased to give him a good old American roughing up. The curtain was hastily drawn on the irate Lyman and his hapless band.

say, King Oliver was so striking as to belie the claim that both were jazz—that earthly and vital musical form which had recently emerged from black popular culture.

The word jazz was deeply misunderstood at the time but, whatever it might mean to different people, it was as the 'King of Jazz' that Whiteman rose on a tidal wave of public acclaim and there is no doubt but that it was largely through his efforts that a jazz-based form of music was popularised.

THE KING OF JAZZ

To some extent Paul Whiteman's music was a bland apology for what was being offered by black jazz bands of the day but he was responsible for giving jazz and other syncopated music a veneer of respectability. Whiteman's arranger, Ferde Grofé used 'jazz effects' such as trumpet growls and slurs (mostly played by Henry Busse) and strident clarinet wails (by Ross Gorman) but by no means was this really jazz. Whiteman succeeded in welding an effective link between jazz and the light classics. In its overall form, this musical hybrid created by Whiteman and Grofé is with us today and can be heard daily in an updated but often unimproved form on the concert platform and on radio and TV.

A tall, burly young man, Paul Whiteman came from Denver, Colorado, where his father was a distinguished music teacher. In later years, Paul's bulk turned to fat and with commendable flair he turned this into a trademark. He took a highly commercial view of the music business, yet was as dedicated as Jim Europe.

In 1923, when he was 33, Paul took his band to London for an extended engagement and on his return was met by an ecstatic welcome culminating in a special reception at the Waldorf-Astoria Hotel.

The following year Paul played at New York's Aeolian Hall with a 23-piece band. Billed as 'An Experiment in Modern Music' it was subsequently hailed, rather inaccurately, as America's first jazz concert. One piece played at this concert was the first performance of a work by New York-born pianist-songwriter George Gershwin. 'Rhapsody-in-Blue', arranged by Grofé and with solo work by Busse, Gorman and the composer at the piano, met with little approval, although in retrospect it was by far the most significant event of the evening.

Even in its early, relatively small and sedate form, Paul Whiteman's band was big with nineteen pieces being commonplace. To a great extent this was a show band although it did play dance dates. Despite its size many of the band's recordings display a remarkably light feel given the somewhat pedestrian arrangements it was usually saddled with playing.

Paul's love for jazz and his appreciation of jazz musicians is often overlooked. He hired many important white jazzmen, among them the guitar-violin duo of Eddie Lang and Joe Venuti, trombonist Jack Teagarden and saxophonist Frankie Trumbauer. While jazz fans can be forgiven for listening only to their work and especially to the crystalline cornet solos of Bix Beiderbecke, big band enthusiasts often give Whiteman's band much less than its due.

If viewed by the standards it set itself, rather than some externally imposed values, Whiteman's band, at its best, offers an interesting and evocative indication of what one highly popular strand of big band music was like in the mid and late 1920s.

There can be little doubt that for all his divergence from the path of jazz and the manner in which later big bands played, Whiteman sanitised

Musicians on Paul Whiteman:
'... whereas most musicians were interested in the Goldkette band, they never did go much for Whiteman's.'
Benny Goodman
'Paul Whiteman and his arranger, Ferde Grofé, visited the Cotton Club nightly for more than a week, finally admitted that they couldn't steal even two bars of the amazing music.'
Ned E. Williams
'All the musicians looked up to bandleaders like Leo Reisman and Paul Whiteman in those days.'
Max Kaminsky
'Bix told me, "It's the greatest experience I ever had—working under a baton and learning—it's been the greatest training I ever had." '
Jack Teagarden
'Whiteman had everybody, Trumbauer and Joe Venuti, and they all say the same thing—that was the greatest training they ever had.'
Jack Teagarden

Uptown in New York was the Home of Happy Feet, Harlem's showplace, the Savoy, where Chick Webb reigned. One flight up from street level was 'the Track', the dance floor that witnessed the birth of the Lindy Hop and the Susie Q. Outwardly, the frontage on to Lenox Avenue changed little between 1935 when Chick and Jimmie Lunceford shared billing and 1947 when the bands of Lucky Millinder and Dizzy Gillespie were on stage.

Paul Whiteman used an elongated baton which had a light on the end of it. One night, perennial practical joker Joe Venuti, who was playing opposite Whiteman, took the long electric light bulb out of his music stand and used it to conduct his little band. His own musicians were highly delighted—maybe even Whiteman saw the joke.

WGN

Coon-Sanders Nighthawks at the Blackhawk Restaurant, Chicago, 1929. Joe Sanders seated at the piano and Carleton Coon at the drums.

Band on the wall. The ebullient Joe Venuti was a featured soloist with Paul Whiteman. Here he strikes a demonic pose from high above his band at the Rainbow Room, Rockefeller Center, NYC, in 1935. (L to R) Elmer Beechler, Bob Romeo, Murray Williams, Ernie Striker, Carl Orech, Chuck Evans, Johnny Owens, Ruth Lee, Kit Reid, Noel Kilgen, Tony Giannelli, Vic Engle, Joe White, Venuti, Buss Michaels.

Down among the sheltering palms the Paul Whiteman Orchestra entertains holiday-makers at Coral Gables, Florida, in 1926.

the music for the wider public. If in so doing he misjudged the true nature of jazz this should not detract from his enthusiasm, the encouragement he gave to young musicians and, particularly, from the manner in which he gave jazz a publicly acceptable face at a very early stage in its development. Trumpeter Max Kaminsky observed that 'Whiteman tried to make jazz acceptable and respectable by attempting to raise it to a symphonic level...' Two of Duke Ellington's long-serving stars, trombonist Lawrence Brown and baritone saxophonist Harry Carney, are among many important jazz artists who have acknowledged Whiteman's role in popular and big band music, confirming Kaminsky's comment that it was Whiteman who effected the transition of concert hall music from the symphony to dance music. Carney observed, perhaps with some irony, that Whiteman had 'made a lady out of jazz'.

During the first quarter of the twentieth century the American popular music scene was one of hyper-activity. Dance bands and emerging jazz bands were everywhere: musicians were influencing their peers and being influenced in their turn, promoters were keenly aware of the profit potential of the new musical style, the public wanted music and yet more music.

As Paul Whiteman's star waned, due in part to his failure to move with the changing musical times, among those who gave the public what it wanted as the Roaring Twenties gave way to the Troubled Thirties were Fletcher Henderson and Duke Ellington.

Most important of the developments musicians were generating were several which dramatically affected America from the mid-1930s onwards. The signs and portents of these changes could be discerned long before that date, however, and nowhere were they more obvious, nor more significant, than in New York City.

Several big names of 1920s big band music featured in the Jean Goldkette band, seen here at the Graystone Ballroom, Detroit, in 1926. (L to R) Russ Morgan, Fred Farrar, Doc Ryker, Ray Lodwig, Bill Rank, Jimmy Dorsey, Chauncey Morehouse, Spiegle Wilcox, Lou Longo, Howard Quicksell, Don Murray, Steve Brown.

Sam Lanin's 1928 band in Atlantic City. (L to R) Tommy Dorsey, Harold Peppie, Frank Teschemacher, Larry Tise, Charlie Jondro, ? Levy, Lanin, Phil Napoleon, Ray Eberle, Jimmy Mullens, ? Waner, Smith Ballew.

THE ARRANGER'S TOUCH—1

The work of the arranger is of paramount importance in the continually evolving world of big band sound.

Whereas the layman can identify the role of the composer, the work of the arranger-orchestrator is not so readily understood nor easily defined. Arranging music well requires flair and imagination although orchestrating can at times be a chore. Irksome or not, orchestration is a skill and at the very least requires a high degree of competence and is an essential ingredient in band work.

From necessity, bandleaders rely heavily upon their arrangers for musical and commercial success yet, inevitably perhaps, it is the jazz soloists who gain rave responses from many fans. For these enthusiasts, improvisation is the essential spark which ignites a band performance, but from the arranger's point of view improvisation is a measured thing which must not upset the overall balance of a piece. Indeed, it is often the arrangement which projects the soloist's performance either inspiring him to greater heights or simply making him sound better than in truth he is.

Ideally, the attributes of a good big band arranger are that he, or she, should be a musician who can read and write music fluently; a musician who knows about harmony and the voicing of chords. It is also advantageous for the arranger to know something of the limitations of the instruments and of the individual musicians who will be playing them. Certainly it is advisable that the arranger is aware of each musician's strong points and weaknesses when writing for a specific band. It is, after all, in their performance that the arranger's own work is brought to life.

Viewed in basic terms an arranger's job is to take a theme, whether his own composition or not, and embellish it and voice it for the entire band or orchestra. He will score sections for brass and reeds, notating each part, trying to create variations upon the original melody line, enhancing it with subtle harmonic and rhythmic qualities. In short, the arranger brings musical order to an assembly of perhaps fifteen or more highly individual musicians.

Frank de Vol, one of the busiest studio arrangers of the 1940s and 1950s, offered young musicians interested in arranging the following advice: 'Make as thorough a study of classical scores as you can.' Contrary to this view is the fact that many of the finest jazz arrangers began their craft without any formal knowledge of arranging. Don Redman, Duke Ellington, Sy Oliver and Gil Evans, four of the greatest and most personally styled arrangers in the business, worked out their own musical theories from the practical end of the business, using the band as a sounding board and in the process developing writing techniques uniquely their own. This intuitive element in big band arranging, so essential in most creative forms of art was expounded upon by Billy Strayhorn, himself no mean stylist, 'Write it down—hear it played—once you've heard it you will not require anyone to tell you what is wrong—you'll know...'

The element of self-teaching, seemingly inherent in big band arranging, has in the past ensured that a variety of differing band styles has developed. This healthy situation leads to much discussion, argument and controversy. Musician, arranger and A & R man Teo Macero's positive views were expressed to Sinclair Traill. 'You learn to take two saxophones to equal one trumpet, in the terms of intensity. One trombone equals one trumpet, or two saxophones. If you use a mute than one trumpet becomes one saxophone. Then it all balances itself out, and you can write the dynamics into the parts.' Macero described why this balance was necessary. 'When you go into a concert hall the saxophone section will be heard properly. But if you write with two to a part and a baritone, the only thing you'll hear is the baritone and the brass. You never get to hear the middle parts—and you might as well send those guys home and save yourself the money... You don't write for ten brass, with five of the saxophones playing: nor do you write for the five saxophones and sort of overlay the trombones and the trumpets.

Macero's views directly contradict the working methods of Stan Kenton and vividly illustrate the point that the thoughts of arrangers are many and varied.

In general, arrangers divide between those who use the basic concepts first crystallised in the work of Don Redman, Fletcher Henderson and Sy Oliver and those who seek new harmonies, new techniques and new instrumentation.

In the first category, slick section work, blistering brass, precision saxophones and crisp rhythm, are everything. With the latter, smooth and accurately voiced section work is of secondary importance; individuality is supreme. The more jazz oriented bands gravitate towards the latter grouping whereas the staightforward swingers naturally belong to the former. It is therefore quite futile to draw comparisons between, say, the innovatory skills of Gil Evans or George Russell and the tasteful expertise of Nelson Riddle or Billy May for they seek different goals and, in these particular examples, are equally successful in what they do.

CHAPTER TWO

NEW YORK, NEW YORK

'AIR CONDITIONED JUNGLE'

'Jazz is not the music of the land. It is the music of new cities. It blows across the American prairies, but does not come out of them. It is the music of hot-dog wagons and elevated trains, the music of morning papers published at nine in the evening, the music of the quick lunch and the signboard and the express elevator.'

Alfred Frankenstein, 1925

The New York scene:
'[New York]makes *all* musicians sound kind of funny when... they first come *here*; I don't care what they were in their home towns, when they come *here*, they get cut.'
Coleman Hawkins

In 1959 a famous landmark was closed to the public. Located in New York City on Lenox Avenue between 141st and 142nd Streets, the building was a piece of America's cultural heritage: the Savoy Ballroom.

Although just one of many dance halls, one of countless venues for big bands, the Savoy was a symbol. Every band of note played there.

The Savoy, along with such dance halls as the Roseland on Broadway, clubs like the Famous Door, Connie's Inn and the Cotton Club, theatres like the Apollo, plush hotel ballrooms like the Madhattan Room at the Hotel Pennsylvania or the Terrace Room at the Hotel New Yorker, were all part of the New York music scene. That scene was itself a part of the wider world of popular entertainment which had its hub in the city.

Between the closing years of the nineteenth century and the start of the Great Depression New York built an unparalleled reputation as an entertainments centre. It was here that the recording industry had its base; radio, which mushroomed dramatically during the late 1920s and early 1930s, was also based in the city. New York's Tin Pan Alley was home to the music publishers; even the motion picture companies in Hollywood answered to head offices 'back East'. For theatregoers Broadway was still the Great White Way, the most important street in the world. Even in later years, when television nosed out radio and induced paranoia in the motion-picture industry, the TV companies were centred there.

For entertainers of most kinds, New York has always appeared to offer endless opportunities for work. Music halls like Tony Pastor's or Weber and Fields operated nightly in the late 1890s. Restaurants, such as Rector's and Bustanby's or the Reisenweber Café off Columbus Circle where Tim Brymn played and where, in 1917, the Original Dixieland Jazz Band first told the world that they were the 'creators of jazz', catered for the after-theatre crowd. At less pretentious eating-places revellers could delight in the sounds of smaller, less formal dance orchestras.

But it wasn't all elegance and sophistication. Notorious dance halls

Over on the west coast, while the exterior glories of the Casino on Catalina Island took some beating, there were few places to rival the interior magnificence of El Patio in Los Angeles. This ballroom was followed by the Rainbow Gardens during the Depression before becoming the Palomar where, for all its palm tree-lined interior, it was possible for a couple to dine and dance all night, see the cabaret and have a drink or two and still take home change from a five dollar bill. The Hollywood Palladium, seen here in 1951, was another noted California venue whose architecture matched preconceptions of street scenes in the movie capital of the world.

DINE AND DANCE IN COOL COMFOR

In Addition To Pleasurable Dancing On The West's Largest Floor . . . .

. . . . You May Enjoy The Luxury Of Palomar Cuisine At Our Always-Moderate Prices . . . .

. . . . Treat Yourself To A Delightful Evening With The Stars On The

NEW TERRACE

Enjoy A DELICIOUS PALOMAR DINNER During 'Dining-out Weather' . . . . Served, Full Course, By Our Courteous Staff

DELUXE DINNER ON THE TERRACE . . . 90c

No Cover Charge—Dinner Served From 7:30

COMPLETE A LA CARTE and MIXED DRINK SERVICE

Minimum service at tables 50c per person

Three Cocktail Lounges

Mixed Drinks From The Finest Ingredients, Mostly at 25c

TWO FLOOR REVUES

NIGHTLY AT 9:30 and 12:15 with ALL-STAR VAUDEVILLE ACT and the HUDSON-METZGER GIRLS

ADMISSIONS NIGHTLY

Ladies .... 40c Men 55c
(plus tax)
Includes Dancing, Loges, and Entertainment
Table Service Optional
Saturdays
Ladies .... 55c Men .... 90c — (plus tax)

AMPLE FREE PARKING SPACE FOR DINNER PATRONS — JUST DRIVE UP TO MAIN ENTRANCE

VERMONT at 2nd and 3rd LOS ANGELES Telephone FItzroy 3106

Ben Pollack's Californians Victrola recording band played Chicago's Southmoor Hotel in September 1926. (L to R) Glenn Miller, Benny Goodman, Gil Rodin, Harry Green, Ben Pollack, Fud Livingston, Al Harris, Harry Goodman, Vic Bredis, Lou Kastler.

Improvisation *v.* arrangements—2: In the early days, when jazz musicians and arrangements were still uneasy bedfellows, leaders sometimes found it difficult to control the enthusiasm of their sidemen. In the late 1920s Jelly Roll Morton sternly rebuked his musicians, 'You'd please me if you'd just play those little black dots—just those little black dots that I put down there. You don't have to make a lot of noise and ad-lib.'

like the Haymarket, the Sans Souci and the Egyptian Hall along Sixth Avenue, bawdy Bowery cabarets, and seedy concert gardens, entertained the pleasure-seeking masses with popular music. Theiss's Alhambra Music Hall featured a 26-piece orchestra which played Viennese waltzes for the delectation of carousing and highly voluble audiences.

In more respectable areas 50-piece brass bands played for concerts throughout the summer, ending each evening with dancing. Brass bands regularly entertained on excursion steamers, at Coney Island or Manhattan Beach. Music was everywhere.

The early 1920s were heady days for bands in New York. Listening to jazz was the 'in' thing although the music that Scott Fitzgerald's 'Jazz Age' flappers danced to was rarely jazz in the true sense of the term.

But, like the times themselves, popular music was changing. Some changes resulted from the influence of visiting bands. There were territory bands of the Northeast which played the fringes of the city and there were often out of town bands, from as far afield as New Orleans, Chicago and Kansas City.

Despite the successes of some black New York bandleaders during the first quarter of the twentieth century, white musicians undoubtedly had the best of it.

Most prominent among the white big band leaders of the early years were Paul Whiteman and Jean Goldkette, a young French-born entrepreneur working out of Detroit.

Paul Whiteman came to New York attracted by the large salaries being offered musicians. Thanks to a band he formed in 1920 the Palais Royal on Broadway did capacity business. The following year he was a smash-hit at the Palace Theatre in Times Square. A combination of giving the audience what it wanted, a sharp business sense, good publicity and pleasing yet, for the times, adventurous music gave Whiteman a measure of popularity that remained unequalled in New York until Benny Goodman doubled at the Madhattan Room and the Paramount Theatre in 1937.

Among the numerous ballrooms the biggest and best in Downtown New York were the Arcadia and the Roseland. At the Arcadia in 1921 dancers enjoyed the music of Joe Kayser's band which featured saxophonist Frankie Trumbauer. That same year, at the Roseland Ballroom on Broadway, between 51st and 52nd Streets, the Sam Lanin orchestra entertained the crowds with hot solos from trombonist Miff Mole and cornetist Phil Napoleon. Lanin's popular band stayed at the Roseland for a number of years, eventually leaving, so it was rumoured, as a result of protests by some of his sidemen at having to play opposite the black bands of Armand J. Piron and Fletcher Henderson.

The Sam Lanin orchestra was followed into Roseland in 1926 by a Jean Goldkette band under the management of Charlie Horvath and featuring the 'modern' arrangements of Bill Challis and the solo prowess of such sidemen as Bix Beiderbecke, Frankie Trumbauer and clarinetists Don Murray and Danny Polo.

It is difficult today to fully comprehend the effect this Goldkette outfit had upon the dance band world of the late 1920s. The few available records of the band give little indication of its zestful spring. Bill Challis, who wrote arrangements for both Goldkette and Whiteman, has stated that the band was restricted in what it could record by decision makers in the recording company's offices. As a result, what later generations hear are frequently dull, ineffective popular novelty songs usually featuring doleful vocals. Only occasionally does the excitement of a Beiderbecke chorus shine through.

The brilliance of the band which took Roseland by storm in 1926 was described evocatively by cornetist Rex Stewart in a *down beat* article in 1967 (and reprinted in his book *Jazz Masters of the 30s*). 'We in the Fletcher Henderson band were amazed, angry, morose, and bewildered as we sat on the opposite bandstand waiting our turn to go on—and it was a long wait ... because everything this band played prompted calls for encores from the crowd. This proved to be a most humiliating experience for us, since after all, we were supposed to be the world's greatest dance orchestra. And up pops this Johnny-come-lately white band from out in the sticks cutting us... The facts were that we simply could not compete... Their arrangements were too imaginative and their rhythm too strong ... and Frankie Trumbauer's inspiring leadership as he stood in front wailing on his C-melody saxophone... We learned that Jean Goldkette's orchestra was, without any question, the greatest in the world and the first original white swing band in jazz history.'

For all Rex Stewart's generous praise, however, it was the orchestra of which he was a member, Fletcher Henderson's, that was to have the most telling, and longest-lasting effect upon the big band years.

HOTTER THAN 'ELL

A distinguished-looking man, Fletcher 'Smack' Henderson was something of an enigma. Although Jim Europe, Whiteman, Lanin and others had reached the top thanks due largely to being shrewd businessmen, Henderson attained a comparable place without any such qualities and with seemingly little effort.

Spike spiked:
In 1933 British bandleader Spike Hughes spent three days in New York recording with leading American jazzmen including Red Allen, Chu Berry, Benny Carter, Sid Catlett, Wilbur De Paris, Coleman Hawkins and Dicky Wells. Convinced that anything he did afterwards would be anticlimactic Hughes decided not to continue playing this kind of music.

***

'No matter how much talent or experience a player brings here, there are things to learn when he sits down with a seasoned band... No matter what they bring here, New York shakes them.'
Cannonball Adderley

***

Royal Lanin:
Sam Lanin was one of three bandleading brothers. Howard achieved little distinction but Lester became a major band contractor and the darling of New York society. He played for American presidents from Eisenhower to Reagan. In the 1980s Lester Lanin was in London playing his brand of bland, inoffensive music at weddings, engagements and birth-days of various members of the British royal family.

A singularly important figure in the story of big band music, Fletcher Henderson not only set the standards by which his contemporaries were measured, he also employed leading jazz players of the day. Most significantly, the arrangements he and Don Redman wrote for the band created the format which was popularised by all but a handful of big bands during the following thirty years.

In his early years as a bandleader, Henderson followed the stylistic trend of Paul Whiteman. In his adherence to Whiteman's style, Henderson was not alone. Ironically enough many black bands of the mid-1920s took up the blander aspects of Whiteman's music, seemingly unaware that he was playing music adapted from the syncopated styles of pre-1920s black bands.

Henderson drifted into the music business almost by accident. A highly intelligent and well-educated man, he came to New York in 1920 having already gained a degree in chemistry at Atlanta State University. Drifting into working for the Pace-Handy Music Company as a means of supporting himself while he continued studying he became a manager for Harry Pace's Black Swan record company. His pianistic abilities were used to good effect in-house and on tour with Black Swan artists and at one point he formed a band to accompany singer Ethel Waters. By chance, he found himself leading a ten-piece band at a New York nightclub, the 'Club Alabam' (actually the Little Club on West 44th Street near Broadway).

According to Don Redman, in conversation many years later with Felix Manskleid, the band was only a loose collection of musicians who were not really a formally assembled band. 'We had a meeting,' Redman

The Big Reunion:
In 1957 the Fletcher Henderson band was recreated as the Fletcher Henderson All Stars for the Great South Bay Jazz Festival. A hit of the festival, they reassembled and recorded in the studios of RCA Victor. The music is powerful, exciting and the excellent ensemble passages are shot through with sparkling solos. The collective personnel reads like a who's who of the New York big band scene of the 1930s: Rex Stewart, Emmett Berry, Taft Jordan, Joe Thomas, Dick Vance, trumpets; Benny Morton, J. C. Higginbotham, Dicky Wells, trombones; Buster Bailey, Garvin Bushell, Hilton Jefferson, Coleman Hawkins, Ben Webster, Haywood Henry, Norman Thornton, reeds; Red Richards, piano; Al Casey, guitar; Bill Pemberton, bass; Jimmy Crawford, drums. All the soloists shine, urged on by Stewart's enthusiasm and crackling drumming from Crawford, but, just as he was the leading soloist in the 1931 Henderson band, Hawkins is outstanding. But the real star of the album, 'Big Reunion', is a man who had died 5 years earlier, in 1952, and is on this record only in spirit—Fletcher Henderson.

recalled, 'and we decided that Fletcher Henderson should be the leader... He made a nice appearance and was well-educated and we figured all that would help in furthering our success.'

Later that same year, 1924, Henderson took up a residency at Roseland where the band remained under contract for four years. The offer could not have come at a more convenient moment. At the Club Alabam, the band's star soloist, tenor saxophonist Coleman Hawkins, was asked to feature as accompanist to singer Edith Wilson. He demurred, asking for more money. Sacked for his temerity, Hawkins and his colleagues were pleased when Henderson took up the offer of the Roseland gig.

Henderson's connection with Roseland continued, on and off, for the next ten years. Playing for the dance hall's white patrons, the band's repertoire included tangos, waltzes, popular songs and light classics played in dance tempos, usually employing the stock arrangements available to any bandleader. There is, therefore, a marked resemblance between what the band does and the kind of music being played by white bands of the period. Billed as 'the coloured Paul Whiteman', Henderson gave only a passing nod at jazz idioms. When Louis Armstrong joined the band's ranks in September 1924 (he stayed until late in 1925) his presence dramatically changed the direction of the Henderson band and forced Don Redman to revise his conception of arranging. From Louis's solo style and from the few scraps of sheet music he brought with him from the King Oliver band in Chicago, Redman devised his visionary arranging technique of playing one section against another while still utilising the solo skills of the musicians, simulating the New Orleans polyphonic style.

'... nobody could beat our band...'
Leora Henderson

The bandstand at the Roseland Ballroom on Broadway, NYC, at Christmas 1928 with the Fletcher Henderson band in residence. (L to R) Henderson, Buster Bailey, Benny Carter, Clarence Holiday, Coleman Hawkins, Kaiser Marshall, Cootie Williams, Jimmy Harrison, Bobby Stark, Charlie Green, Rex Stewart.

At this time the trumpet was the dominant jazz instrument although reed sections had been introduced by the bands of Art Hickman and Paul Whiteman. With Redman's arrangements for the Henderson band reed sections came into their own, the clarinet trio becoming a noted Redman trademark.

By 1927 the band included such important soloists as Joe Smith and Tommy Ladnier with lead trumpet Russell Smith completing its three-piece trumpet section. The trombonists were Jimmy Harrison and Charlie Green while the reed section included Buster Bailey and Coleman Hawkins. It is this section which most obviously demonstrates the changes which were still to come in formulating the accepted sound of the big bands of the swing era. Bailey was primarily a clarinetist, doubling on alto and soprano saxophones; Hawkins, the most distinguished tenor saxophonist of his generation, also played clarinet or baritone saxophone.

The easy-going Henderson was nevertheless ambitious but, like so many bandleaders, encountered financial problems. Even so, he might well have achieved success on a level comparable to that found by Basie and Ellington had he not been severely injured in a road accident in 1928, an accident which affected his personality. Fletcher's wife, Leora, later observed, 'That was the only accident he ever had, and after that—why, he just changed... He never had much business qualities anyhow, but after that accident, he had even less.'

In place of the two contradictory elements in his make-up, his casualness and his ambition, Henderson now was merely easy-going. As many others would discover to their cost, this was no way to run a big band although his talent for music, and especially his arranging skills, appear not to have diminished.

In 1929, the band's members were infuriated when Henderson failed to back them up when many were fired from an out-of-town assignment playing for a white revue. Several long-term sidemen quit and Henderson was forced to dissolve the band, eventually reforming the following year.

Henderson was by then his own chief arranger, Don Redman having moved on. Although largely following the guidelines laid down by Redman, Henderson had advanced his arranging technique. Even though the reed section was still only three-pieces, he had clearly learned a great deal about instrumental voicing and the band plays with marvellous sonority on such tunes as his re-arrangement of 'Sugar Foot Stomp', recorded in 1931. However, when playing arrangements by others, for example Bill Challis who wrote for Goldkette and Whiteman, the thin earlier sound is still in evidence.

In 1931 Henderson took up a residency at Connie's Inn on 131st and Seventh. By this time Fletcher's band had a formidable array of talent: Russell Smith, Bobby Stark, Rex Stewart, trumpets; Claude Jones, Benny Morton, trombones; Russell Procope, alto and clarinet, Edgar Sampson, alto and violin, Coleman Hawkins, tenor and clarinet; and a four-piece rhythm section which was hampered by the fact that John Kirby had not yet switched to bass and was playing tuba.

Even in a band as star-studded as this, there is no doubt that Coleman Hawkins is the major jazz presence. Henderson's brother, Horace, contributed excellent arrangements for the band (not always receiving credit through confusion of names), and if on some, 'Big John Special' for example, the band occasionally sounds hesitant, the overall vibrancy and the marvellous solos make amends. But without question it is

Don Redman and McKinney's Cotton Pickers

McKinney's Cotton Pickers was a band which had few equals in its time.

Don Redman was invited to front McKinney's Cotton Pickers in 1927. Until then, the band, originally formed by drummer William McKinney, had a reputation for lots of flashy showmanship but not much else. As drummer Cuba Austin observed, 'We were a pretty scrubby bunch'.

Immediately on joining the Cotton Pickers, Redman dumped the funny-hat approach of the band, brought in a number of fine musicians, including trumpeter Joe Smith and trombonist Claude Jones, and set about rewriting the band's book. Redman's growth as an arranger can be studied from the superb recordings made by this band over the next few years.

The band recorded many excellent sides featuring tight arrangements and brief solo outings by sidemen buoyed by a crisp, light rhythm section which in its early days included pianist Fats Waller.

1940s bandleader Gene Krupa remembered them well, especially when asked about the antics of 'jitterbugs and so-called ickies'. He always tempered his replies, remembering how, as a youth, he 'stood open-mouthed, completely awed and fascinated, and cheered more lustily, grew far more excited than any of the most obnoxious ickies that ever got in the hair or became a general nuisance to a performing band. No indeed, I'll never forget the Cotton Pickers...'

Trumpeter Doc Cheatham was never in doubt about the band's quality, observing that the 'Cotton Pickers played *together*, that's why the band was so great. We played opposite Fletcher [Henderson]several times in Detroit and washed them clean off the bandstand.' ▶

The Chick Webb Band with Johnny Hodges in the reed section.

Fletcher's own work which is most striking. The band's style and sound on such tunes as 'Down South Camp Meeting', 'Wrappin' It Up' and 'Hotter Than 'Ell' is beginning to take on the characteristics by which the soon-to-dawn swing era would be recognised.

But by 1939 Henderson had had enough. His band was playing to declining audiences, and his easy-going attitude towards the band had degenerated almost into indifference. In June 1939 he joined Benny Goodman as an arranger and pianist. In 1941 and at various other times through the 1940s he formed a big band for short residencies and tours, continuing to write for Goodman and others. In 1950 Fletcher Henderson fell in the street, apparently as a result of a severe stroke and thereafter was largely incapacitated until his death in 1952.

Although New York City did not become the creative centre of the jazz world until the 1940s, it was always the place in which to make a mark. If the 1920s and 1930s did not see much in the way of revolutionary creativity, the city certainly saw the honing and polishing of creative gifts forged elsewhere.Musicians toured clubs and dance halls, listening, sitting-in where they could, and learning. Always they were learning. For the growing number of musicians employed in the big bands, the place to learn most, and to compete in popular 'band battles', were the dance halls.

When the Savoy Ballroom opened on 12 March 1926 the music was provided by three of the best black bands of the period: Fletcher Henderson,

▶ Duke Ellington was in full agreement, recalling that 'there was a lot of talk about McKinney's Cotton Pickers up in Detroit. They were another bunch that made a gang of musical history, and their records had everybody talking about them.'

After leaving the Cotton Pickers, Don Redman opened in New York in 1931 with an orchestra under his own name. This was at Connie's Inn and the band was made up partly from disaffected Cotton Pickers and young men from Horace Henderson's band who had started out together at Wilberforce University. Of the records made by this band 'Chant of the Weed', with its genuinely orchestrated conception and its full, rich texture, is generally regarded as outstanding.

The Don Redman band was one of the very few black bands of its time to benefit from radio sponsorship, playing on the 'Chispo' show in 1932.

When the band folded at the end of the 1930s Don wrote arrangements for other leaders including Harry James, Jimmie Lunceford and Count Basie. Clearly he found this no hardship, observing, 'I always liked to write and liked that part of the business best.'

He occasionally raised bands again, including one which he brought to Europe in 1946–7. In the 1950s Don Redman became musical director for singer-entertainer Pearl Bailey and continued writing arrangements for New York bands until his death in 1964.

Chicago had its Savoy, located on South Parkway at 47th, which implemented a big band policy in 1936 featuring the best of the bands four nights each week. A year later, when Erskine Tate was providing music for visitors to the city which was staging the heavyweight boxing match between Joe Louis and Jim Braddock, bands played only on Sundays. This Savoy closed on 6 July 1948.

'The Cotton Pickers wasn't a solo band but a unit. I was trying to get a sound and a style a little different from the other bands.'
Don Redman

***

'Without Fletcher [Henderson] I probably would have had a pretty good band, but it would have been something quite different from what it eventually turned out to be.'
Benny Goodman

***

The neglected ones:
One of Harlem's unsung bands was the Renaissance Ballroom house band led by Vernon Andrade. The band never recorded but musicians speak favourably of it. Featuring many top players, including Louis Metcalf, trumpet, George Washington, trombone, Happy Caldwell, tenor, Al Morgan, bass, and Zutty Singleton, drums, the Andrade band defeated many better-known bands in battles in the 1930s. Andrade's victims included the supposedly unbeatable Chick Webb, the top Kansas City outfit of Bennie Moten, and the Missourians.

guesting for the first three evenings (after racing there from the band's regular gig at Roseland), the Charleston Bearcats and Fess Williams and his Royal Flush Orchestra.

The Bearcats, soon known as the Savoy Bearcats, were a 10-piece group plus violin-playing front man, Leon Abbey. Strongly jazz-oriented, this well-disciplined band had no major soloist but in pianist Joe Steele had an adept arranger.

Fess Williams was already an established musician by the time he moved to the Savoy although his qualities as a player were less significant than was his showmanship. A vaudevillean by inclination, on the bandstand he wore a diamond-studded suit. Williams did not match the Bearcats when it came to driving ensembles, his band's music being angled towards amiable hokum. Initially the favourite, Willams's band was gradually overhauled by the Bearcuts.

The Savoy was a lavishly appointed hall. Marble staircases and glass chandeliers abounded. The decor mixed gold and blue, and there were numerous tables, chairs and settees spread across a carpeted area from where customers could relax and watch the other dancers.

The dance-crazy patrons who went there each week to jump and jive had the joy of performing their steps on a polished maple floor, 10,000 square feet in area—so big that it earned the nickname 'the Track'. A twin bandstand and a disappearing stage meant that there need be no pause in the music once the evening was under way. Dancers, several thousand at a time, pounded the dance floor all night long and the Savoy's management was obliged to replace the dance floor every two years.

Just as Fletcher Henderson was boss at the Roseland so, eventually, Chick Webb became King of the Savoy. A drummer, who overcame grave physical handicaps to reach the peak of his profession, Webb was crippled from birth and suffered from tuberculosis of the spine which resulted in his being hunchbacked. He came to New York in 1925, while in his mid-teens and for the next few years worked extensively in clubs and dance halls. In 1931, now with a big band, Chick took up a residency at the Savoy and from then until his death in 1939 woe betide any band coming there intent on cutting him.

The Webb band geared its book to suit the requirements of the Savoy's dancers and together they helped put on the vernacular dance map such spectacular offerings as the Lindy Hop and the Suzie Q. From 1935 the band's featured vocalist was a young girl named Ella Fitzgerald. Perhaps understandably, the band is today often thought of as merely an appendage to the fortunes of the twentieth century's finest female singer of American popular song. This is unfortunate for the band played with great swing and displayed a high level of musical ability. Thanks to the presence of such musicians as trumpet players Taft Jordan and Bobby Stark, trombonists Jimmy Harrison and Sandy Williams and, among the reeds, Louis Jordan, Chauncey Haughton and Wayman Carver, the band had a striking selection of solo talent.

Chick was a combative musician who took great delight in 'band battles' which had become a feature of the Savoy. Although the mid to late 1930s was the great period for these musical contests, with famed confrontations between Erskine Hawkins and Count Basie, Webb and Benny Carter, Webb and Basie, Don Redman and Duke Ellington, they had been a feature from the Bearcats-Fess Williams days. Duke, Basie, Jimmie Lunceford and other visitors competed with the ballroom's regular

Uncle Fess:
In 1962, the distinguished modern jazz master Charles Mingus invited his uncle to a concert he was directing at New York City's Town Hall. Mingus's uncle was Fess Williams, former leader of the Royal Flush Orchestra which had played at the opening of the Savoy Ballroom 36 years earlier.

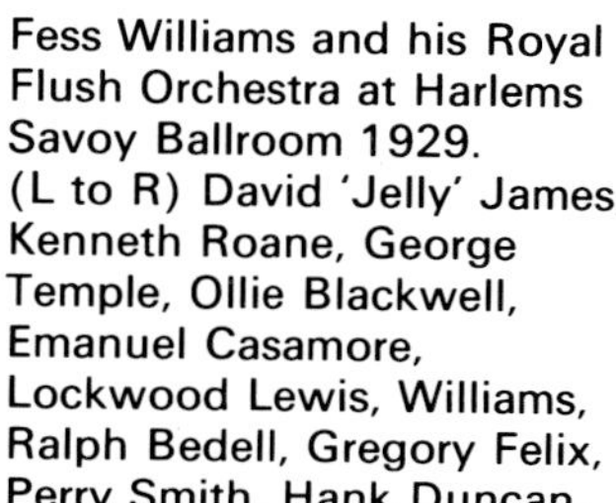

Fess Williams and his Royal Flush Orchestra at Harlems Savoy Ballroom 1929.
(L to R) David 'Jelly' James, Kenneth Roane, George Temple, Ollie Blackwell, Emanuel Casamore, Lockwood Lewis, Williams, Ralph Bedell, Gregory Felix, Perry Smith, Hank Duncan.

groups which were never an easy ride. Many a name band crept home licking its wounds after tangling with Webb or Al Cooper's Savoy Sultans, the other feared resident. Top white bands, too, enjoyed the experience although they knew they were likely to be bested. Gene Krupa, who openly modelled his drumming style on Chick Webb's, played there with Benny Goodman in 1937 and afterwards never failed to acknowledge that that night 'he was cut by a better man'. White musicians might have gained the fame and financial success, but in Harlem it was trumpet virtuosos like Taft Jordan with Webb and Sam Massenburg with Cooper who gathered the glory as they swung high above the screams and cheers of the delirious crowd.

The man chiefly responsible for the Chick Webb band's book was Edgar Sampson who also played alto saxophone and violin. Although much less praised than either Henderson or Don Redman, Sampson's contribution to the sounds of the swing era both by way of arrangements and by his compositions was significant. Among his compositions were 'Stompin' at the Savoy', 'If Dreams Come True', 'Blue Lou' and 'Don't Be That Way' (which became Benny Goodman's theme tune).

For all the undoubted skills of Sampson and the other members of the Chick Webb band, it is the leader himself who was the dominant force. A dynamic drummer with great solo ability, he concentrated on driving his band along with a relentless swing, never losing sight of the needs of the Savoy's dancers for a stimulating, fluid yet solid beat.

The Savoy became known as the 'Shrine of the Public Dance' and, less formally but much more appropriately, as the 'Home of Happy Feet', and swung for more than thirty years. Competitors of the Savoy Ballroom included the Rockland Palace, originally known as the Manhattan Casino, where Jim Europe held sway before World War I, and which continued its policy of employing big bands well into the 1950s. Harlem's Renaissance Casino was another long-serving ballroom of distinction as was the Central Plaza over on the Lower East Side.

Although far from being the only New York venues for bands during the 1930s, the Savoy and Roseland dance halls were the most important of their kind. There were also countless nightclubs among which the leaders in Harlem were the Cotton Club, Ed Smalls' Paradise and Connie's Inn. The Cotton Club was the base for several fine bands, notably the Missourians originally led by Andy Preer but which metamorphosed into Cab Calloway's band, and those led by Duke Ellington and Jimmie Lunceford.

Al Cooper's Savoy Sultans

Sharing a piece of Chick Webb's glory in Harlem was Al Cooper's Savoy Sultans. From their first appearance at the Savoy in 1937 until the band folded almost ten years later, the Sultans retained a remarkably consistent personnel. The size of the band, usually eight pieces (two trumpets, three reeds, three rhythm) places it outside the context of big bands but the Sultans swung with such dedicated and infectious urgency that they drubbed many bigger, powerhouse units which ventured to the Savoy for a band battle. Apart from the fiery trumpet playing of Sam Massenberg, the main solo attraction was alto saxophonists Rudy Williams whose stomping style helped make the Sultans one of the jumpingest bands ever to hit the Home of Happy Feet.

Bands could also be heard in theatres, usually in the pit but sometimes on-stage too. The principal theatre for black artists, and by a considerable margin, was the Apollo, on 125th Street in Harlem, which had a reputation for having the toughest audience in the world. The bands of Ellington, Count Basie, Lionel Hampton and Claude Hopkins are just a few that played the Apollo and won over that hard-to-please crowd.

A host of fancy hotels featured bands, usually white, as part of their appeal during the 1930s and 1940s. There was the Starlight Roof at the Hotel Astor, the Roosevelt Grill, and the Park Central where Ben Pollack played with great success.

Regular broadcasts from these venues became a major factor in presenting the music of the times to the nation. The movie theatres offered patrons a full-scale show including a name band as well as a movie. It was at such a movie theatre in New York, the Paramount, that Benny Goodman set the seal on his success at the close of the return

THE WORLD'S GREATEST
COLORED STARS COME ONLY TO THE

APOLLO

AMERICA'S
FINEST
COLORED
STAGE
SHOWS!

125th ST.
NEAR 8th AVE.

TELEPHONE
UNiversity 4
4490

ONE WEEK
ONLY
BEGINNING
FRIDAY
OCT. 1st

A GREAT SHOW with BOB HOWARD
VIZARD OF THE IVORIES

MILLS
ARTISTS, inc.
present

LUCKY MILLINDER

And the MILLS
BLUE RHYTHM
BAND

AND
REVUE
CAST OF
FIFTY

GALA MIDNIGHT SHOW SATURDAY

RESERVED SEATS
NOW ON SALE

EXCLUSIVE VARIETY RECORDING ARTISTS

IN PERSON

"fats"

WALLER

VICTOR RECORDS

AND *his* ORCHESTRA

One hundred miles south of New York, on the New Jersey coastline, stands Atlantic City. Today the atmosphere may resemble that of Las Vegas but back in the 1930s the boardwalk at Atlantic City was where fashion conscious holiday-makers strolled by day and danced by night in several ballrooms, most famous of which was the Steel Pier.

leg of his 1935–7 tour which launched the swing era in the public's consciousness.

New York's 52nd Street was a very special haunt for musicians where they could jam and where big band musicians could momentarily relax from the continual grind of one-night stands and listen or, perhaps, if the spirit moved them, sit in. For the most part 'the Street' was a small band scene but in some instances big bands were employed there. In 1938 Count Basie's band could be found crammed onto the undersized stand at the Famous Door.

Despite poor pay and long hours, the 1930s were fine times for big band musicians in New York. Thousands of young hopefuls scuffled around the city, some becoming respected sidemen or bandleaders in their own right.

'The Savoy, the Golden Gate, and the Renaissance ballrooms battled for the crowds—the Savoy introduced such attractions as Thursday Kitchen Mechanics' Nights, bathing beauty contests, and a new car given away each Saturday night. They had bands from all across the country in the ballrooms and the Apollo and Lafayette theaters. They had colorful bandleaders like 'Fess Williams in his diamond-studded suit and top hat, and Cab Calloway in his white zoot suit to end all zoots, and his wide-brimmed white hat and string tie, setting Harlem afire with 'Tiger Rag' and 'hi-de-hi-de-ho' and 'St James Infirmary' and 'Minnie the Moocher'.

Malcolm X

* * *

'Of the 30,000 members of New York's Local 802, American Federation of Musicians, perhaps 3,000 work fairly regularly.'

Nat Hentoff

The opportunities for playing jazz in New York were relatively few and many musicians found work in pit bands and in radio. Working in radio, the real boom area of the entertainment industry of the late 1920s and 1930s, meant temporarily (and in some cases permanently) dousing the jazz flame. For those who preferred eating by playing sentimental pap to playing hot jazz and starving it was a way out. Indeed, it could prove more than merely a grub-stake. Working in radio meant seven days employment a week with musicians rushing between studios from one show to the next, churning out Hawaiian music here, Eastern European polkas there, now Latin American rumbas, next some hack arranger's idea of a hot jazz number.

Inevitably, times changed but New York retained its importance as a centre and as the place in which a musician had to prove himself.

After World War II the New York big band scene was still thriving even if the names were somewhat different. In March, 1946, New Yorkers could hear bands led by Charlie Barnet at the 400, Randy Brooks at the Hotel Pennsylvania, Cab Calloway at the Strand, with Xaviar Cugat taking over from Sammy Kaye at the Capitol Theatre. Up in Harlem Duke Ellington was following his former sideman Cootie Williams into the Apollo. The same Spring, Benny Goodman was back at the Paramount and his former sideman Lionel Hampton had a band at the Aquarium while Erskine Hawkins had the Lincoln Hotel residency and Herbie Fields was at the Palladium. At the Spotlite on 52nd Street Dizzy Gillespie was enlarging his band to seventeen pieces and Vincent Lopez was at the Taft Hotel. Over at the Commodore there was Ray McKinley while Buddy Morrow was offering the dancers at the Roseland very different fare to pre-war years. Leo Reisman was at the Waldorf-Astoria and Georgie Auld and Billy Butterfield, apparently deaf to forecasts of impending doom for big bands, were both in town forming new bands.

In the late 1950s the emerging rehearsal bands made their first real impact in New York. One, led by pianist Nat Pierce played the Savoy just before the hall finally closed its doors in 1959.

The activities of recording bands, important clubs and festivals, and the prestige of playing Carnegie Hall for any surviving name band, means that New York remains an irresistible lure. Entertainers of all kinds know that however highly regarded they might be in Los Angeles or Chicago, until they have played New York and made an impact there, they haven't made it at all.

That, certainly, was the way it was in the 1920s and 1930s when, for jazz artists of most persuasions and for the emerging big bands, New York was Mecca.

Guy Lombardo And His Royal Canadians

For jazz fans, Guy Lombardo is merely a curious anecdote in the Louis Armstrong story; for big band fans he is rarely even a footnote. Yet for decades, the 'Sweetest Music This Side of Heaven' was danced to by moonstruck young couples who forever afterwards credited (or, maybe, blamed) Lombardo for starting them off along the path of matrimony.

The band is pictured here at the Roosevelt Hotel, NYC, shortly after their 1929 opening. Apart from holidays and short tours, this was where they stayed for the next 40 years.

The Royal Canadians' brand of predictable undemanding music was performed with consummate musicianship. However blandly unimaginative it might be their music was certainly well-played.

LUIS RUSSELL AND HIS ORCHESTRA

Pianist Luis Russell became a bandleader without really meaning to. A member of the George Howe band at New York's Nest Club, he was elevated to leadership by the club's owner. Born in Panama, Russell lived for a while in New Orleans and inclined towards that city's more traditional style of music making. Luis's band had a strong affinity with the New Orleans groups—simple arrangements with a powerful rhythm section anchored by Pops Foster's steel bass and allowing soloists like Red Allen, trumpet, J. C. Higginbotham, trombone, Albert Nicholas, clarinet, and Charlie Holmes, alto saxophone, great scope for their improvisations.

Luis mostly used his own arrangements although Barney Bigard's reminiscences suggest that these were somewhat informal. Luis's band was hired to accompany Louis Armstrong for whom he had made some special arrangements when the trumpeter appeared in New York in 1929. Eventually, Armstrong became the nominal leader of the band and, thus, Luis Russell, who had become a bandleader without meaning to, ceased to be one in much the same off-hand manner.

Luis Russell and his 'Old man River' Orchestra Stepping up from the bottom left are Percy 'Sonny' Woods, Rex Stewart, Nat Story, Paul Barbarin, Charlie Holmes, Henry 'Moon' Jones, Leonard 'Ham' Davis, Bingie Madison, Greely Walton, Lee Blair, Jimmy Archey, Pops Foster, Gus Aiken. (Russell inset.)

CHAPTER THREE

DUKE ELLINGTON

'ELLINGTON MOOD'

'I am a piano player, a rehearsal piano player, a jive-time conductor, bandleader, and sometimes I just do nothing but take the bows ... and I have fun. My, my, my. My thing is having fun.'

Duke Ellington

One day in 1928 a teenager in New York discovered that station WHN had moved its antenna and he could no longer pick up the music of his favourite band which was broadcasting regularly from the Cotton Club. Young David Sternberg wrote to the bandleader telling him of his difficulties and when no reply came, with all the innocence of youth, 15-year-old David walked across town to the club intent on putting his problem personally. 'I'd never been into a place like that before in my life but since it was four hours or so before their regular playing time, it was easy to walk upstairs and I just introduced myself to Duke Ellington.'

'Hello everybody. Welcome to our famous Cotton Club. Great to see so many friends here tonight enjoying themselves in spite of the cover charge and if you can spare a minute from your merrymaking I'd like to have the pleasure in introducing the greatest living master of jungle music. The rip-roaring harmony-hound, none other than Duke Ellington. Take your bow, Dukey.'
Announcement by *Irving Mills*—1929

Had David Sternberg known a little more about the Cotton Club he might well have been somewhat less sanguine at wandering in there so casually. Although the Cotton Club had quickly become the in-place for New York's smart set it was owned by a tough character named Owney Madden, a hardened gangster.

The flamboyance of the Cotton Club's decor, the exotic floor shows, the obvious wealth and sometimes shady connections of the patrons all added to the legendary status the club achieved.

For any black band, being chosen to play at the Cotton Club was a major coup. For a band to become resident there was as close as anyone could come in such an unpredictable business to a guarantee of success.

The music demanded by the Cotton Club had to match the exoticism of the surroundings and the shows. Andy Preer, whose Cotton Club Orchestra (later known as The Missourians) was resident at the club for two and a half years from the end of 1924, initiated the use of 'jungle sounds', mainly created with mutes which were particularly evident in the plunger work of trumpeter R. Q. Dickerson.

When Preer died and The Missourians left in 1927 the job was turned down by King Oliver, who wanted money to match the prestige. Auditions were called and among the bands trying out for the job was one which, in later years, appeared to make a fetish out of being late. The Cotton Club audition was no exception; it was almost as if Duke Ellington was starting as he meant to continue.

Ellington had been playing at the Kentucky Club, off Times Square, for some years and had established a solid, if limited reputation. On the day of the audition Ellington was working an out of town gig at a theatre in Philadelphia and by the time he had returned to New York and rounded up additional men needed for a Cotton Club band was late.

Chicago's exotic Regal Theatre in 1932 provides the backdrop for a happy Duke Ellington band. (L to R) Freddie Jenkins, Wellman Braud, Cootie Williams, Harry Carney, Artie Whetsol, Juan Tizol, Johnny Hodges, Joe Nanton, Barney Bigard, Sonny Greer, Freddie Guy, the Duke.

Fortunately, so was Harry Block, currently the manager of the Cotton Club. Block had agreed to listen to the band after being pressed by songwriter Jimmy McHugh, who was responsible for most of the club's shows. In the event it was largely academic. By the time Block arrived at the audition every band except the tardy Ellington had been and gone. Block liked the band and Ellington was hired, but there was still a problem to overcome. Ellington was contracted to Gibson's Standard Theatre in Philadelphia and the management there refused to release him. Harry Block resolved the impasse with a telephone call to Owney Madden. Several phone calls later, the Standard's manager was made an offer: 'Be big,' he was told, 'or you'll be dead.'

Duke began playing music early in life and by his mid-teenage was earning money as a piano player and showing the early influence of the ragtime professors. It was not long before he was leading his own hot band which included Artie Whetsol, trumpet, Otto Hardwicke, saxophone, Sonny Greer, drums, and Elmer Snowden, banjo. By no means was this band a trail-blazer and it was not long before they all joined clarinetist Wilbur Sweatman for a New York date where Sonny and Duke augmented their meagre earnings hustling in local pool rooms.

After returning to Washington the core of the band was persuaded back to New York in 1923, picking up jobs at various clubs including Barron Wilkins's. The band was nominally Snowden's with Duke by now regularly writing music. With a few personnel changes, guitarist Freddie Guy replacing Snowden and Whetsol quitting to study medicine, the band succeeded in landing a residency at the Hollywood Club, later known as the Kentucky Club. The group was joined by growl trombonist Charlie Irvis who was noted for his 'jungle style'. Irvis was followed into the band by Joe 'Tricky Sam' Nanton and trumpeter Bubber Miley both of whom excelled at the creation of 'jungle' effects. 'Our band changed its character when Bubber Miley came in,' Duke later observed. 'That was when we decided to forget all about the sweet music.' The arrival in its ranks of Nanton and Miley transformed a competent but undistinguished group of musicians into a startlingly new and original unit.

An important arrival in the band was Harry Carney who joined in 1927. Originally a clarinet player, Carney moved to alto saxophone then on to baritone where he stayed, becoming a keystone of the Ellington band. It was Carney's skill which established a permanent place for the baritone saxophone in the jazz orchestra. With Ellington, Carney's counter melodies added a deep and sombre contrast to the growling menace of the brass players. The saxophonist's long tenure with Duke was mutually beneficial as Carney commented to Stanley Dance: 'It has not only been an education being with him, but also a great pleasure. At times, I've been ashamed to take the money.'

Among further newcomers over the next couple of years were trumpeters Freddie Jenkins and Cootie Williams, who replaced Miley, and there was a colourful addition to the brass with the arrival of valve trombonist Juan Tizol. Clarinetist Barney Bigard joined as did Johnny Hodges, a childhood friend of Harry Carney's. An alto saxophone player of superbly romantic depths and with an elegant, creamy sound, Hodges set standards which remain a yardstick by which all players of the instrument are at some point measured.

All of these musicians were strikingly individualistic voices which Ellington eagerly wove into the fabric he endlessly revised throughout

Fallen idol:
'I was a clerk and errand boy with Mills Artists, a booking agency... My job for Duke was that I had to look at the contracts and then report to him... with a digest of contracts opened in his absence. Also I had to tell him of any "suspicious" bills that were paid in names other than the corporation. Anyway, in 1934, I was being paid $10 a week and I went up to Duke and said, "Look, I'm doing a pretty good job and I think I deserve a raise. Shall I ask Irving Mills?" Duke said, "Yes, by all means." So I went up to Irving Mills and asked him for a raise on the basis of my performance [as clerk and messenger boy]and he said, "I don't think we can afford it." I said, "I think you should be able to afford it," and he replied, "No, we can't. You're fired!" I laughed, inwardly perhaps, but I laughed all the same. You can say it, but you can't do it, I thought. After all, Duke is my boss. So I went back to Duke and told him Mills's answer. I was amazed at Duke's reply! He didn't say boo; he didn't come to my defence. He just took it for granted that if Irving had said it, then that was the way it was. I was thunderstruck. I couldn't speak. I was out of a job. I suppose with hindsight it wasn't just me. Duke didn't, or couldn't, stand up to anyone; he was afraid of a battle... Although it didn't change my love for his music, I lost my respect for him as a man.'

David Sternberg

***

'Some of the guys used to tell him he was a fool to give in so much to management, but Duke knew what he wanted, and I guess to get what you want, you have to compromise.'

Louis Metcalf

Longest serving Ellingtonian—Harry Carney, baritone sax.

his career. Unlike other bandleaders within the mainstream of big band progression, Duke Ellington considered the individual sounds of each sideman to be of crucial importance. This concentration on seeking out the individualism of his musicians made Ellington's band quite unlike those which sought section evenness and precision to the detriment of individual expression.

The Kentucky Club residency lasted four years during which time Duke extended the scope of his writing. The effects of this period of Ellington's life remained a constant part of his work throughout his career, long after the departure of those original musicians for whom it was created. Thereafter, the band went from strength to strength as equally individualistic soloists joined. It was not, however, simply the presence of soloists which gave the band its uniqueness but Ellington's genius at utilising their strengths and disguising their weaknesses by carefully framing them with an infinite variety of apt tonal shadings and backgrounds.

The band had been taken in hand by Irving Mills, an energetic promoter with a sharp eye for business and the ability to carve himself a corner in any promising deal, be it a band or a show or even a song. Under Mills's management the band began to find favour with the public and at the end of 1927 was successful in landing the Cotton Club residency, opening there on 4 December.

Cat on a hot tin horn:
Stratospheric trumpet playing was Cat Anderson's forte, his piercing notes were a spectacular finale to many of Duke Ellington's finest charts. When Cat joined the Ellington outfit both Duke and Billy Strayhorn could write trumpet lines well and truly above the staff, knowing that Cat's marvellous range and splendid articulation would cover it. But to consider 'El Gato' simply as a high-note specialist would do this exceptionally talented musician a grave injustice. A fine example of his work comes on the Ellington band's 1956 version of 'Stompy Jones' when he blows a scorching solo against the full might of the orchestra.

There is also a great deal of fine feline blowing on a record made in 1958 by an Anderson-led studio band. An album of scintillating sounds resulted, 'Cat on a Hot Tin Horn'. Perhaps not surprisingly, the album was outstanding with Cat leading such talented performers trumpeters Ray Copeland, Reunald Jones and Ernie Royal, trombonists Henderson Chambers, Jimmy Cleveland and Frank Rehak, a reed section including Sahib Shihab, Earl Warren, Ernie Wilkins and the exceptional Jimmy Forrest, and the rhythm section of Jimmy Jones, George Duvivier and Panama Francis.

Another eastern dance hall noted in the engagement books of all leading bands was Glen Island Casino at New Rochelle. It was here that Glenn Miller was truly launched on the road to his huge success; and it was where the Dorsey brothers had their climactic flare-up in 1935.

Explaining his role in these events, Mills might have added a touch of exaggeration when he stated: '... I was producing a new show for the Cotton Club, I built as much of it as possible around Duke's band and his music. The budget, incidentally, did not provide for a band as large as Duke felt he needed—ten pieces. I paid the salaries of the additional musicians out of my share of the project. I did it gladly, because I had complete faith in Duke Ellington and firmly believed that together we were launching something more than just a dance orchestra.'

For all the undoubted merits of the Ellington band at the Cotton Club, the great boost to the band's fortunes was directly attributable to the regular radio broadcasts the band made from the club. David Sternberg, from just across town, was not the only listener. Millions heard the band and because, for most of them, a visit to a nightclub, *any* nightclub least of all the Cotton Club, was next to impossible, they listened to their radios and dreamed and bought records.

For those who lived outside America there was not even a chance to hear radio broadcasts; for them there were just the records. This different setting in which Ellington's music was heard in Britain had a profound effect upon audiences and, in time, on the musicians themselves.

Duke Ellington's awareness of his growing importance in the world of music came in 1933 when he visited Britain. There, instead of being regarded as an 'entertainer' who played while audiences ate and drank and talked and danced and waited for the floor show, he was listened to in an atmosphere of studied critical approval.

The previous year the same thing had happened to Louis Armstrong but the long-term effect was much greater on Ellington. A British classical musician, Constant Lambert, likened Ellington's works to classical composers, some of whom were probably then unknown to Ellington. Unwittingly, he had been affected by classical composers through the influence of men like Will Vodery and Will Marion Cook, both of whom had assisted his musical progress.

Lambert was unstinting in his praise in his book, *Music Ho!*, published

Ellingtonian appetites:
'He may be a genius, but Jesus how he eats.'

Tricky Sam Nanton

***

'I remember many times we would stop in a diner after travelling all night and we would sit—Duke would be on my left and Quentin Jackson on my right—and the waitress would come over and say, "What would you have", and Duke would say, "I'll take a loaf of bread, toasted, a dozen eggs and a pound of bacon. That's just for me." ...Then Quentin would say, "The same for me." '

Louie Bellson

the year after Ellington's visit. 'I know of nothing in Ravel so dextrous in treatment as the varied solos in the middle of the ebullient "Hot and Bothered" and nothing in Stravinsky more dynamic than the final section... The exquisitely tired and four-in-the-morning "Mood Indigo" is an equally remarkable piece of writing of a lyrical and harmonic order, yet it is palpably from the same hand.' In the same passage in his book, Lambert went on to commend this ability of Ellington's to maintain the same style, doing so in a manner which implied Ellington's superiority, in this respect, to Franck, Hindemith, Stravinsky and Vaughan Williams.

True, Lambert did go on to suggest that beyond the limits of the three minute composition, designed to fit onto one side of a gramophone record, Ellington might not have the same success. But, then, this was 1934 and, apart from such slightly longer works as "Creole Rhapsody", Ellington had yet to show real signs that this was the way he wanted to go.

Such minor qualifications apart, the visit to Europe and especially to Britain, was a huge success. Most importantly for Ellington was the revelation of how his music was received. Many years later, Duke recalled his impressions of that visit for Henry Whiston of the Canadian Broadcasting Company: 'They recognised the word "jazz" as a form of art ... and took it very seriously. I'll never forget that when we played our first concert in England ... Spike Hughes wrote the critique after the concert but he didn't criticise us! No, he criticised the audience for applauding at the end of solos and in the middle of numbers. It was just that serious.'

The 1930s saw further changes in the Ellington band's personnel but while some important figures left their replacements were usually their musical peers. Virtuoso trombonist Lawrence Brown, who joined in 1932, brought a hitherto absent sophistication to the band while Wallace Jones brought a distinctive swing feel to the band in these pre-swing era days, and there was also the dazzlingly audacious cornetist Rex Stewart. All these new talents were accommodated by Ellington as his writing skills continued to develop.

1939 was a good year for new faces with the sensational young bass player Jimmy Blanton, the sensuous and unpredictable tenor saxophonist Ben Webster, and an arranger, composer and pianist named Billy Strayhorn who became Duke Ellington's *alter ego*. Strayhorn joined Duke as a lyric writer with Duke observing, 'I don't have any kind of position for you. You'll be my protégé'. Strayhorn immediately showed his worth arranging for a number of small group record dates which have since become acknowledged classics. Strayhorn had a special touch for pastel shadings and subtle, delicately balanced arrangements. What is immediately obvious is Strayhorn's ability to score in identical fashion to Duke. Such is his ability that few can say precisely where his contribution begins and Ellington's ends. As a composer, Strayhorn provided many of the orchestra's finest pieces including the moody 'Chelsea Bridge' and, most famous of all, 'Take the A Train' which became the Ellington theme tune.

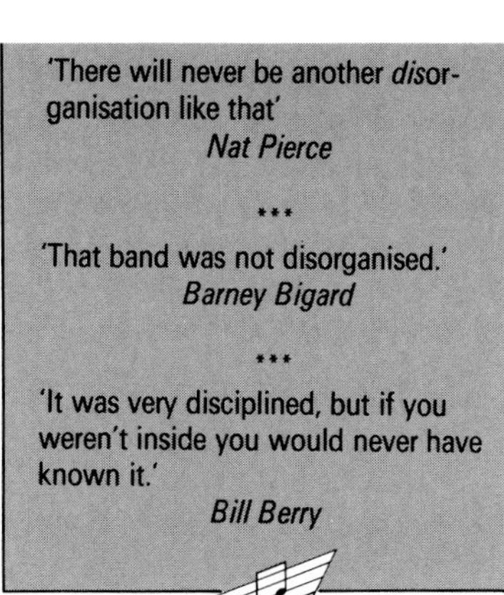

As the 1930s ended Ellington's music adopted a more modern sound and he presented more ambitious compositions. Yet, amazingly enough for music that was built around the personalities of individual sidemen, it remained identifiably Ellingtonian in character. Soloists might change but the essential sound continued.

Ellington's commercial success appeared assured and to a great extent this is attributable to Irving Mills. Although he has been criticised for

Hiring and firing—1:
'I was at home one evening, when Duke rang and asked if I could play a broadcast with him, just for this one night. Well I played that one night, and here I am, twenty years later still with him!'
Russell Procope
'I started that Friday and ended fourteen years later.'
Barney Bigard
'While I was shaking hands with Duke, his road manager was asking, "Would you be willing to leave town with us?" I said, "What does it pay" and "Yes!". He never answered my question but now that I know what I know, I would have paid *them* anything.'
Bill Berry
'It's funny, I never knew Duke to fire anyone. But I'll tell you, he was a slickster. He would make life so miserable on the job that you would just quit.'
Barney Bigard

the manner in which he cut himself a piece of the action, and Duke himself instigated their split over the manner in which his financial affairs were managed, there can be little doubt that, for whatever motive, Mills worked assiduously to promote the band during its formative years. Quite clearly, a man with Ellington's talent could not have been kept down but had he not had Mills behind him, had he not enjoyed the benefit of the broadcasts from the Cotton Club, had he not been late for that all-important audition, Duke's career might well have followed a very different pathway towards his eventual success.

One benefit Duke enjoyed was the ability to hold on to sidemen. In later years he disarmingly told British bandleader and broadcaster Humphrey Lyttelton that this was due to his 'gimmick'; he paid them a lot of money.

ELLINGTONIA—1

From the earliest days, Duke's music included numerous works of distinction which remained in the band's book for decades.

The broodingly intense 'East St Louis Toodle-oo' became the band's first theme tune. Featuring Bubber Miley's growl trumpet, it demonstrates the influence the trumpeter had upon Duke at this time. 'Black and Tan Fantasy', 'Creole Love Call' with its unearthly instrumentalised vocal by Adelaide Hall, and the elegant 'Black Beauty', featuring the muted trumpet of Artie Whetsol, are early examples of the emotional depths Ellington's music could probe. These recordings, and such other minor masterpieces as 'The Mooche', with moodily dramatic solos from Whetsol, Hodges and Barney Bigard, and the energetic 'Stevedore Stomp', came in the 1920s while the early 1930s saw such classics as 'Mood Indigo', 'Rockin' in Rhythm' and 'Creole Rhapsody'.

In 1936 there came a string of miniature concertos, each written with one particular musician in mind. These included 'Cootie's Concerto' (later retitled 'Echoes of Harlem') for Cootie Williams, 'Barney's Concerto' ('Clarinet Lament') for Barney Bigard, 'Lawrence's Concerto' ('Yearning for Love') for Lawrence Brown, and for Rex Stewart 'Rex's Concerto' ('Trumpet in Spades').

1940 found the band's personnel settled and ready for its most glorious period of recordings. Obviously, no band is perfect but it is hard for even the harshest critic to discover anything that is less than good while most of the band's records made between February 1940 and February 1942 are little short of miraculous. Almost half a century later, they stand out as a marvellous series of miniature masterpieces.

Among the tunes recorded in this period are new versions of 'Solitude' and 'Mood Indigo', with the remarkable teaming of Harry Carney's baritone, Johnny Hodges' alto and Cootie Williams's trumpet. There are also definitive versions of such classics as 'Jack the Bear', a feature for Jimmy Blanton's brilliant talents, 'Ko-Ko', one of Ellington's most striking compositions of the period, 'Morning Glory', a bright and gently rocking ballad with simply scored saxophones behind an elegant Rex Stewart solo, and 'Conga Brava', a Latin-tinged piece written by Juan Tizol which echoes the same composer's 'Perdido'.

'Concerto for Cootie', a new feature for Cootie Williams, is a work of unsurpassed brilliance in which orchestra and soloist are perfectly united. Duke once explained, somewhat lightheartedly, why he liked having Cootie Williams in the band: 'It's done for my ear health. I am addicted to certain zesty sounds, of which Cootie's is certainly one. My ear health

The Apollo's chief rival in Harlem was the Opera House which featured such bands as those of Tiny Bradshaw with Ella Fitzgerald low down on the bill, and Cab Calloway, the latter topping a bill of Cotton Club artists including the dancing Nicholas Brothers and Lena Horne.

ONE WEEK — BEGINNING FRIDAY, FEBRUARY 15TH

Tiny Bradshaw

And His Sensational **BAND**

MAE ALIX—EDDIE HUNTER—BILLY HIGGINS
3 SAMS—GEORGE BOOKER—ELLA FITZGERALD

Special Added Attraction
MAE WHITMAN Presents
POPS AND LOUIE
WITH ALICE WHITMAN
in a wonderful new act

On the Screen **"MENACE"** Mystery Melodrama | First Chapter "Rustlers of Red Dog"

ONE WEEK ONLY — BEGINNING FRIDAY, FEB. 22ND

GREATEST EVENT IN THEATRICAL HISTORY!

with the great COTTON CLUB Cast:

Nicholas Bros.
Meers & Meers
Lethia Hill
Swann & Lee
Dynamite Hooker
Bill Bailey
Lena Horne
Cora La Redd
Cotton Club Chorus

AND THE ENTIRE
COTTON CLUB
REVUE

> 'As Bach says, "If you ain't got a left hand, you ain't worth a hoot in hell!" '
> *Duke Ellington*

is very important. It is so near my mind and that gets a little diluted by the wrong sound.' (With lyrics added later, 'Concerto for Cootie' was retitled 'Do Nothin' Till You Hear From Me'.)

Another glorious moment of Ellingtonia comes on 'Cottontail', a feature for Ben Webster who plays a tenor saxophone solo of breathtaking originality. 'Bojangles' and 'A Portrait of Bert Williams' followed and then, in July, came 'Harlem Airshaft', one of the best examples of what Ellington called his 'tone parallels'. Demonstrating the sounds that could be heard in the high, narrow spaces between Harlem's buildings, this tune's inspiration was eloquently evoked by the composer:

> So much goes on in a Harlem airshaft. You get the full essence of Harlem in an airshaft. You hear fights, you smell dinner, you hear people making love. You hear intimate gossip floating down. You hear the radio. An airshaft is one great big loudspeaker. You see your neighbours' laundry. You hear the janitor's dogs. The man upstairs' aerial falls down and breaks your window. You smell coffee. A wonderful thing, is that smell. An airshaft has got every contrast. One guy is cooking dried fish and rice and another guy's got a great big turkey. Guy-with-fish's wife is a terrific cooker, but the guy's wife with the turkey is doing a sad job. You hear people praying, fighting, snoring. Jitterbugs are jumping up and down, always over you, never below you. That's a funny thing about jitterbugs. They're always above you, never below you. I tried to put all that in 'Harlem Airshaft'.

Immaculate in their white ties and jackets, the Duke Ellington band poses for the camera during an engagement at the Congress Hotel, Chicago, in 1935. (L to R) Sonny Greer, Arthur Whetsol, Juan Tizol, Ellington, Hayes Alvis, Billy Taylor, Johnny Hodges, Freddie Guy, Barney Bigard, Harry Carney, Cootie Williams, Lawrence Brown, Joe Nanton, Otto Hardwicke, Rex Stewart.

Top rank New York hotels favoured lush decor but even the flamboyant excesses of the canopies over the bandstand at the Essex House failed to overpower the smooth swing of the Casa Lomans.

Before 1940 was out the band had added 'In a Mellotone', 'Warm Valley' and Billy Strayhorn's 'Take the A Train'. All these foregoing masterpieces came amidst a flurry of recordings which occupied only the first half of this glorious two-year period in the band's history.

Duke's ability as a composer never stopped growing. Although the miniature masterpieces of the 1940s were already enough to secure his place as a giant of jazz, there was much more yet to come.

His longer works of the late 1950s included 'A Drum Is a Woman' and 'Such Sweet Thunder', suites which contain passages that display his talent at its brightest. 'Such Sweet Thunder' evokes with witty inventiveness and warm beauty such Shakespearean characters as Lady Macbeth and the witches ('Lady Mac' and 'The Telecasters'), Romeo and Juliet ('Star Crossed Lovers'), and Henry V ('Sonnet to Hank Cinq').

In the 1950s Duke Ellington was as dynamic as ever, even if he continued to hide his boundless energies beneath a cloak of studied nonchalance.

Throughout the decade new soloists arrived in the band, each a master craftsman bringing with him his own clear identity and yet capable of blending into the ensemble. Each gave Duke new challenges as he sought to introduce their special qualities into his overall vision. Among the newcomers were trombonists Quentin Jackson and Britt Woodman, tenor saxophonist Paul Gonsalves, and trumpeters Cat Anderson, Willie Cook,

Clark Terry and Harold 'Shorty' Baker, a player with often overlooked crystal clear lyricism.

For a short spell at the beginning of the decade Ellington's band came closer than usual to the broader concept of the big band sound. This came about when Duke poached two sidemen from Harry James: lead alto Willie Smith and drummer Louie Bellson. The immaculate Smith, who never worked in any saxophone section which did not benefit greatly from his presence, helped give the band a more cohesive sound while Bellson kicked things along in a manner never achieved by any other Ellington drummer.

Yet the influences of these newcomers, however much they improved the band's standing in the eyes of big band fans, seemed momentarily to divert Duke from the Ellingtonian path.

It was in the middle of the new decade that Ellington's renaissance began; at least that was how the media saw it. With the oversimplification that can simultaneously illuminate and obscure an event, the spotlight falls on the Newport Jazz Festival on 7 July 1956. Placed last on a bill which was already running late, the band found itself playing to dwindling numbers as members of the audience began making their way home. Then Duke announced that the band would play a tune he had composed almost twenty years before, or, rather, two tunes, 'Diminuendo in Blue' and 'Crescendo in Blue', which would be bridged by a tenor saxophone solo from Paul Gonsalves. The band was in good form and built up a rhythmic urgency which inspired Gonsalves and caught the attention of the audience, many of whom were already out of their seats and on their way to the exits. By the time Gonsalves was into his stride a vibrant yet mysterious alchemy had communicated the feelings of the band and the soloist to everyone present. Those who had remained in their seats came out of them and now the rapport was two-way as the audience's excitement infected the band and, in particular, the soloist. Gonsalves's playing of his 27 choruses was nothing less than the flowering of his errant genius.

Clark Terry, who was in the band at Newport, later remarked with commendable understatement, 'It was a good night'.

Paul Gonsalves, tormented genius: At the 1956 Newport Jazz Festival, tenor saxophonist Paul Gonsalves's fearsome solo, which bridged the two parts of 'Dminuendo and Crescendo in Blue', 27 choruses of driving, swinging excitement, helped set the seal on Duke Ellington's 'come back'. They also doomed Paul to repeating this triumphal performance over and over at the insistence of audiences and Duke. To a great extent this single moment in Paul's career overshadowed the fact that his was an eloquently inventive talent. He had a capacity for introducing to ballads an exquisite lyricism that was in striking contrast with the dramatic Newport performance yet was simultaneously a perfect match to his warm and gentle personality. Everybody loved Paul, and yet there were those who took advantage of his vulnerability, or at best failed to sway him from falling prey to those flaws which in the end proved fatal to this talent and his life. Overall, Paul's tenure with Ellington was 24 years but there were periods when he was kept away by his addiction to drugs and alcohol.

For all his offstage problems, in his playing Paul Gonsalves retained those distinctive qualities which led many fellow musicians to rate him in the top handful of truly great tenor saxophonists.

Inevitably, Paul's long years of succumbing to the temptations placed before him by those who, perhaps, believed they were helping a friend finally took their toll. When he died in London in 1974, ten days before Duke died in New York, Paul Gonsalves was 53.

ELLINGTONIA—2

From the late 1950s onwards, with Ellington's personal stock rising ever higher, his composing entered a period of intense activity which saw him tackling ever more complex works with increasing confidence. In 1959 he wrote the score for a movie, *Anatomy of a Murder*, observing that all he sought to do was write fitting background music. Far from background music, 'Suite Thursday', was commissioned for the Monterey Jazz Festival of 1960 and evoked events in John Steinbeck's novel, *Sweet Thursday*. 1959 also saw the composition of 'The Queen's Suite' written for Queen Elizabeth II. Through the 1960s came a steady stream of important works: 'The Far East Suite', 'The Virgin Islands Suite', 'The Latin American Suite'.

In the mid-1960s Ellington entered the final stage of his life as a composer. It would be facile to suggest that his career had always built towards the sacred music which graced his last decade, yet it is impossible not to see in his long-evident ability to compose music which reached to the heart and emotions a series of musical stepping-stones to the powerful majesty of the work he now undertook. In 1965 he was invited to perform a concert of sacred music at Grace Cathedral, San Francisco and

The leading theatre in Harlem was the Apollo on 125th Street where, in 1935, Blanche Calloway's band played, where Charlie Barnet set the chorus line afire in 1939, and where Jimmie Lunceford and Eddie Vinson had them lining up for admission in the 1940s.

Little Eddie—the Maestro

from then onwards similar concerts were held in various parts of America and elsewhere in the world.

Sacred music was not Ellington's sole preoccupation in these closing years; he composed 'The New Orleans Suite', music for a ballet entitled 'The River', 'Afro-Eurasian Eclipse', 'The Goutelas Suite' and 'Toga Brava'. Yet, for all these other, major works, none of which has been fully exposed to public attention, it was sacred music which continued to occupy Ellington's mind. In 1973, as his life drew to its close, he prepared a third Sacred Concert, this one to be presented at Westminster Abbey in London on United Nations Day. Later in the year, on 23 December, this final Sacred Concert was given its second performance, at St Augustine's, a church in New York's Harlem.

It would be unwise to attempt here to summarise the musical output of Duke Ellington. Indeed, at best such a task would require not one but several summaries of his career: as writer of melodies which have become standards of American popular song; as creator of jazz classics of several decades; as composer of important longer works which strain against those boundaries which seek to hold apart jazz and classical music; as composer of sacred music which redefined an area of music which had long lain dormant and which he now brought into step with contemporary attitudes towards religious belief.

What cannot be disputed is that as a composer, Edward Kennedy 'Duke' Ellington, is assured of a place in the pantheon of twentieth-century music regardless of style, personal taste, or any other limiting definition.

'The wit, taste, intelligence and elegance that Duke Ellington brought to his music have made him in the eyes of millions of people both here and abroad, America's foremost composer. His memory will live for generations to come in the music with which he enriched his nation.'
President Richard M. Nixon—1969

ELLINGTON TRUMPETS

The Ellington brass sections always had an incredible amount of talent within their ranks and it was Duke's appreciative consideration for the individual which allowed each to flourish during his time in the band.

The line of growl and wa-wa trumpet stylists began with the bizarre Bubber Miley, the finest of them all, and afterwards no other trumpeter ever produced the same variety of tonal effects. Freddie 'Posey' Jenkins was a brilliant if erratic soloist, equally at home playing in a tightly muted or in a broad open style, and often displaying flashes of humour. Artie Whetsol's sensitivity was always evident and his distinctive, soulful tone added an exquisite delicacy to many early Ellington classics. Brought into the band to replace Miley, Cootie Williams did so splendidly using his plunger to telling effect and giving his role a sense of dramatic urgency and power while his open horn was impressively majestic.

In 1934, Rex Stewart's unique half-choked style of cornet playing gave further variety to the trumpet section. A talented individual, Stewart's intense and audacious playing enriched an already outstanding line-up of musical extroverts. Ray Nance, who replaced Cootie in 1940, purveyed some of the flamboyance and showmanship the section had lacked since Posey Jenkins left. Nance also touched his ballad playing with a sweetness somewhat akin to the early sounds of Whetsol although occasionally showing a sentimental streak Artie had always avoided. Perhaps more in keeping with the Whetsol role was Harold Baker whose delicately phrased solos offered quiet contrast to the stratospheric spiralling of Cat Anderson.

One of the most skilled of all Ellington trumpeters was Clark Terry whose impish sense of fun is always evident in his solos. One of the most underrated Ellington trumpet soloists was Willie Cook whose extremely effective and powerful playing enhanced many of the band's finest performances of the 1950s.

CHAPTER FOUR

ON THE ROAD

'AT A DIXIE ROADSIDE DINER'

'I made $7 a night and slept on the bus.'

Bill Berry

SCENARIO FOR A 'B' MOVIE:
A bus lurches along an unpaved road, dust clouds swirl from beneath its wheels. The dust almost obscures lettering painted along the side of the bus:
JOE CAYMAN'S SENSATIONAL BROADCASTING BAND.
A sign by the roadside announces that a bridge ahead has been washed out by flooding. The bus turns to follow diversion signs and its engine whines protestingly as it begins to climb a mountainside. Then another sound rises above the engine note: from inside the bus a band can be heard playing 'Darktown Strutters Ball'.
CUT TO:
Inside the bus the musicians playing the song are happy and oblivious to anything happening outside. All their attention is on their music. But then the bus grinds to a stop and tilts alarmingly to one side. After a moment the music falters.
CUT TO:
The musicians are helping push the bus out of a ditch. The spinning rear wheels throw up dirt which covers some of the men but all this does is bring a barrage of wisecracks from the unscathed members of the band.
CUT TO:
It is a few moments later and the bus is rattling on up the mountain track and as it goes we can see another sign across the back window:
TONITE AT LANSING DREAMLAND
JOE CAYMAN'S RHYTHM KINGS.
The music starts up again and continues to echo as the scene fades.

That, more or less, is how Hollywood has chosen to depict life on the road in the hey-day of the big bands: musicians jamming in the aisles, fun and high spirits abounding, love affairs blossoming between sidemen and girl singers. Outside there are broken axles, boiling radiators in summer, snowdrifts in winter. Bands arriving late for gigs, bookers running off with the money. Throughout these hazards and diversions, the band plays on.

Given Hollywood's propensity for telling it like it never was, it is tempting to regard this view as hopelessly inaccurate. Yet most elements of this romantic fiction really did feature in the lives of musicians during the big band years—an exception being those carefree jam sessions in the aisles.

When touring became a fact of life for dance bands in the 1920s the

Life on the road—1:
'Musicians are just people, they have problems like everyone else... Maybe a guy's the greatest musician of all time but if his wife's giving him some heat the last thing he wants to do is play music... Maybe the drummer's drunk, or the bass-player broke a string, or the piano's bad (which it usually is). Maybe some guys wife is in the hospital having a baby; or another's wife has run off with somebody else. But somehow you have to overcome your personal problems. You've got to project to the audience and what you project must not be your troubles.'

Nat Pierce

***

Learning on the road—1:
'The best part of working in the [Phil Harris]band was playing second saxophone to the best lead alto player in the business, Les Robinson. I had heard him on records he made with Artie Shaw, had met him a few years before, and now was sitting beside him listening to every marvel-lous sound he made. The fact is, most players make the alto sound like flies buzzing. I had never liked the sound of an alto sax until I heard Les Robinson...'

Drew Page

Johnny Hodges—artistry in alto

Learning on the road—2:
'I was playing with a cornball band, trying to sound like Wayne King, when Shaw happened to hear me. He told me I sounded so bad he just wanted to see if he could teach me to play right. He had to hire me to do that.'

Les Robinson

***

Learning on the road—3:
'When I was a teenager, there were always classified ads in *down beat* for what were called 'territory bands', which worked within a certain geographical area. They were professional, working, making-a-living bands, and they would run an ad like: "Need second trumpet player, second saxophone player, drummer needed, etc." In fact, they really needed hundreds of musicians because they had dozens of bands. I wrote them a letter when I was 17 and got my first job—no audition or anything—just come on and go to work. That was with Don Strickland. We played places like Strawberry Point, Iowa, and the band bus was always in trouble. Through the winter, the drinking water we carried stayed frozen. I made seven dollars a night and slept on the bus. I kept a room for two dollars a week in the town where we were headquartered. In those days you could get a good meal for 75 cents. All I wanted was to play my horn, so I figured life was great. I did that for a year although now it seems much longer. Those territory bands were fantastic training grounds, so valuable for kids like me who were coming up, or hoping to, because we were working with guys who had been in the name bands and for one reason or another hadn't made it. But they could teach us kids a lot.'

Bill Berry

bands mainly travelled by road. If they were lucky enough to be playing only major cities they might manage journeys by rail. Often, a band had to travel as much as 500 miles overnight to the next gig on the itinerary.

In his autobiography, Benny Goodman recalled how the band would play until the small hours. 'What happened after that depended on the distance to the next booking. If the jump was a fairly short one, say two hundred miles or so, we spent the night at a hotel in the same town, and made the trip the following day. If it was closer to three hundred or anything up to four hundred, we piled into the bus when the job was finished, and made the jump at night, when we could make better time, and allow for any incidents that might come up on the trip... There are more towns in America that I have only seen after dark than I care to think about.'

Doris Day has similar memories from her days with the bands of Bob Crosby and Les Brown, recalling her most vivid sensation as 'that of awakening in a hotel room and not being able to remember what city I was in.'

For most bands, faced with playing a string of one-nighters in towns and hamlets too remote to warrant a railroad, they had no choice but to travel by car. In his fascinating reminiscenses, trombonist Dicky Wells recalls working with a ten-piece band which somehow crowded into one Packard.

Some bands had it better: at the height of their popularity every member of the Coon-Sanders Nighthawks had his own matching and personalised automobile and drove in convoy from town to town.

Travelling by car had its dangers. Bandleader Hal Kemp died following a road accident. Joe Smith fell asleep at the wheel and the resulting crash killed his best friend, singer George 'Fat-Head' Thomas. Cab Calloway's superb tenor saxophonist Chu Berry also died in a car crash.

Not surprisingly, given the problems of travelling by car, most bands sought the ideal of their own bus but this could be an economic impossibility. If a band could afford a bus of its own, the vehicle quickly became a more important part of a musician's life than his home. For some it really was home, often for as much as sixteen hours a day. For many musicians, the bus was where they slept; a few extra dollars and there might be enough for a hotel room, provided there was enough time before the gig. Bill Berry recalled, 'We used to live on those sleeper buses and check into the Loyal Hotel in Omaha on Mondays just to take a bath.'

But even bus travel could be hazardous. In 1935 Earl Hines sideman Cecil Irwin died and other musicians were injured when the band bus crashed in Iowa.

One side effect of time spent on the bus was that it became a place for learning. The tyro musician might learn about music on the stand but on the bus he learned about life. Tommy Dorsey's singer, Frank Sinatra, observed that working in a band was like attending 'a sort of cross-country college'. Bill Berry concurred: 'The bus was two-thirds of our lives, often 16 hours a day. What I learned on the bus with Duke I couldn't have gotten anywhere else. With the other bands, all the guys were my own age. In Duke's band, everybody was old enough to be my father and were already on the bus when I was born. Those guys *really* knew what was going on.'

The reality of life on the road was a hard, bone-shaking, sleepless matter of consuming hundreds of miles before fulfilling the expectations of audience, and bandleader, with a performance of impeccable musicianship. In addition the musician had to be clean-shaven, well-groomed, and keep his pants pressed. It was far from easy. At the end of the 1930s superior motor coaches were designed but even they were well short of the luxurious vehicles of today. More than half a century ago road surfaces were not freeway smooth, breakdowns miles from anywhere were commonplace and complaining vehicles had to be cajoled over bad roads (Dicky Wells recalls helping push that Packard up a mountain).

As for the fleeting glimpses of lights in people's homes; they simply underlined what the musicians were missing. As Gene Krupa observed, 'I used to look at the lighted windows of the houses and yearn for the same kind of life.' Many felt the same way but covered their emotions with a mask of assumed indifference which fooled nobody. Gerry Mulligan told *down beat*'s Bill Coss about a 1960s trip through Pennsylvania: 'We were hungry and cold, completely miserable. As we rode along, we could look into the lighted windows of the houses along the roads, see the kids running up and down the stairs, the husbands reading the newspaper, the wife out in the kitchen. Somebody in the back of our bus ... saw our whole scene for what it was, "Look at the squares," he said.'

Getting the band back on the road after an overnight stop could be a problem. In her autobiography, Anita O'Day recalled one such experience when she joined Gene Krupa's band. 'When it came time for the bus to pull out, everybody started shouting, "Murph's not here", "Where's Murph?" "Anybody seen Murph?"—whatever. Norman Murphy, a trumpet player, was missing, so the driver shut off the motor and the band boy ran back to the hotel looking for the missing trumpet player. Half an hour later, he came trudging down Randolph Street carrying Murph over his shoulder, passed out drunk. The guys threw Murph on the back seat, piled the drums around him and we finally took off.'

Similar things happened with Duke Ellington's band, although one such tale, told by Bill Berry, has a hint of the apocryphal about it. 'One night in Cincinnati, Jimmy Campbell showed up and went out on the town with Paul Gonsalves. Next morning, we have to drive to Cleveland—that's, oh, 300 miles—and we can't find Paul Gonsalves. Like, *nowhere*. Everybody's on the bus, we've looked under the bed, we've called Jimmy Campbell, and we look and look, and we knew Paul didn't have a dime and couldn't have gotten there alone. And we had to leave, so we thought we'd take one more look. Bobby Boyd, the band boy, went up into the room, looked under the bed—he's gotta be there somewhere—opens the closet door and there's Paul. He had tried to hang up his coat, but fell asleep before getting out of it.'

Even when drinking was not an issue, getting the Ellington band mobilised was still a major logistical problem as Bill Berry remembers. 'If the bus was supposed to leave at 4 I would leave my house at 4, and I was *still* the first to arrive.'

The horrendous overnight hauls of 500 miles which bedevilled bands of the 1930s eventually disappeared. Matters improved, but not much, when an American Federation of Musicians ruling limited such hops to a mere 400 miles. The outbreak of World War II and the consequent rationing of fuel for cars and rubber for tyres brought in more stringent limits. But even 200 or 300 miles was a massive distance for bone-weary musicians after a late-night gig.

For many musicians the touring life was just a job; for others it was a vocation. Some loved it, others hated it; most loved and hated it

Life on the road—2:
'The dreariest, loneliest life you can imagine. Band wives didn't hang around the band. We went on opening night, or when there was something special, but most nights I waited at the apartment... I had to stay up to do the cooking. It would be three or four when we got to bed, and by the time we got up the following day, there wasn't much time until my husband had to go back to work.'

Doris Day

***

Life on the road—3:
'I stayed with Herb Alpert for two years during which time we rehearsed, performed or recorded every day with the exception of a few Sundays when we were in Los Angeles and not travelling. It was a very intense social, financial and musical experience for two years. I loved it, it was the most fun I'd had, and with a great bunch of musicians and a marvellous bunch of guys to travel with. We travelled all over the United States, and we went to Europe in 1975 and played several dates in England. That was the first time I've ever really had a chance to see any place outside the United States. It was a great thrill for me. The band was sensational. It had very little to do with the original Tijuana Brass except for the fact that we played the hit repertoire from the old days. Herb was interested in a more modern approach and he had hired some of the best solo and ensemble players I've ever had the pleasure to play with. It was a hot band and a slick, professional band. I got a solo spot on the show and played some of my Jelly Roll Morton stuff and ragtime piano.'

Dave Frishberg

***

'Travelling with a band on tour is the next thing I can think of to moving a circus.'

Benny Goodman

simultaneously. Some would not have traded it for anything else even if, from time to time, they found it necessary to take a well-deserved break from the ceaseless travel.

Contrary to popular opinion musicians are just ordinary guys, ordinary in all respects except their special talents and how they earn their living, even if most bands have their 'characters'. On the bus, musicians did what other ordinary men do in greater comfort; they spent their time reading, writing letters, talking, playing cards, telling jokes, arguing, fighting and, possibly most often, just sleeping. For a few, the band bus was the place, the only place, where they could catch up on their composing and arranging chores.

The band bus, this romantic image of the big band years, might have been home to musicians but it was also a prison from which their only escape between bandstands was at a roadside diner or to answer calls of nature. Even these natural breaks could be denied at the whim of the bandleader. Tommy Dorsey saw no reason to slow progress for the sake of those with weak bladders. To Tommy's credit, however, as his sidemen later recalled with gratitude, if they were ever near to his family home he would detour so that the band could enjoy a home-cooked meal provided by his mother.

For black bands the problems of life on the road were even more intolerable. For them, the 'greasy spoons', cheap cafés and roadside diners, did not always offer an opportunity to leave the bus. As many black bands found to their cost when touring in the Deep South, leaving the confines of the band bus also meant losing the security it offered against violent racism. When a black band arrived in a town they would immediately head for the black section looking for accommodation; if the town did not have a black section, they stayed on the bus.

Black musicians were rarely allowed to drink at the bars of clubs they played, and had to use rear entrances. Relations with audiences were also potentially fraught with problems. In the South and often elsewhere, too, audiences were customarily segregated. Where black bands played for black audiences an evening's work could be free of the dangers inherent in this split-level society. But it was by no means uncommon for a black band to play for whites. In such circumstances fraternisation between musicians and audience was at best frowned upon and at worst a signal for violence.

As bad as times could be for all-black bands, and some musicians tell grim tales of mutilation and even murder, there were special problems for solitary blacks touring with white bands. Roy Eldridge encountered blatant hostility during his time with Gene Krupa's band. On one occasion he was refused admission to the hall even though his name was on the marquee as the featured attraction.

There were similar problems for the occasional instances of a solitary white musician appearing with a black band. When trumpeter Toby Butler was a member of the Darlings of Rhythm in 1946 she was detained by the authorities in Milledgeville, Georgia, because the state laws prohibited her from associating with the other musicians in the band, all of whom were black. As late as 1961, Bill Berry, then the only white man in the Duke Ellington band, was the only one allowed off the bus at some Southern roadside diners and would have to 'buy 15 hamburgers and 15 Cokes to go'.

For all its problems, life on the road went on. Indeed, for many bands it was their only way of survival. There was also financial advantage in

Life on the road—4:
'In those days, when you did one-night stands with a black band, you were half beat from the beginning. You couldn't get decent accomodation, there was no place to eat, transportation was impossible and the money was nothing.'
Marshal Royal

***

Sideman—Joe Smith:
In New York from around 1923–4, trumpeter Joe Smith led the pit band for one of Sissle and Blake's revues before joining Fletcher Henderson's band where he remained for three years. Joe also worked with McKinney's Cotton Pickers but failing health repeatedly interupted his career. His distinctive style set him apart from his fellows and he was in great demand as an accompanist by the finest blues singers, among them Mamie Smith and Bessie Smith with whom he made several superb records. Joe died in New York's Belle Vue Hospital in 1937 at the age of 35.

Atlantic City ballrooms served as a backdrop for numerous publicity picture calls by the big bands including Fletcher Henderson in 1932 and Bob Crosby in 1935.

DANCELAND
FLETCHER
HENDERSON
DANCE
EVERY NITE
in this
BALLROOM
to
Americas
Greatest
Sylvia
SIDNEY
Herbert
MARSHALL
Accent on YOUTH

touring. Some one-night stands were worth as much as a week's work in a prestigious New York residency. Additionally, there were advantages in getting out into the sticks and letting the fans who bought the records see and hear the band in person and observe at source what went over best and what new trends were worth pursuing.

Inevitably, the pressures of touring proved too much for many musicians and they quit, or were fired for behaviour probably brought on by those pressures.

For all the potential financial loss of a residency at a club or hotel it had the luxury of a bed every night, although some hardened travellers found it difficult to sleep in a stationary environment. Trombonist Henry Coker remarked on this to Valerie Wilmer: 'I find now that I can sleep better on a bus sometimes than in a bed.'

When in residence, the musicians might be able to live at home (if they had one and if the residency happened to be in their home town). Often, they roomed at places which entered big band lore. The Whitby Hotel in New York City rented out apartments and became a haunt of musicians during the big band years. The Whitby even became the first home for some musicians. When Gene Krupa was first married he brought his new wife to the Whitby; some years later the Whitby was where Doris Day, then singing with Les Brown's band, set up home with her first husband, a big band sideman.

Home life, especially as transient as that offered by rooming houses, was essentially unstable. Not surprisingly, whether on the road or off, some musicians succumbed to temptations which offered an appearance of respite from the relentless grind. Among these temptations were drink, drugs and women, and even if they were not a major fact of the touring musician's life they certainly were the most spectacular of diversions and appealed to the sensationalist press.

While the use of both drugs and drink has been largely overstated in the story of popular music, drink has produced a substantial number of

Leapin' with Lionel:
Lionel Hampton's dislike of alternative means of travel surfaced when he was offered his first European tour. 'I won't fly,' he said. He was told that the band could travel by boat. 'I won't sail,' he said. Understandably puzzled, and not a little irritated by this, the promoter asked how Hampton proposed getting to Europe. 'You want me there,' Lionel said, 'you figure it out.'

New York movie theatres like the Strand and the Paramount on Broadway at West 43rd Street, where Benny Goodman had them jitterbugging in the aisles, regularly featured bands. Charlie Barnet was at the Strand in the mid-1940s while in 1938 and again in 1939 Chick Webb was at the Paramount with Ella Fitzgerald, and Gene Krupa's name lit up the skyline there in 1938.

victims. Even in the days of Prohibition liquor was easy to obtain. The links between jazz, crime, booze and prostitution have also been heavily overemphasised, but they existed and a musician could always find a bottle. Indeed, late at night, and especially for black bands in the South, it was easier to find a drink than it was to find a place where they were allowed to eat. Drinking after the gig and on the bus helped bring sleep; for some it became a habit that became a problem. Some spectacular drunks made headlines and helped elaborate the myths and legends.

Drug-taking among musicians in the 1920s and 1930s was far from widespread. With only few exceptions, users in those days were smoking marijuana and were not on hard drugs. Then, marijuana was used, like liquor, as a means of shrugging off discomfort and daily pressures rather than as a means of supposedly enhancing performances.

Women were a somewhat different hazard and for young men on the loose the attention of female fans could prove welcome; or it could make life even more uncomfortable than it already was. Some fans offered friendship, free drinks, maybe food and companionship, in return for nothing more than an autograph. Some offered their idols a rather more intimate form of worship.

For the women in the bands, touring had all the same problems as their male companions or counterparts plus some others which made their life even harder to endure. All-girl bands, like the International Sweethearts of Rhythm, Ina Ray Hutton and Her Melodears, and the Darlings of Rhythm, were faced with the same difficulties as men arising from having to travel by bus over hundreds of miles. Although men were expected to look smart and clean on the bandstand, and give a performance, women had to offer more. Given the prevailing attitude towards women in entertainment (which hasn't changed much since), their performance had to be better than good and they also had to look glamorous.

> 'Rather than have the uniform fit, the sideman should fit musically.'
> *Si Zentner*

In those early years it was rare to find a woman playing an instrument

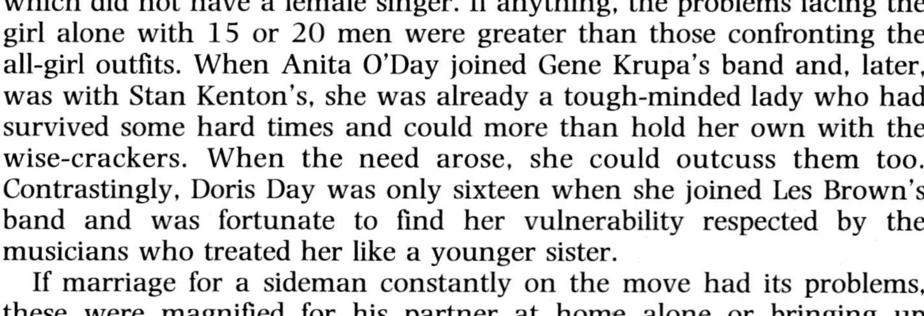

in an otherwise all-male band but it was equally rare to find a band which did not have a female singer. If anything, the problems facing the girl alone with 15 or 20 men were greater than those confronting the all-girl outfits. When Anita O'Day joined Gene Krupa's band and, later, was with Stan Kenton's, she was already a tough-minded lady who had survived some hard times and could more than hold her own with the wise-crackers. When the need arose, she could outcuss them too. Contrastingly, Doris Day was only sixteen when she joined Les Brown's band and was fortunate to find her vulnerability respected by the musicians who treated her like a younger sister.

If marriage for a sideman constantly on the move had its problems, these were magnified for his partner at home alone or bringing up children perhaps thousands of miles away. These marriages required a considerable measure of tolerance, understanding and strength on both sides, particularly from the wife who may have faced less temptations but had more day-to-day problems to overcome.

Conversely, as Marshal Royal recalled to Stanley Dance, marriages could cause problems if the wife did not understand the peculiar lifestyle of a musician. 'A lot of guys I worked with in the early years who were very good musicians, were told by their wives: "I want you at home. If you're going to be a married man, you've got to be at home with me." Well, the only reason the girl was attracted to the musician in the first place was probably because he was sitting up there on the bandstand playing music.'

Some bandleaders allowed wives to travel with them but this was often a source of disharmony within a band. It was not unknown for wives to provoke their spouses into demanding more time in the solo spotlight, pay increases, or to seek recompense for real or imagined slights.

Such hassles were an unwarranted additional burden for bandleaders and, wisely, most prohibited wives. The motive for such bans was neither trivial nor misplaced. Loyalty and a measure of comradeship could be of signal importance for a band's survival, to say nothing of the quality of its music.

Loyalties within bands could be complex affairs. While some sidemen were loyal only to a close friend, others developed a profound measure of group loyalty which cannot have done other than enhance the band's performances. And for every leader, like Benny Goodman or Glenn Miller, who earned the hostility of his men there were others who earned respect, admiration and a remarkable level of affection. It is rare to find a sideman with unkind words for Woody Herman, Harry James or Les Brown, and even the fiery-tempered Tommy Dorsey could be generous to a sideman going through hard times.

Some bands became battle-grounds. The ranks of the Boyd Raeburn band in 1944 were burdened with more wild men than most bands. Two cliques developed within the band and each noisily heckled the other during performances. Not surprisingly, the band suffered and when they reached New York Raeburn fired all but a few key men and started over.

Such animosity was unusual and most sidemen found warmth and companionship within a band. Prolonged proximity always causes some awkward moments but a great number of lasting relationships were formed. Some were born of similar musical ideas, others from shared pleasures and habits, many lasted a lifetime. As Eddie Miller confided to

'The first trumpet player and the drummer control the band. The man out front wielding the stick, you can't hear that... The trumpet player and the drummer can make all the difference in the world. You can kill them or make it good.'

Bobby Rosengarden

***

Life on the road—5:
'We'd be on a bus trip and stop for something to eat and Basie would tell us, "All right, men, 45 minutes". We'd pile out of the bus and everybody would eat. With about five minutes left Freddie [Green]would saunter in, very cool, and check out the menu. We'd always wait for him... after all, even Basie admitted the band wouldn't sound too good without Freddie.'

Buddy Tate

***

Learning on the road—4:
Hired by Claude Thornhill for a date at Glen Island Casino, John Graas considered: 'That was my first education in jazz, and what a teacher I had—Conrad Gozzo. I played an octave apart from him so I just followed his lead.'

***

Life on the road—6:
'One-nighters were very rough. Many times there were halls with no windows and inside there were thousands of people shouting and fighting. And it was very rough when you had to go over mountains to make another town and you'd skid on ice. Man, there were some long hauls between states... Many times we'd get into town, check into a hotel, and we'd actually hear them planning how they were going to start fights and shootings where we were going to play that night.'

Gene Sedric

Max Jones, his seven years with the Bob Crosby band 'were the happiest I ever had... Matty [Matlock]and I are real buddies. He was in the Ben Pollack band when I joined, back in 1930, and we've been close ever since.' Milt Hinton, talking to Steve Voce, concurred with this view of band life. 'All of us from the [Cab]Calloway band, in mass, we're like a family. This band hasn't been together in many years, but we're still looking out for each other... Our love for one another ... doesn't change.'

These companionships also accounted for how some musicians changed bands. A sideman might well move for no reason other than an old friend was in another band and had recommended him to the leader.

In later years, life on the road became a very different affair to how it had been in the 1930s. Travelling became much simpler. Bands took to the air but even then there were problems. An army aircraft carrying six members of the Boyd Raeburn band in 1944 developed landing gear trouble and had to circle for three hours before attempting a successful landing. An earlier flight by Benny Goodman's band, when such means of travel was new and frightening, had a happy outcome when Lionel Hampton's nervous whistling of a little tune attracted Benny's attention. 'What is that?' Benny asked. 'I don't know,' Lionel told him. Benny suggested he should work on it; Lionel did, and the resulting composition became his theme tune, 'Flyin' Home'.

Later still, European tours and the round of festivals changed the face of big band travel. A band, in some cases assembled especially for the tour, would play several days at a time in one location with the hops between festivals or major concert venues in different countries being

Brothers in brass. The Candoli brothers, Conte (L) and Pete (R) have graced many fine orchestras including those of Stan Kenton and Woody Herman. (Photo: C & P Candoli).

'It hasn't been easy for me, as a jazz player, to devote 50 years of my life to playing with society bands, especially since I'm only 28...'
Whitey Mitchell

'I slept more hours in my bus seat than I did in a bed.'
Doris Day

***

'The bands were awful, but I was fortunate to have been involved.'
Bill Berry

***

"Pittsburgh, as a music town, stinks.'
Bunny Berigan

made by air. On occasions when the journey was within the same country the old days of bus travel would be revived but now with the undreamed of luxury of hot food and drinks prepared on the coach, videos, reclining seats or even beds and, luxury of all luxuries, and one for which a Tommy Dorsey sideman of old would have sold his soul, on-board lavatories.

The differences in means and ease of travel was not necessarily all for the good. Basie band drummer Jo Jones recalled his 50 years in show business to Graham Colombé, explaining how few latterday musicians, especially drummers, had the benefit of experience he had enjoyed. 'They never saw the people, they weren't on the circuses and carnivals, they didn't hit the forty-eight states—villages and hamlets, you know. After World War II it got so they could get in an aeroplane and they never see nothing. I say, "Where are you guys going?" They say, "California". They get on a plane. "What did you see?" They didn't see nothing. "It sure was a rough trip—five hours and five minutes". That's a rough trip! It used to take us days to get to California, and from Chicago to New York with Basie's band. We were playing one-nighters and we'd puddle-jump. They didn't have those beautiful highways then and the Clipper service didn't come in until 1939.'

Yet for all the real or imagined benefits of experience gained this way and the sometimes superficial excitement of those early years, and however much the outsider might view the scene through Hollywood-tinted glasses, there can be little doubt that life on the road was mighty tough.

THE ARRANGER'S TOUCH—2

The Jean Goldkette band's arrangement of 'My Pretty Girl' is an example of collective arranging. Adapting it from a stock chart, Bill Challis and some of the band's musicians re-worked the arrangement providing plenty of solo space for Danny Polo, clarinet, and Joe Venuti, violin. Bix Beiderbecke's cornet chorus is adapted into a three trumpet chorus with the ending worked out by Jimmy Dorsey, and with Steve Brown's solid New Orleans bass all the time propelling the group along.

Another early example of collective arranging was recalled by Paul Mertz when he spoke of an incident when alto saxophonist Jimmy Dorsey took a liking for a Frankie Trumbauer solo on the Benson Orchestra's recording of 'I'll Never Miss the Sunshine'. Dorsey learned Trumbauer's solo chorus and played it with the Goldkette band. His section partner, Don Murray, played along in harmony and later wrote a third part for Doc Ryker. Eventually, the Trumbauer solo formed a three part harmony for the Goldkette saxophone section.

After Don Redman left the Fletcher Henderson band his former boss was obliged to resume the role of arranger and in 1935 Henderson's own arrangements were a major factor in the success of the Benny Goodman band. Goodman's success was sustained with the subtle and swinging arrangements of Edgar Sampson and the stomping 'killer diller' writing of Jimmy Mundy. Another Goodman arranger, Eddie Sauter, gave some indication of what the working life of a Goodman arranger was like during those hectic days. 'There never was an arranging staff as such, no main arranger. Benny needed—as he would say—notes to play. The band's appetite was voracious, keeping up with seven or eight new pop tunes that seemed to surface each week. Fletcher didn't like to do them—I don't know why. Jimmy Mundy and Edgar Sampson, who had been doing some, no longer did and I was too young to question them about it. I wanted to study composition and needed a constant stipend, which Benny supplied me with. When I brought in 'Clarinet A La King', Benny used it straightaway. He always said if band numbers don't play right away, they're no good! Mind you, he always thought my scores tended to be too classical—like in 'Benny Rides Again', there's some 'Caucasian Sketches', a little 'Sing, Sing, Sing' and 'Clarinet A La King', together with some country Brahms and very bad Vaughan Williams!'

CHAPTER FIVE

SWING IN: BENNY GOODMAN

'STEPPIN' INTO SWING SOCIETY'

'For all that Benny did for music, for jazz, for musicians, and for me, I, for one, doff my cap in a salute of sincere appreciation.'
Gene Krupa

A 1938 issue of *Life* magazine included a long article on a current musical phenomenon, swing music, which left the writers somewhat out of their depth. Elsewhere in this issue were the customary selection of articles on a wide range of subjects. Among the picture essays, for which the magazine was justly famed, is a light-hearted one about people using shooting sticks, while other pieces are rather more sober, covering such topics as the refugee problem in Czechoslovakia, the efforts of Mao Tse-tung and his army in their struggle against the Japanese and a new production of Sinclair Lewis's *It Can't Happen Here*. There were also features on fashion, sports, health, and one about the latest Andy Hardy movie starring Mickey Rooney and Judy Garland.

The fact that *Life* couldn't quite get to grips with swing is not very surprising; better qualified people, writers, fans, and even the musicians themselves, didn't find it an easy subject to define.

The swing era, that imprecise number of years from the mid-1930s to the late 1940s, is one of the most misunderstood periods in the history of popular music—overpraised by some, underrated by others.

Most of the difficulties of perception lie in the tendency to divide the music and the bands that played it into broad categories: white and black, 'hot' and 'sweet'.

To some extent the first of these divisions can be justified. Although some black bands enjoyed great success, none achieved the same measure as that which attended Benny Goodman and other white bandleaders. Only a handful of top-flight black bands were able to secure engagements at the more prestigious venues. On radio, sponsorship was decidedly rare. Sponsors were concerned that their products were not associated in the public mind with the black race. There was also a marked difference in the style of the black bands which were much more jazz-oriented.

As a result, this black-white division is largely justified; the swing era was, substantially, a phenomenon enjoyed by white bands playing to white audiences.

The second division, into hot and sweet playing styles, does not stand up so well. All the white big bands of the swing era maintained a proportion of sweet music in their programming. It was essential to include a degree of sweet corn to temper the spice of 'killer-diller' swing.

There were many dance bands during the swing era and later years

'I'm probably the best guy to tell about those swing days because I'm probably the only one who was ever sober.'
Johnny Guarnieri

***

That old gang of Benny's:
'When we started the band, the only purpose we had was to play music, and Gene Krupa, Teddy, Hampton, Jess, Hymie, and the rest, they had a purpose. It was their life, it was important to them.'
Benny Goodman

***

The individual Bud Freeman:
'The big bands *needed* individualists—they *needed* stars... Certainly, leaders might have had trouble with some of us, but we believed what we were doing, we grew up with jazz, felt strongly about our music, and each of us developed in his own way, becoming both distinct individuals and *soloists*. We weren't just another sideman!'

***

Benny's blues:
'... something happens when you find out that what you're doing is no longer music—that it's become entertainment. It's a subtle thing and affects what you're playing. Your whole attitude changes.'
Benny Goodman

(L to R, from top) Don Cowan, Victor Halpric, Jack Blanchette, Dick Kissinger, Don Henniman, Leo Murphy, Sterling 'Red' Ballard, Eddie Stone, Johnny Carlson, James Basil Dupre, Harold Moeller, Isham Jones, James 'Jiggs' Noble, Wally Lageson.

CHICAGO AMUSEMENT SERVICE CORPORATION
Presents
ISHAM JONES
and his Brunswick Recording Orchestra

Nightmare:
'The bigger our success, the more dissatisfaction there seemed to be in the band... Instead of a bunch of guys that were happy to be struggling towards a common objective, we became a bunch of cliques, and I gradually became estranged from the men.'

Artie Shaw

***

Paying for the piano:
According to popular legend, three of Isham Jones's best-known songs were written in one night, his 30th birthday. Following the gift of a piano from his wife, Jones was so worried at having received such an expensive gift that he sat down to write something which would help pay for it. The three songs, any one of which would have paid for a hundred pianos, were 'It Had to Be You', 'The One I Love Belongs to Somebody Else' and 'Spain'.

which qualify for the unfortunately perjorative term, 'sweet'; but there were many which played with verve and which swung as well as any of the hotter bands. Conversely, Charlie Barnet, Goodman, Woody Herman, Artie Shaw, and others, had numerous ballads and sweetly sentimental songs in their books. They didn't play 'Cherokee', 'Roll 'Em', 'Apple Honey' and 'The Carioca' all the time.

A glance through the titles recorded by such bands reveals at least as many soft-centred songs as there were hardcore flagwavers. In short, the hot bands did play sweet and the sweet bands sometimes played hot.

Although artificial, this division into hot and sweet bands cannot be entirely ignored. Clearly there is a world of difference between the music

Artie Shaw at New York's Paramount Theatre in 1939. (L to R) Georgie Auld, Hank Freeman, Harry Rodgers, Les Robinson, Les Jenkins, Chuck Peterson, Bernie Privin, Tony Pastor, George Arus, Johnny Best, Shaw, Buddy Rich.

of Sammy Kaye and that of Woody Herman. Artie Shaw commented upon this problem in a magazine published in 1939 by the Tommy Dorsey organisation:

> The two outstanding types of swing that are now being played often merit the ridicule and somewhat harsh criticism directed from more erudite circles. The first type of swing is that which attempts to blast off the roof... Offensive to most ears and definitely of the musically punch-drunk variety, it is an out-and-out menace. The second classification bears the alliterative titles of 'smooth' or 'sophisticated' swing. For sheer monotony I don't believe this type of music can be surpassed... Instrumentalists can almost doze off on the bandstand and it would have no effect on their playing. Swing—and I mean real swing—is an idiom designed to make songs more listenable and more danceable than they are in their original form. It is, in sum, the creation and sustenance of a mood. In it, there is blasting, purring, subtlety, obviousness—all in their proper places naturally.

The bands for which the term 'sweet' is a not entirely unreasonable soubriquet had certain things in common. Often they played with a rich and full sound. While the tendency to batten down the hatches and avoid all suggestions of aggression was a recipe for blandness, in a curious way some bands found that this approach gave them a measure of musical swing that some of their hotter fellows lacked. The fact that the sweeter sounding bands chose to adopt a musical style which did not call for featured jazz soloists does not mean that they also lacked a distinctive sound. Thanks to the skills of their arrangers, a surprisingly high number achieved a recognisable sound and style.

Bandstand broadside—1:
[Benny Goodman]doesn't know how to explain what he wants. He acts dissatisfied, yet can't put into words what he'd like to hear. He just knows that whatever they *are* doing—he *doesn't* want that.'
Teddy Wilson

Doin' the new low down:
'All Artie [Shaw]ever wanted was for you to tell him how good he was, or more, how much better he was than Benny [Goodman].He lived to cut Benny and Benny lived to cut him. But they were both great musicians. Each was great in his own style.'
Johnny Guarnieri

***

Elliot Lawrence and his Orchestra:
In July 1946 the new Elliot Lawrence band attracted a great deal of attention thanks to an engagement at New York's Hotel Pennsylvania and the extensive airtime this gig gave it. Musicianly and showmanly though it was, the band lacked a distinctive style but press and public alike felt that this 21-year old newcomer was here to stay. Ten years later, when the big band business was at a low ebb, Lawrence formed a band for a set of recordings using arrangements by Gerry Mulligan, Johnny Mandel and Tiny Kahn. Featuring such top-class musicians as Ernie Royal, Eddie Bert, Urbie Green, Al Cohn and Zoot Sims, the dynamic style of the new band blew hope into mid-1950s hearts that the end of big band music was not yet in sight.

The Casa Loma Orchestra was an interesting and largely overlooked pathfinder for the bands of the swing era. They could blow up discreet storms in a manner which would have been beyond the powerhouse tactics of, say, the Gene Krupa band a decade later; although, needless to add, Krupa's crew could do things the Casa Lomans could barely imagine.

There were many other early white bands which helped shape the sound and style of the swing era. Few of them played jazz; most settled for a more orthodox, but new, musical style drawing heavily from the concepts which had contributed towards the success of Jean Goldkette and Paul Whiteman. Few could approach the Whiteman flash and spectacle and settled instead for a refined if often unimaginative form of music making which made its priority the needs of the average dance hall customer: correct tempo, and not so loud the dancers couldn't talk to one another. Out of this kind of band emerged a style which the musicians themselves derisively tagged 'Mickey Mouse music'. For all the derision, mickey bands could often find work more readily than the bands some musicians longed to be in.

While the mickey bands proliferated, a few hardy souls bravely stuck out for playing music a little closer to their sidemen's hearts.

The California Ramblers, like the Coon-Sanders Nighthawks, are indelibly associated with the Jazz Age. Originally made up mostly of college graduates, the Ramblers were a popular dance band of the 1920s. The band opened at Rector's in New York at the instigation of promoter Ed Kirkeby (who later became Fats Waller's manager) and despite a constantly shifting personnel, maintained a personable identity. At one time or another the band had a number of good jazzmen (including Adrian Rollini and the Dorsey brothers) in its ranks which gave it a slightly hotter sound than many of its rivals. Musically, the Ramblers were very much of the 1920s but offered that period's dance music at its best. Indeed, the band's highly professional musicianship rivalled the leading bands of the day. Eventually, the Ramblers' commercial appeal faded and the musicians moved on to other bands.

Ben Pollack's band began as a strongly jazz-oriented outfit. From its California origins in 1925 the band moved to Chicago (the home town of its leader and of Benny Goodman, a 16-year-old clarinet player Pollack had hired) where it attracted much favourable comment and a Victor recording contract. Late in 1927 drummer Pollack brought the band to New York for an extended engagement at the Park Central Hotel. Alongside the young Benny Goodman in the band during this period were Chicagoan cornetist Jimmy McPartland, trombonists Glenn Miller and Jack Teagarden, and saxophonist Gil Rodin. Pollack maintained a jazz-oriented policy until the mid-1930s when he folded the band. At Rodin's instigation, the jazz players stayed together, forming a new cooperative band. They named themselves after the personable young singer they hired to front the band, Bob Crosby. Pollack's own new band was much more commercially oriented although he still hired jazz players, including future bandleaders Harry James and Freddy Slack.

An outstanding dance band of the 1920s which continued into the next decade with greater success was that led by Isham Jones. Despite a sombre personality, Jones was a first-rate musician and set the highest standards for himself whether playing piano, saxophones, bass, arranging or composing. He saw to it that his sidemen also maintained similar standards. Jones built a band which provided dance music of the highest

Lew Stone and his Orchestra, perhaps the most jazz-orientated of the British dance bands of the 1930s. (L to R) Ernest Ritte, Nat Gonella, Albert Harris, Jim Easton, Stone, Monia Liter, Harry Berly, Tiny Winters, Joe Ferrie, Joe Crossman, Lew Davis, Alfie Noakes.

quality with faultless musicianship. He played an engagement in London in 1924 and by 1928 was one of the foremost American dance bands.

In 1930 Jones recorded Hoagy Carmichael's 'Stardust' which until then had not generally been treated as a ballad. Jones's version changed popular perceptions of the tune and was hugely successful both as a record for Jones and as a future pointer to Carmichael's enormous success as a songwriter. In the years immediately preceding the swing era Jones continued to enhance his already substantial reputation as a musician of taste and as the leader of a band of considerable merit. He was also a songwriter of great ability.

The band Jones led in the 1930s was superb, being described as 'one of the finest all-round dance bands in the history of the music'. Using his own arrangements and those of Gordon Jenkins and Victor Young, Jones built an extensive library of melodic numbers. Until the freewheeling sounds of the Page-Moten-Basie bands emerged from Kansas City in the mid to late 1930s, Isham Jones had one of the most rhythmically relaxed bands in America. Their rich and powerful ensemble sound was achieved in part by having Saxie Mansfield's tenor saxophone scored an octave below Johnny Carlson's strong trumpet lead. This resulted in what George T. Simon called 'a gutsier, more masculine version of the Glenn Miller ensemble sound...' Thanks to its sound, and the quality of its arrangements and sheer musicality, the Isham Jones band was admired not only

The King swings on—Benny Goodman in the 1950s

by audiences but also by many rival bands. In 1936, as the big band business leaped into the swing era, Jones perversely called it a day.

The end of the Isham Jones band prompted some of its jazz-minded members to form their own band. Thus began Woody Herman and 'the Band That Plays the Blues'. It is sad that today Isham Jones is remembered, if he is remembered at all, as a recondite footnote to Woody Herman's story when, musically, there was little to connect the two. The Isham Jones band was an excellent aggregation of musicianly musicians and by any standards must be regarded as one of America's outstanding dance bands.

By the mid-1930s the strand of big band music the Isham Jones band represented was about to be overwhelmed in the public mind by the sounds of swing. Yet, musical matters were only one of the factors which shaped the swing era.

The ending of Prohibition in 1933 was followed by the mushroom growth of clubs, hotels and other venues which offered live music to their customers. More and more bands were needed, but even so, many more musicians sought work with the bands than could ever hope to be employed. The reason was simple: the nation was in the grip of the Great Depression.

With unemployment rife the areas in which men outnumbered jobs included the entertainment industry. Club owners, hotel management and promoters of all kinds demanded size and spectacle in order that they could attract customers away from the spiralling number of alternative venues. The fact that they did not have to pay more for a bigger, more spectacular-looking show was a great incentive.

A significant factor in the changes which came over big band music lay in their new alliance with the worlds of advertising campaigns, sponsorship and big business. Commercial attitudes dictated many things. Bands were packaged and their leaders groomed for a kind of demi-stardom. Soon the norm was a group of smartly uniformed musicians sitting behind scrolled and initialled music stands and fronted by an immaculately dressed figure in a white tuxedo. A manufacturer of hair tonic, automobiles or hand lotions would not countenance anything less. As a result of such pressures the music was 'sanitised' often to the point of blandness. When a band was broadcasting, either from a studio or, more often, by a remote line from a dance hall, the music played during airtime was a reflection of what the sponsor wanted.

The concentration upon white bands allowed the press an opportunity to write about jazz without writing about blacks and largely without the patronising putdowns that had marked most 1920s newspaper and magazine accounts. Unfortunately, apart from a tiny handful of specialist critics writing in a few journals, the Fourth Estate was singularly ill-equipped and utterly unprepared to handle the swing era.

The article in the 8 August 1938 issue of *Life* magazine was an illustrated piece on the subject of swing music which by this date was attracting so much interest and excitement that it could no longer be ignored by the popular press.

> It was the fashion two years ago, and a year ago, and six months ago to say that the form of jazz called 'Swing' was on the way out. It is still the fashion to say that Swing is on the way out. Maybe so—but the fact is that, as of August 1938, Swing is the most popular kind of popular music.

The bands within the bands: Paradoxically, a lasting musical memory of the big band years is the sound of small groups—the bands within the bands. The gently swinging music of the Benny Goodman Trio—Benny, Teddy Wilson and Gene Krupa—was first heard on record in 1935. The following year Lionel Hampton was added and his extrovert personality dramatised the mood of the small group's music. Popular though the BG Trio and Quartet were, it was the Benny Goodman Sextet which made the most significant of Benny's many contributions to jazz. Star of the Sextet was Charlie Christian whose long, fluent electric guitar lines brought out the best in Lionel and inspired Benny to performances he seldom bettered.

The popularity of the Goodman small groups prompted other leaders to form their own versions. The Dorsey brothers inclined towards Dixieland; Tommy had his Clambake Seven, a light-hearted band which featured Pee Wee Erwin and Johnny Mince. Brother Jimmy's small band, the Dorseylanders, was also a fun band but neither was ever a serious contender for the crowns worn by the classy Goodman groups. ▶

SPRING
ALIN
WINS
"IT'S ONLY
THE BEGINNING
SAM

So far, not too bad but the article then tries to define swing and attempts a potted history. What emerges is an inaccurate survey of the story of jazz in which the word 'jazz' is replaced by the word 'Swing'. White musicians are extolled while their black counterparts are all but ignored. Thus Louis Armstrong gets a 21-word sentence by way of an introduction to 500 words on Bix Beiderbecke.

Other passages in the article detail the behaviour of jitterbugs who are, according to *Life*, 'the extreme swing addicts who get so excited by its music that they cannot stand or be still while it is being played. They must prance around in wild exhibitionist dances, or yell and scream loudly. In their quieter moments, they discuss Swing with weird words like *jive, gut-bucket, dog-house, push-pipe, agony-pipe*.'

Agony-pipe?

There is a parallel between the manner in which *Life* magazine describes this world it clearly finds so alien and how the popular press in Britain greeted the arrival in 1956 of Bill Haley and His Comets, or the reaction a few years later when the Beatles first came to town. Both groups of journalists exhibit patronisingly amused tolerance coupled with an almost complete lack of understanding.

Life was on slightly stronger ground when it got down to figures. Just as the cost to the public of someone's suicide was faithfully recorded elsewhere in this issue so too did *Life* announce the earnings of Benny Goodman: 'He and his band earn $400,000 a year, a third of which goes to Benny, another third to his players.'

When set against the earning capacity of even the best jazz musicians of the day these figures are staggering. Like so many of the pop-stars of later years, few bandleaders were equipped to handle the sudden riches which came their way and there were always massive expenses, advisers and hangers-on, and the tax man to accommodate.

Benny Goodman was one of the fortunate exceptions. He made millions, and he kept millions. His fame lasted and in time he became one of a handful of names instantly recognised outside the world of jazz. Although Goodman might not rank today in the general public's consciousness as highly as such other jazz world figures as Louis Armstrong or Ella Fitzgerald, or such other swing era stars as Glenn Miller, his name still evokes an era that is for many fans the highest point of the big band years.

▶ Also Dixie flavoured, and much more successful than the Dorseys, were Bob Crosby's Bob Cats. The size and personnel of the Bob Cats varied but in their peak years and on their best records they featured Yank Lawson's trumpet, Warren Smith, trombone, Matty Matlock, clarinet, Eddie Miller, tenor, and the rhythm section of Bob Zurke, Nappy Lamare, Bob Haggart and Ray Bauduc whose snappy, two-beat drumming was as distinctive in the Bob Cats as it was in the full band.

Not surprisingly, Benny Goodman's arch-rival, Artie Shaw, came up with a band within his band which rivalled Benny's with its elegance. The musical and popular success of Artie's Gramercy Five was helped in no small part by Johnny Guarnieri's twinkling harpsichord which provided an unusual and highly appropriate backcloth for the leader's decorative clarinet and Billy Butterfield's eloquent trumpet.

Woody Herman's Four Chips were followed by his Woodchoppers, a band which enjoyed a number of successful recordings. This band, which featured Sonny Berman, Bill Harris, Flip Phillips and Red Norvo, had a whole string of record successes.

The small groups, formed most often rather casually to give jazz-minded soloists a chance to play more than their occasional solo spots, became and have remained a much loved facet of the big band years.

THE KING OF SWING

Benny Goodman had gained experience at leading big bands thanks to his work as contractor for, among others, Ben Selvin, a highly popular bandleader who made uncountable numbers of dance music records during the 1920s and early 1930s.

Encouraged by the wealthy entrepreneur and jazz enthusiast John Hammond, Benny formed his own band in the early 1930s and by 1934 had a competent if unexciting group which was enhanced by the hiring of some young and upcoming jazz talents, notably trumpeter Bunny Berigan and drummer Gene Krupa.

Although still only 25, Benny was a serious, faintly scholarly-looking individual whose demeanour fell well short of the flamboyance exuded by that earlier so-called King of popular music, Paul Whiteman. Benny's talents lay elsewhere than in putting on a show-biz front. He was a dedicated, hard-working musician who had long been his family's principal bread-winner. With hard times barely out of sight around the

Above: Harry James—survivor
Below: Ex-Ellingtonian – Willie Cook. (*Courtesy: Bob Charlesworth*)

last corner Benny saw no reason to take life lightheartedly. By the time he was a runaway success, his dourness had become habitual, occasionally alleviated by a mile-wide streak of eccentricity.

With his new and enhanced band Benny won a spot on a radio show sponsored by the National Biscuit Company. The show, 'Let's Dance', was broadcast nationwide from New York between 1 December 1934 and 25 May 1935 and featured three bands playing contrasting styles of dance music: 'sweet', Latin American, and 'hot'. Benny's was the hot band.

After the 'Let's Dance' show Benny and the band went on tour, only to discover that they were not what the mid-West public wanted. The band suffered various indignities as irate dance hall proprietors objected to their style of playing. On the west coast, first in San Francisco, then in Los Angeles, things suddenly looked up. The time zoning of the North American continent meant that the 'Let's Dance' programme had been heard at a time of night when the teenage audience was at home listening to their radios. Primed by this, and fuelled by the efforts of Al Jarvis, a local disc-jockey who had been playing Goodman records for weeks prior to the band's appearance on the Coast, an audience of enthusiasts was ready and waiting.

Dejected by their reception elsewhere on the tour, and with their spirits flagging, the band reckoned they were at the end of the road. On opening night at the Palomar Ballroom, Pasadena, Benny decided that if this really was the end of his band then they would go out in style, playing the kind of music they wanted to play in the way they wanted to play it.

It turned out to be exactly what the fans wanted too. They erupted in roaring enthusiasm, the band was a smash-hit, and their two-week engagement at the Palomar was extended for several months before the band began a triumphal return passage across the continent.

The date of the opening night of the Palomar engagement was 21 August 1935 and although the kind of music played that night had been played earlier, elsewhere, by other bands, and sometimes to better effect, this date has become, in tradition if not in fact, the beginning of the swing era.

On the return journey from California, an engagement at the Congress Hotel, Chicago, was renewed for months on end before the band finally made it back to New York City. Here, they had a gig at the Hotel Pennsylvania, doubling at the Paramount Theatre where they gave Claudette Colbert's latest movie some serious competition.

The kind of music offered by Benny Goodman's band that night at the Palomar and at the Congress and the Paramount, and which so attracted the fans, was from the hotter end of the band's book and included many arrangements by Fletcher Henderson which he had used for his own vibrant band a few years earlier.

In the hands of Benny Goodman's musicians Fletcher Henderson's arrangements may not have sounded as exciting as the Henderson band but Benny's musicians, collectively and individually, found them to be a marvellous springboard which helped many of them achieve enormous fame and, comparatively, great riches. Benny, for one, never failed to acknowledge the debt he owed Fletcher Henderson and continued to employ the arranger and in later years hired him as a piano player in his small groups.

Jack Teagarden And Bunny Berigan

The poised, unhurried trombone of Jack Teagarden brought style and quality to every ensemble he ever graced. Yet this greatest of all trombone talents never succeeded with his own band.

Another great talent, trumpet soloist supreme, Bunny Berigan, was able to lift the quality of performance of any band with which he was involved but when it came to leading a band of his own, Bunny was another failure. However glorious his playing might have been on 'I Can't Get Started', the tune's title all too accurately reflected his bandleading career.

Both Teagarden and Berigan preferred to simply blow their horns, take a belt or two with the boys, and forget the day-to-day problems of running a band.

Even the weather was against Bunny. The band was booked into the prestigious Ritz Carlton Roof in Boston in 1938 but a hurricane blew the bandstand off the roof of the hotel and the job was cancelled. That finished Berigan's bandleading ambitions, even if it took a hurricane to do it.

After a short but magnificent career as a trumpet player of great distinction, Berigan succumbed to chronic alcoholism. Although a big drinker, Teagarden had a stronger constitution and was able to enjoy an extended career, but not as a big band leader.

For all their failure as big bandleaders, nothing can ever detract from the brilliance of Bunny Berigan and Jack Teagarden as solo performers and few musicians in jazz can equal the wealth of marvellous music they left behind on records, and in the hearts and memories of their many fans.

The BG 3 on the set of the 1937 movie, *Hollywood Hotel*. Teddy Wilson, Benny, Gene Krupa.

Early records by the Goodman band display a raw urgency with good solos. The record sessions which produced the titles played by the LA deejay were made between April and July 1935 and include a splendid 'King Porter Stomp' featuring Bunny Berigan's searing trumpet and powerhouse drumming from Gene Krupa behind soloist and ensemble. This was a Fletcher Henderson arrangement, as were 'Blue Skies' and 'Sometimes I'm Happy', while 'Dear Old Southland' came from Fletcher's brother Horace.

During the following months the band recorded numerous flagwavers, among them Jimmy Mundy's 'killer-diller' arrangement of 'Bugle Call Rag', Edgar Sampson's smoothly swinging 'Stompin' At the Savoy' and Spud Murphy's 'Get Happy' amidst a string of Henderson swingers. But throughout these recording sessions runs a steady stream of lyrical ballads all of which, like the uptempo numbers, feature Benny Goodman himself.

So many great names of the swing era are associated with Benny Goodman that it is easy to lose sight of the fact that the principal soloist with the band was Benny himself.

A stern and humourless taskmaster, Benny wanted perfection from himself and from the men in his band. From himself he got that perfection he craved, from others it was a permanent problem for him. His attitude towards his sidemen resulted in a rapid turnover of musicians, unlike some bands which stayed together and built an appropriately homogeneous sound.

Musicians on Goodman:
'Had Benny thrown in the towel before his first great triumphs at the Palomar in Los Angeles and the Congress in Chicago, there's little doubt [that]many of us who have enjoyed success, prominence, and considerable financial reward since the late 1930s would have never attained those heights.'
Gene Krupa

Relaxing during a 1941 Columbia recording session, Benny Goodman laughs at something Cootie Williams has said. They are surrounded by several well known names in jazz and big band music including Helen Forrest, Charlie Christian (behind Benny), Johnny Guarnieri (facing Benny), Billy Butterfield (peering around Cootie), Lou McGarity.

Among the trumpet stars who worked at one time or another with Benny were Ziggy Elman and Harry James and, before them, the brilliant Bunny Berigan. Later, when it was possible for a white band to have a black musician in its ranks, Benny hired Cootie Williams. Benny's trombone players were sound section men rather than exceptional soloists. His reed section was similarly filled with solid musicians rather than outstanding jazz artists. Although not really a soloist with the Goodman band, Krupa was a flamboyantly spectacular drummer and, along with James, the most charismatic of the men in the band. The real stars Benny hired were for the small groups rather than the big band: Charlie Christian, Lionel Hampton, Teddy Wilson.

Even in later years when he hired such notable artists as Stan Getz, Zoot Sims and Bob Wilber to play in his big band the principal soloist with the Benny Goodman band was Benny himself.

On ballads, medium tempo dance numbers and torrid flagwavers, it is Benny's transcendent clarinet that weaves most magic. His seemingly effortless fluidity betrays no signs that this was the end product of many years' careful study and selfless dedication. Indeed, the ease with which he demonstrates his mastery of his instrument has led to criticism of his playing which is patently unjust.

With Benny's clarinet riding high above the crisp trumpet section, the solid trombones and reeds and the thundering rhythm section, the Goodman band came to epitomise the swing era which was itself the epitome of contemporary American popular music.

Usually evoked as the high point of Benny's reign as King of Swing is the Carnegie Hall concert on 16 January 1938. Although just about everything the band played that night was played better on other occasions, there was an undeniable atmosphere of excitement which communicated itself between audience and band and back again, building towards a climax of enthusiasm that was less demonstrative than displayed at the Palomar or the Paramount but was no less genuine. Importantly for future generations this concert was recorded in its entirety and released in 1950 after Benny had found the master discs in a cupboard.

The release of this concert on long-playing records proved that for once the memories of those who were there had not been tinged with the rosy glow that often inhibits accurate critical assessment of past delights.

All the way from the opening tune, Benny's theme song, 'Don't Be That Way', through a piece featuring members of the Ellington band, a jam session with members of the Basie band, spots by the Trio and Quartet, and superb playing by James, Krupa, pianist Jess Stacy, and above all by Benny, to a rousing 'Sing, Sing, Sing' (followed by two ill-advised encores) the concert was a triumph. For Benny Goodman, who had grown up poor in Chicago, this was a moment to savour. Not yet thirty, he had almost fifty more years of music making ahead of him but in terms of public acclaim, this was his finest night.

Shortly after the Carnegie triumph Benny and Gene Krupa parted company and Gene formed his own band. A few months later, Harry James formed a band and before long so too did Lionel Hampton and Teddy Wilson. The Benny Goodman band was just as good as ever with the replacements Benny found. Indeed, thanks to such drummers as Dave Tough and Sid Catlett the band often swung more and certainly with greater subtlety than when Krupa was at work. But some of the steam had gone out of the Goodman bandwagon and Benny folded his band in the early 1940s.

During the next few years Benny periodically re-formed then folded again. In the late 1940s he flirted with bebop and made interesting records with such outstanding modernists as trumpeter Fats Navarro, tenor saxophonist Wardell Gray, and even shared the spotlight with another clarinet player, Stan Hasselgärd. But Benny's heart was never in this new form jazz was taking and he never made any concessions to the idiom in his own playing.

From the 1950s onwards the big bands Benny led were assembled only for special occasions. Mostly, the last thirty years of Benny's life were spent in small group work and in playing classical music (of which form he became an internationally accepted exponent—which probably surprised everyone but Benny who never did anything by halves).

Benny's death, in 1986, was not greeted with the same measure of sadness as had attended the deaths of Louis Armstrong, Count Basie or Duke Ellington. As far as the jazz world was concerned Benny did not belong in the same rank; perhaps not, but he was a major figure in the world of the big bands. Indeed, as far as the general public in that phenomenal decade known as the swing era was concerned, Benny Goodman was the unchallenged 'King of Swing'.

Red Norvo And His Orchestra

Vibraphonist Red Norvo had one of the most subtle and soft-toned bands in an era not renowned for such delicacy. As a consequence, he remains one of the least remembered bandleaders of the swing era. This neglect is unfortunate because the band was particularly musical and in Eddie Sauter had an arranger of extremely advanced and sensitive talents. The band's greatest asset, however, was Red Norvo's wife who was one of the finest vocal stars of that or any other era in jazz. The sound of Mildred Bailey's lilting voice floating effortlessly over the softly swinging textures of her husband's band is one of the most delightful memories of the swing era.

***

Musicians on Goodman:
'I think a guy that can play as well as [Benny Goodman]does is entitled to a few eccentricities.'
Bobby Hackett

***

'That band [Benny Goodman]had in 1935 hasn't ever been topped—Benny really knows how to make a band swing—he had good guys, but it was his know-how that made the thing so great.'
Jimmy Giuffre

BRITISH DANCE BANDS OF THE THIRTIES

The British dance band scene in the years between the wars was vital and exciting, and often at least on par with happenings across the Atlantic. Indeed, the British bands were frequently tighter and their strict tempo playing was greatly enjoyed by dancers.

A number of bands of this period cannot be overlooked. Among these was the band led by Jack Hylton who took over leadership of the Queen's Dance Orchestra in 1920. The band was already well-known among London's smart set for its music in the Paul Whiteman manner, with a smattering of the Original Dixieland Jazz Band thrown in for good measure. Hylton's early recordings, using charts brought in from America, display sound musicianship and if the solos are not particularly lively they are certainly much more than merely adequate. Later, Hylton claimed that he took to amending imported arrangements which he felt were unsuited to the British audience. His enormous success and huge record sales, suggest that if this is so then he had clearly understood a need.

During the next few years Hylton built a formidable reputation with residencies at several top London hotels, including the Piccadilly, but London alone was too limited for him. From the late 1920s until just before the outbreak of World War II he regularly toured Europe. Hylton's popularity and success may be measured from his decision to turn down a year-long residency at the Empire Cinema in Leicester Square, an engagement which would have paid £40,000—no mean sum in those depressed days.

In 1932 Hylton shared the bill during a European trip with Duke Ellington and in 1935 engaged Coleman Hawkins as a soloist. The prospect of an American tour beckoned but the American Federation of Musicians stepped in and killed the tour as the band arrived in New York.

Roy Fox was born in the United States, taking up playing music when still a child and living in Hollywood. As a youth he played in a number of bands including that led by Abe Lyman, eventually forming his own group for an engagement at the Club Royale in Culver City, Los Angeles. He worked in the movies for a while, eventually travelling to England with a small band to take up an offer of an engagement at London's Café de Paris. At various times Roy Fox employed many leading British dance band musicians and singer Denny Dennis, who later worked with the Tommy Dorsey band.

An important band on the London scene in the 1930s was that led by Lew Stone. With records, films and a string of engagements at top London clubs and hotels, among them the Monseigneur, the Café de Paris, the Trianon and the Dorchester, Stone quickly built a reputation for quality. He also played in West End theatres and toured extensively in the late 1930s, during World War II and on through the post-war years, eventually folding his big band in 1959.

Lew Stone's band was among the top handful of British dance bands of the period it spanned and at various times had many excellent musicians in its ranks, among them clarinetist Joe Crossman, trumpeters Nat Gonella, Tommy McQuater and Alfie Noakes, drummer Bill Harty and pianists Stanley Black and Monia Liter (who played together in the 1935 band).

Much more jazz-oriented than many of his fellow dance bandleaders, Stone's rhythmic interpretations always maintained a very high standard of performance in the Casa Loma tradition. Stone arranged many of his band's numbers himself and brought to them a distinctive touch and, heard today, there is sometimes a surprisingly modern sound to them.

For several years, the popular singer Al Bowlly worked with the Lew Stone band and contributed towards its success. However, from the vantage point afforded by half a century, it is the extraordinarily high quality of the band's music, in both the writing and its performance, that Lew Stone's reputation comfortably rests.

A British musician who worked for a while in America was Bert Ambrose. London-born Ambrose emigrated while still a very young man and for a time worked in a pit band in a New York movie theatre, eventually becoming leader of the band at the city's Palais Royale. In 1920 he returned to London then shuttled back and forth before settling down in the winter of 1922/3 to lead the orchestra at the Embassy Club in London's Bond Street where he remained until hired by the Mayfair Hotel in 1927.

Ambrose's New York experience had convinced him of the qualities of the musicians there and he hired several Americans for his Mayfair band, the best known of whom was trumpeter Henry 'Hot Lips' Levine. The American contingent varied as work permits expired and later included the musicianly Sylvester Ahola, trumpet, and clarinetist Danny Polo, both of whom made significant contributions to many Ambrose recordings. Among the British musicians in the band was the extremely fine trombone trio of Lew Davis, Ted Heath and Tony Thorpe while many of the band's best arrangements were written by saxophonist Sid Phillips.

Ambrose continued to lead a band through the 1930s and at the outbreak of World War II had a band which boasted several outstanding British musicians, including the trumpeter Tommy McQuater, trombonist George Chisholm, saxophonist Billy Amstell, pianist Stanley Black and guitarist Ivor Mairants. When many of his musicians were called up for war service (with several playing in the Squadronaires) Ambrose lost a fine band but not his enthusiasm. Throughout the worst days of the war he continued playing at the Mayfair and touring. Sometimes he led a big band, at other times he led a small group featuring his long-time showman-drummer Max Bacon and the West Indian clarinet virtuoso Carl Barriteau.

In the mid-1950s Ambrose gave up bandleading but stayed in show business as an artist's manager until his death in 1971.

The Ambrose band in London in the 1930s. The reed section includes Sid Phillips, Billy Amstell and Danny Polo, with Max Bacon on drums.

GENE KRUPA AND HIS ORCHESTRA

The flamboyant, rampaging drumming of Gene Krupa with Benny Goodman's band made two things certain: one, Benny would eventually fire him; two, Gene would have his own band. When the break-up happened, early in 1938, the fans flocked in their thousands to the new band's opening at Atlantic City's Steel Pier. Highly successful though it was, Krupa's first band was not particularly distinguished. Built upon the leader's drumming and with adequate rather than polished sectionmen and with no soloists to speak of, the band was completely overshadowed by Gene's later band. The difference in Gene's 1941 band was largely the result of his hiring two people, singer Anita O'Day and trumpeter Roy Eldridge. Eldridge's powerful solo work was featured on such numbers as 'After You've Gone', and 'Rockin Chair' and he and Anita joined forces on 'Let Me Off Uptown'. With Anita's throaty jazz singing, so strikingly different from that of any other white big band singer of the time, the band was now highly distinctive and, sparked by the leader's thunderous drumming, seemed assured of a successful future. But, in 1942, Krupa fell foul of a crusading DA in San Francisco and was imprisoned on drug related charges. Before these charges were shown to have been at best highly dubious the band had folded.

After spending time with Benny Goodman's band in 1943 and Tommy Dorsey in 1944, Gene reformed and continued leading a big band until early 1950. At first, Gene's new band was weighed down with strings and Krupa's insistence on conducting, which meant leaving his crucial rhythm section duties to much less able drummers. Fortunately, the strings did not last long and thereafter the band was always efficient and musical, the repertoire varied. The band played such numbers as the swing-style 'Leave Us Leap' and the slightly boppish 'Calling Dr Gillespie', 'Lemon Drop' and 'What's This?'. Although Krupa never adapted his drumming style to accomodate the demands of bop he did employ a number of modernists including trumpeter Red Rodney and the highly effective arranging talents of Gerry Mulligan.

After 1950 Gene played with small groups although he did make records for Norman Granz in 1956 and 1958 with reconstituted big bands. He also played with the reformed 'Benny Goodman band' for an aborted tour and for the movie version of Benny's life story in 1955 and for his own bio-pic in 1959.

Krupa's dark good looks, his dynamic personality, dramatic on-stage presence and the flamboyant manner of his playing made his work with Benny Goodman and his own bands one of the most striking visual images of the swing era.

THE CASA LOMA ORCHESTRA

Canadian tycoon Sir Harry Pellatt had delusions similar to those displayed by William Randolph Hearst. Whereas Hearst's *folie-de-grandeur*, San Simeon in California, gave rise to the Orson Welles movie, *Citizen Kane*, Pellatt's version of San Simeon, the Casa Loma outside Toronto, gave its name to a fine dance band. One of only a few major bands which were not led by a 'name' but were, instead, cooperative ventures, the Casa Loma Orchestra grew out of the old Jean Goldkette Orange Blossom Orchestra which had played extensively in Canada. The Orange Blossoms' home had been the Casa Loma, and when the musicians returned to New York they reformed using the old palace's name as a reminder of happy days.

The band's nominal leader was alto saxophonist Glen Gray Knoblaugh who wisely dropped his last name for show business purposes.

In its early days, the Casa Loma band was considered by both white and black musicians to be one of the hottest bands around. Among several strong sidemen was Clarence Hutchenrider, an outstanding clarinetist. Also important to the band's commerical success were the silky-smooth vocals of Kenny Sargent.

Although it was surpassed in fame by most of the name bands of its time, the Casa Loma Orchestra retained a very high standard of playing, aided in no small part by the arrangements of Gene Gifford. Stylistically, Gifford's work reflected and was in turn reflected by many of the arrangers working with other bands. The band played with slightly mechanical precision and a subtle sense of dynamics (and with more regard for such simple yet important qualities than most of their much better known contemporaries).

Unjustly neglected, the Casa Loma Orchestra was one of the best and certainly one of the most musicianly white bands of the pre-swing era and the one which, more than most early bands, set styles and standards that formed the basis of many swing era success stories.

CHAPTER SIX

SWING HIGH: MORE WHITE BANDS

'DANCING ON THE CEILING'

'They paid $1.75 to get in; let's give 'em $3.50 worth.'
Tommy Dorsey

Despite Benny Goodman's apparent invincibility, there were occasional attempts to usurp his title as King of Swing, often by rather more charismatic leaders whose bands had at least an equivalent standard of musicianship.

Among the leading contenders for Benny's title was Artie Shaw, who also played clarinet. The fans took sides and endlessly argued the merits of their particular favourite, while both band leaders benefited from the additional publicity. As for the press, they loved Artie who was handsome and outgoing; he could be charming when things suited him and acerbic when they didn't. He also displayed a marked penchant for beautiful and usually famous women. If Harry James earned a curious kind of immortalisation by marrying the glamorous movie star, Betty Grable, then Artie qualified for eternity in the marital Hall of Fame by marrying, among several others, such strikingly attractive women as movie actresses Lana Turner, Ava Gardner, and Evelyn Keyes. Such activities gave the popular press a field day and allowed them to write their favourite kind of gossipy nonsense.

Shaw also gave the press good 'copy' by periodically packing it all in at the height of his band's success and taking off for parts unknown, often to the distress of his musicians for whom his departures were as much a surprise as they were to the fans.

Shaw had numerous record hits (unlike Goodman who, curiously enough, made few records that were individually million-sellers even if, collectively, they sold very well indeed). Among Artie's smashes were 'Begin the Beguine', 'Frenesi', 'Adios' and 'Concerto for Clarinet'.

Less spectacular in their private lives and public personas, yet enormously popular with the fans were Jimmy and Tommy Dorsey, Bob Crosby and Gene Krupa (although he, too, had a fling with Lana Turner and later gained great notoriety for a dubious drugs bust).

Also highly successful bandleaders were ex-Goodman trumpet star Harry James and Charlie Barnet. (The latter's forays into marriage were as extensive as Artie Shaw's but somehow escaped the same fascinated attention from the press.)

Encouraged by his circus bandmaster father, by age seven Harry James had given up a budding career as a contortionist to play drums and a year later switched to trumpet. It was clearly the trumpet for which Harry had an affinity and by age eleven he was playing in the band of the Christy Brothers Circus. When his parents decided to settle down

Hal McIntyre and his Orchestra:
In August 1946 Hal McIntyre was playing at Frank Dailey's Meadowbrook, Cedargrove, New Jersey, and offering the public a much looser and more commercial sound than his first band which, in 1942, had missed the masses. The early band used strong brass phrasing, heavily muted but highly effective. The new band allowed more time to his inadequate singers while the arrangements used made every concession to popular taste.

***

Drummer's role:
In midsummer 1950 a drummer in a name band decided to move to another job. So, Tommy Dorsey hired Louie Bellson to replace Kenny John who had joined Jack Palmer where he replaced Phil Sillman who had moved on to the Teddy Powell band taking over from Buddy Lowell who had joined Ray Anthony to replace Mel Lewis who had joined Tex Beneke...

***

Bandstand broadside—2:
'Occasionally the guys in the [Tommy Dorsey] band used to get giddy, so he made a rule that there was to be no laughing on the bandstand. Then he said no *smiling* on the bandstand, and he brought in a $25 fine for that! That was all he had to say! The next show the whole band was doubled over trying to stop laughing!'
Johnny Mince

Jan Savitt And His Orchestra

Russian-born Jan Savitt was classically trained and joined the Philadelphia Symphony Orchestra while still a young teenager but decided to form a band known as the Top Hatters. With its distinctive shuffle rhythm, the band achieved considerable popularity during the late 1930s and had a number of hit records. In hiring singer George 'Bon Bon' Tunnell, Savitt became one of the first white bandleaders to feature a black artist. In the early 1940s Savitt followed a currently popular trend among big band leaders by adding strings but, like all the others who tried this gimmick, he had decidedly mixed results. Later, in dire financial straits, he was compelled to slash the size of his band and embark on a tour to help pay his tax debts. In 1948, while driving to an engagement in California, he suffered a cerebral haemorrhage and died. He was 36.

they picked on a small Texas town where Harry continued playing and even auditioned for Lawrence Welk who happened through on tour. Perhaps fortunately, Harry's playing was too assertive for Welk and he didn't get the job. Later, in Chicago, Harry was heard by bandleader Ben Pollack and hired. Harry's formidable technique attracted attention during his stint with Pollack and in 1936 he was invited to join Benny Goodman's band. The fire and exuberant dash of the Goodman trumpet section was never better than at this time with Harry alongside Ziggy Elman and Chris Griffin (all three sharing lead and solo duties).

When Harry's biting tone appeared on Goodman recordings he began to attract his own substantial following of fans. For all his ability to play controlled and interesting jazz solos, Harry had a tendency to blast off into complex, showy extravaganzas, but he was aware that technique was not enough, a musician needed to know what he was doing.

Harry's popularity with Goodman led him to make a break for personal fame with the help of Benny's moral and financial support. He formed his own band and was a huge popular and commercial success. With only occasional lay-offs he stayed in business as a big band leader for the rest of his life.

Answerable only to himself, Harry's musical extravagance with his own band included several which, when recorded, were massive sellers: 'Concerto for Trumpet', 'The Carnival of Venice', 'The Flight of the Bumble-bee', 'Trumpet Blues and Cantabile'. Although played with astonishing technical skill and great flair, these tunes raised doubts in the minds of jazz fans during the 1940s as did the appearance of such lachrymose hits as 'You Made Me Love You' and 'I Cried for You'. Some fans never bothered to listen to him again and consequently missed out on a series of excellent bands Harry led during the 1950s and 1960s. Harry employed a succession of swing era veterans, including Corky Corcoran, Buddy Rich, Willie Smith and Juan Tizol (while lead trumpeter Nick Buono, who joined him in December 1939, was still there when Harry played Las Vegas on his 40th anniversary as a bandleader). More important than the sidemen were the arrangers Harry used in his middle period and who included Neal Hefti and Ernie Wilkins.

Through the 1970s and into the early 1980s, Harry James continued to lead an always musical big band, spending long residencies in Las Vegas where he died in 1983.

For all the strong jazz content of many of his performances, Harry James has always been regarded as a commercial bandleader. That charge was never levelled at Charlie Barnet although he, too, could turn on the glucose.

Although some jazz and big band musicians started out poor and ended up rich (while many more started poor and stayed that way), Charlie Barnet was a rarity who began rich. Fortunately, he was no dilettante but an accomplished musician and he used his personal inherited wealth to give him a considerable measure of freedom to play the way he wanted. He was also an outspoken critic of segregation and early in his bandleading career broke a number of unwritten rules by playing the Apollo Theatre (this was in 1934) and hiring black musicians including pianist Garnet Clark (in 1934), bass player John Kirby and trumpeter Frankie Newton (in 1935, a year before Benny Goodman hired Teddy Wilson and Lionel Hampton). Later, at different times, Barnet employed black trumpeters Roy Eldridge, Frank Galbreath, Dizzy Gillespie, Peanuts Holland, Al Killian, Howard McGhee, Jimmy Nottingham, Clark

Anita O'Day in 1942/3 with Charlie Ventura to her right and Gene Krupa, left.

Jimmy Dorsey accompanies vocalist Helen O'Connell.

Sinatra sings as Dorsey swings.
Tommy Dorsey accompanies Frank Sinatra, 1940/41.

NBC

VICTOR

Cutting corners:
In the movie, *The Benny Goodman Story*, Harry James appears playing a solo but in the intercut long shots it clearly isn't Harry. Why didn't Harry do more in the movie? Well, during preproduction musicians were being hired and someone asked Benny, 'How much do we pay Harry James?' Benny recalled that the last time Harry had played for him, 16 years earlier, he was paid $125 a week. Benny thought for a moment, then said, 'Okay, pay him $135.'

Terry, Paul Webster and Lamar Wright, trombonist Trummy Young, bassist Oscar Pettiford, drummer Kansas Fields and singer Lena Horne.

Barnet's musical dedication was to Duke Ellington and he openly modelled his band's style on Duke. The band was highly successful with straightahead swingers and had big popular recording hits with 'Cherokee', 'Pompton Turnpike', 'Redskin Rhumba' and 'Skyliner'. Several of the band's most successful numbers were the work of Billy May whose charts helped build the band an identity. Its distinctive sound was also thanks in part to Charlie himself. A multi-instrumentalist playing most of the saxophone family, Barnet favoured the soprano and when he led the reed section it gave his band unique tonal qualities. Typically, Charlie chose not to label the result: 'I don't have a name for my sound. Either it sounds good or it doesn't. Forget labels. Just so long as it swings.' He also sang occasionally, eventually stopping because, as he complained, 'it was beginning to interfere with my drinking'.

At the end of the 1940s Barnet folded his band in common with others facing huge expenses. Given his financial circumstances and the fact that Capitol Records wanted him to follow in Stan Kenton's footsteps as their 'progressive' standard bearer, there were clearly other factors. Charlie did not favour bebop although, like Benny Goodman, Gene Krupa and a few other swing era leaders, he dabbled with it, using such musicians as Al Haig and Dodo Marmarosa. Neither did he like Kenton's style but here again he took a fling before quitting. The results of these bebop and progressive jazz diversions were interesting if not especially profound. Using charts by Manny Albam, Gil Fuller, Tiny Kahn and Paul Villepigue the band turned in good performances of such tunes as

Harry James and his band in 1949. (L to R) James, Don Lamond, Ralph Osborne, Neal Hefti, Ziggy Elmer, Pinky Savitt, Juan Tizol, Nick Buono.

Randall's Island, NY, was the venue for disc-jockey Martin Block's Carnival of Music in May 1938. One of dozens of star names was Gene Krupa with his recently formed band. Here, Gene lays down the beat for Bruce Squires, Dave Schultze and Dalton Rizzotto. At Gene's shoulder is raconteur, wit, club owner and occasional guitarist Eddie Condon. At Eddie's side is Maxine, one of the Andrews Sisters, and behind the man with glasses and hat can be seen surrealist singer and multi-instrumentalist Slim Gaillard.

'Charlie's Other Aunt', 'Claude Reigns' (with good solo piano from Claude Williamson), 'Cu-ba', 'Over the Rainbow' (featuring superb trumpet-playing from Ray Wetzel) and 'Eugipelliv'. A version of Jerome Kern's 'All the Things You Are', featuring Maynard Ferguson's strato-squeaking trumpet, had the dubious distinction of being withdrawn from sale following protests by the executors of the composer's estate.

The problem for Charlie with such musical diversions as these was that, above all else, he loved to swing. The later sexual colloquialism of this term is not inappropriate for Charlie enjoyed life off the bandstand, too, and his drinking and marital exploits guaranteed his autobiography a place on bookshelves inside and outside the big band arena; in conversation with Leonard Feather about his 11 marriages Charlie insisted that 'five of those don't count. They were annulled...'

Not surprisingly, Charlie enjoyed the music and the good times too much to quit forever and periodically he came back with bands through the 1960s and 1970s all of which played with enormous fire and if they were at times a shade overenthusiastic, they were exciting and as much fun to hear as they obviously were to be in.

The fiery zest of bands like Barnet's have a tendency to cloud an important fact, something which is not illuminated fifty years on when re-created bands pop up playing before sedately seated patrons in concert halls. Excepting only when they played in movie theatres, during the swing era the bands played for dancing.

Certainly, the example of Benny Goodman's Carnegie Hall concert was followed by others, including Duke Ellington in 1943 and Woody Herman in 1946, but throughout the swing era the concert hall was not the home of the bands. The dance halls were their main venues and if there were those who simply went along to crowd around the bandstand and cheer their favourite sidemen, most patrons were there primarily to dance.

Butterball:
Trumpeter Billy Butterfield first came to the attention of jazz and big band fans during his stint with the Bob Crosby band and in particular on one of the band's hits, 'What's New?'. Butterball later worked with Artie Shaw and Benny Goodman before entering the armed services. After his discharge in 1946 he formed his own band, employing such arrangers as Ralph Burns, Mickey Crane, Bob Haggart, Neal Hefti, Bob Peck and clarinetist-alto saxophonist Bill Stegmeyer who was co-leader of the band with Billy. Unfortunately, although the fans of the earlier bands with which Billy had worked knew his name, the general public did not and, consequently, for all its undoubted musical qualities, the Billy Butterfield big band was a commercial failure.

Of all the big name bands of the era, one that filled this role admirably was that led by Tommy, the most warlike of the two Dorsey brothers. When the occasion demanded Tommy's band could turn on the heat as well as any, but when it came to providing danceable music they were in a class on their own.

THE SENTIMENTAL GENTLEMAN OF SWING

More than most bands, the one which highlights the irrelevance of pigeon-holing into hot and sweet is Tommy Dorsey's. It is also one of the most musicianly.

'Go and be creative somewhere else.'
Tommy Dorsey
(on firing Buddy De Franco)

***

'I think I was very fortunate to grow up during that time. As a kid I'd go to bed at 10.30, turn on that radio and I had any selection of bands for almost two hours.'
George Masso

***

Fallen star:
In a Los Angeles alimony court in 1961 Ziggy Elman, former Benny Goodman star and one time bandleader in his own right, was asked by his wife's attorney: 'You are known as the world's leading trumpeter?' Elman replied: 'Lots of people think I am, but I still can't get much work.' Ziggy claimed that six of his seven bank accounts had balances between $1.19 and $11.00. The seventh was overdrawn.

The Dorsey Brothers Orchestra broke up in 1935 after the latest in a year-long string of verbal and physical scraps between the hot-tempered brothers. Tommy took over an existing band, that of Joe Haymes, and set about building a band the way he wanted it to be.

Soon to be known as 'The Sentimental Gentleman of Swing', Tommy was a stocky, round-faced individual with the outward demeanour of a country store-keeper. Beneath this facade, however, lurked an irascible, argumentative and sometimes violent individual who somehow contrived to remain likeable. Max Kaminsky recalled: 'Tommy had a truly magnificent unconcern for consequences; he took pleasure in the fight for the sheer love of fighting, and as mad as you could get at him, it was hard to stay mad because he got over it so quickly with no trace of animosity.'

Tommy was an astute businessman and saw that in order to give the public what it wanted it was necessary to concede that the public did not always want the same thing but varied according to place, status, age and taste. He could see no reason why they needed to have Charlie Barnet if they wanted hot music or Glenn Miller if they wanted smoothly swinging ballads. If they hired him, he would give them the best of both worlds.

It is a mark of Tommy's determination and acumen, and his striking musical ability, that he came close to being the best on both counts. At its jazziest best, and featuring at various times such solo talents as trumpeters Bunny Berigan, Ziggy Elman, Pee Wee Erwin and Yank Lawson and reed players Buddy De Franco, Bud Freeman and Johnny Mince, and with Dave Tough, Cliff Leeman, and Buddy Rich occupying the drum chair, the band could swing with the best of them. When it came to ballads, nowhere was there a better trombone technician than Tommy himself. His playing set extraordinarily high standards of accomplishment.

When playing for dancing, the Dorsey band set strict tempos but, thanks to excellent arrangements, still swung. The band had a very big hit with 'Marie', using a novelty arrangement which combined the singing of Jack Leonard and a vocal chorus by the band. Dorsey had heard this arrangement of the song while engaged in a band 'battle' in Philadelphia with Doc Wheeler's Sunset Royal Serenaders, a black band going through hard times. Dorsey traded eight of his band's arrangements for this one of Wheeler's. By any calculation, it was a good deal for Dorsey and apart from the huge sales of this particular record it led to a string of similar arrangements on tunes like 'Who?' and 'Yearning'. Equally as popular as 'Marie' was the other side of the same record, 'Song of India'. Like 'Marie', 'Song of India' started a succession of hit arrangements, this time of classical tunes.

For all the enormous success of the band's ballads and his own impeccable trombone playing, Tommy's love of jazz meant that he

Tommy Dorsey and his Orchestra entertaining the crowds at the Commodore Hotel, NYC, in 1937.

occasionally turned a blind eye to musicians whose personal characteristics made them something of a liability: Bunny Berigan, Pee Wee Erwin and Dave Tough were three such individuals. Johnny Mince recalled an occasion when Pee Wee turned up very drunk and fell asleep on the bandstand. The band's manager angrily asked Tommy why he didn't fire him. 'I can't fire him,' Tommy replied, 'he plays too good.'

Despite his extraordinary skills as a trombonist, Tommy could display remarkable humility, especially when faced with playing alongside Jack Teagarden. At one session George T. Simon suggested Tommy should play a solo but Tommy would have none of it: 'Ridiculous, when you've got Jack here.' In fact, the admiration was mutual, with Teagarden remarking, 'There's never been such a tone out of any horn as beautiful as his.'

Tommy Dorsey's musical ability was such that it had a long-term and unpredicted effect upon American popular song. This came about when he tempted Frank Sinatra away from the Harry James band. Sinatra was young, impressionable and, although good, still had a lot to learn. From his new boss Sinatra learned how to phrase a song, he corrected his breathing and he developed his taste for the best of twentieth-century American popular song.

The most outstanding of Sinatra's recordings with Dorsey, whether measured in terms of sales or by the remarkable quality of performance from singer, backing vocal group, band and instrumental soloists, is 'I'll Never Smile Again'. Recorded in May 1940, this demonstrates Sinatra's growing mastery and his singing blends superbly with the Pied Pipers, while the band's pianist, Joe Bushkin, turns to the celeste for an appropriately limpid sound. As for Tommy's trombone solo, it is hard to imagine any way in which it could have been improved upon.

Dorsey's fine ear for vocal talents was also demonstrated by his choice of girl singers. Not content, as were some bandleaders, to hire a pretty girl in a party dress to warble away in front of the band, Tommy had Connie Haines and Jo Stafford, another outstanding interpreter of American popular song.

An important acquisition for the band was Sy Oliver, whose arrangements had done so much to assure the success of the Jimmie Lunceford band. Although Tommy had been using Fletcher Henderson arrangements to good effect, Oliver gave the band a boost with his highly individualistic work. Oliver had decided to quit the music business to study law but when Tommy came along and offered him $5,000 a year more than he had earned with Lunceford, not surprisingly Sy took the job. He had already written a few charts for the band during 1939, including 'Stomp It Off' and 'Easy Does It' but now began to turn out a stream of smoothly swinging classics. After Oliver joined the team in 1940 the band enjoyed a string of hits, several of which had a distinctive 2-beat sound reminiscent of the Lunceford band. Among the most popular numbers were 'Swing High', 'Well, Git It!' and, an enormously successful record, 'Opus No. 1'. On all of these records the band swings mightily, propelled by Buddy Rich's dynamic drumming.

In the mid-1940s Dorsey had a succession of strong jazz soloists passing through the band as he, like all leaders, wrestled with the problem of losing sidemen to the draft. Yank Lawson and Charlie Shavers were around, as was Buddy De Franco; Dorsey also employed trumpeter Pete Candoli and tenor saxophonist Vido Musso. For a spell in 1943 and most of 1944 the drum chair was occupied by Gene Krupa whose own band had folded following his imprisonment on drugs-related charges.

Apart from Sy Oliver Tommy had several other experienced arrangers including Paul Weston and Axel Stordahl, whose pretty ballad style would later complement the singing of Frank Sinatra so well. Dean Kincaide also worked for Dorsey although his best work is to be heard with the Bob Crosby band. This use by Dorsey of a multitude of arrangers made his band's repertoire one of the widest ranging among swing bands, contributing towards the great commercial success he achieved.

But, like all the big bands, Tommy Dorsey's was feeling the pinch and his was one of several which folded during the bad times of late 1946. Far from finished, Tommy came back two years later with another fine band. Once again he had a good if occasionally erratic trumpet soloist in Charlie Shavers and a strong drummer in Louie Bellson. The band was successful but times were hard and Tommy had to provide his own financial backing. He found work touring and on TV where he appeared on the Jackie Gleason show.

In 1953 Tommy buried the hatchet with brother Jimmy, who had been obliged to fold his own band. Tommy showed the generous side of his nature by inviting Jimmy to join his band which he promptly renamed: the Dorsey Brothers Orchestra.

But time was fast running out for both brothers. Jimmy had terminal cancer although it was Tommy who went first. In November 1956, at the age of 51, he choked to death in his sleep.

Seger Ellis And His Choirs Of Brass

An early and noble attempt at restructuring the accepted big band ensemble occurred in 1937 when crooner-pianist Seger Ellis formed his Choirs of Brass orchestra. The band comprised eight brass and one clarinet, plus piano, bass and drums. The arrangements were compiled by Spud Murphy and Stan Wrightsman and although doomed to almost immediate failure, the band had a pleasantly enthusiastic sound with solos by Nate Kazebier and Benny Strickler, trumpets, and Irving Fazola alternating with Pancho Villa on clarinet.

***

Rippling rhythm:
Millions loved the sound of the Shep Fields band which mixed solo viola with an accordian, a flute and clarinets all backed by a clickety-clack temple block accompaniment from the drummer. The band's publicity tag, 'rippling rhythm', was coined for them by their radio audience.

The Sentimental Gentleman—Tommy Dorsey in 1944

BOB CROSBY AND HIS ORCHESTRA

Unusual among the big bands of the swing era was that fronted by Bob Crosby, younger brother of singer Bing. Two reasons make it stand out, one administrative, the other musical. Administratively, the band was a cooperative organisation of musicians who rallied together after the Ben Pollack band folded in 1934. Musically, the band had a high proportion of Dixieland numbers in its book, tunes which were usually played in 2/4 time instead of the more customary 4/4 time of swing era bands.

The ex-Pollack musicians included Gil Rodin who became the musical director of the new band. Hiring Bob Crosby to front the band was a marketing decision. Bob had already achieved a small measure of popularity from stints as singer with the Anson Weeks band and the Dorsey Brothers Orchestra. A relaxed and charming man, he proved an ideal choice for the job of fronting the band. As a cooperative unit, the Bob Crosby band managed to avoid many of the usual hassles with beset bands whose leaders were also the man with the capacity to hire and fire. The musicians could relax and concentrate simply on playing music.

Several members of the band originated from New Orleans and it was their presence, especially Nappy Lamare, banjo, and Ray Bauduc, drums, in the rhythm section, which gave the band its distinctive 2-beat flavour. When the band played in the more orthodox 4/4 time there was still a strong jazz feel thanks to tenor-saxophonist Eddie Miller and clarinetist Irving Fazola, both of whom hailed from New Orleans, and trumpeters Yank Lawson and Billy Butterfield. The snappy rhythm section was rounded out by Bob Zurke, piano, a boogie woogie specialist, and Bob Haggart, bass.

In its recorded performances, both from studio sessions and airshots, the immediately obvious quality of the Bob Crosby band is its cheerfully loose sound. While the ensemble passages never achieve the powerful swing of their major competitors, neither do they ever become victim to the rigidity which beset many. The band's relaxed drive provided an excellent springboard for soloists and with the unusually high number of good jazzmen in its ranks there is always something of interest in its performances.

The band enjoyed several successful records, notably 'South Rampart Street Parade' (written by Haggart and Bauduc), 'I'm Praying Humble', 'What's New?' (both by Haggart) and a version of Meade Lux Lewis's 'Honky Tonk Train Blues' which featured Bob Zurke. When the band moved away from its Dixieland style and played such tunes as Phil Moore's 'Black Zephyr' and 'Blue Surreal' it ably demonstrates its considerable versatility.

The Pollack-Crosby tradition lived on through the work of alumni Haggart and Lawson who, in the 1970s and 1980s, co-led the World's Greatest Jazz Band.

Maybe Bob Crosby's Bobcats were posing for the camera at Atlantic City's Steel Pier in 1936, but there was no faking the admiration they felt for pianist Joe Sullivan. (L to R) Irving Fazola, Sullivan, Gil Rodin, Bob Haggart, Nappy Lamare, Crosby, Eddie Miller, Ray Bauduc.

Above: Sixteen men swing—the Count Basie band (*Photo: Chuck Stewart*)
Below: Spotlight on the tragic genius of Paul Gonsalves—with Duke Ellington and his Orchestra (*Photo: Chuck Stewart*)

JIMMY DORSEY AND HIS ORCHESTRA

Although outwardly more placid, Jimmy Dorsey was just as quick-tempered as his brother. Jimmy was an equally dedicated perfectionist and his liquid alto saxophone, revered by many musicians, was the sound which most identified the band.

Unwillingly picking up the reins of the Dorsey Brothers Orchestra after the final bust-up when Tommy stormed off the stand at Glenn Island Casino, Jimmy took quite a while to achieve a level of fame comparable to that enjoyed by his brother. Eventu-ally, thanks to his dedication, he made it.

On taking over, Jimmy's first and most difficut task was to find a trombone player to replace his brother. He surprised many by choosing an unknown 16-year-old named Bobby Byrne. Thanks to an astonishing virtuosity for one so young, Bobby didn't stay unknown for long.

Jimmy used some good jazz-inclined musicians including Byrne, drummer Ray McKinley who didn't stay long, tenor saxophonist Herbie Haymer and trumpeter Shorty Sherock.

Jimmy attracted great loyalty from his musicians and singers. Most notable in this respect must be Bob Eberly. He repeatedly turned down offers to make a solo career, preferring to stay with the band.

The most striking musical memories of the Jimmy Dorsey band came from a series of records which featured Jimmy and the band's two singers. Faced with packaging the band's principal assets in one three-minute radio spot, arranger Tutti Camarata came up with the bright idea of the three-in-one arrangement. He started off the song as a pretty ballad languidly sung by Bob Eberly, then segued into an up-tempo section featuring Jimmy's alto in jazzy mood, and finally the band's other singer, the extrovert Helen O'Connell, entered at a slowed-down tempo, wailing where Bob had crooned.

The routine was a sensation. The first songs performed and recorded this way were 'Amapola' and 'Yours' but the third, 'Green Eyes', was a runaway hit. Later, the same treatment was tried with similar smashing success on 'Tangerine'.

By the mid-1940s, Jimmy's band was out-polling brother Tommy but the early 1950s were hard times and Jimmy folded. He rejoined his brother who showed there were no lasting hard feelings by promptly renaming his band, the Dorsey Brothers Orchestra.

ARTIE SHAW AND HIS ORCHESTRA

Although Benny Goodman's was the success story *non pareil* of the swing era, for a while he was given a run for his crown by another highly talented clarinet player. This was Artie Shaw who had worked in the dance bands of Vincent Lopez, Paul Specht and Roger Wolfe Kahn before forming his own big band in 1936. Thanks to a string of highly successful records including 'Nightmare', 'Begin the Beguine' (arranged by Jerry Gray), 'Indian Love Call' (which aped Tommy Dorsey's success with 'Marie'), 'Carioca' and 'Frenesi', the band became hugely popular. Although there were other clarinet-playing leaders it was Shaw who was pushed into the position of challenger to King of Swing Benny Goodman.

Both men had enormous talent on their chosen instrument and while Goodman had a considerable edge in terms of sheer virtuosity, when the mood was on Shaw he could play with great elegance and natural swing. At various times Artie's band had several good musicians including John Best and Bernie Privin, trumpets, Jack Jenney, trombone, Georgie Auld and Tony Pastor playing tenor saxophones, and a succession of fine drummers in Cliff Leeman, George Wettling and Buddy Rich. Artie also broke delicate ground by hiring Billie Holiday as his singer in 1938. Artie made many of his own arrangements and was also well served by the highly proficient Jerry Gray.

Outspoken about critics and fans, none of whom he appeared to like very much, Artie was highly opinionated and more capable than most bandleaders of expressing himself verbally. Max Kaminsky recalled Artie's technique for getting the best out of musicians. He would make a little speech about 'how he felt it was too hard for us, too much to ask of us. Of course, we insisted on doing it.'

Artie's great problem, and one he never overcame, was that he was too aware of the undercurrent of sharp business practices in the entertainment industry. He was a success in a business he despised. Several times he quit, walking away from the band and leaving his baffled sidemen to pick up their severance pay and find another job. Had he persisted he might have usurped Benny Goodman in reality and not just in the imagination of publicist's; but, then, had he been able to stick it he would not have been the man he was—a fine musician and, now and again, leader of one of the most musicianly bands of the swing era.

CHAPTER SEVEN

SWING ON: GLENN MILLER

'ALWAYS IN MY HEART'

'Glenn Miller was experimenting constantly.'

George T. Simon

The post-war popularity of Glenn Miller is a show business phenomenon akin to that which later surrounded such artists as Buddy Holly and Jim Reeves and which, at times, comes close to overshadowing the real worth of the individual concerned. Nevertheless, while anyone might be forgiven for adopting a cynical view of record company hyping which capitalises upon the work of dead men, to use this as a reason for putting down the real lifetime achievements of the artist concerned is unfair.

In the late 1940s and on through succeeding decades, there were several 'Glenn Miller' bands and others which adopted his musical style. Some have continued playing in a largely unchanged Miller manner through to the present day. Ex-Miller sideman Tex Beneke and Ray McKinley led such bands, so too did Glenn's brother Herb (who had a band during his brother's lifetime but with little popular success), and there were others including an 'official' band led by Buddy De Franco. Former Miller arranger Jerry Gray, who also helped create the distinctive Artie Shaw sound, was another who led a band in the Miller mould.

The popularity of the musical style of the pre-war and wartime Glenn Miller bands was not confined to America and much of the band's posthumous popularity is as a result of acclaim in Britain.

This may well be due to the simple historical fact that he was the only important American swing era bandleader Britain saw in the flesh. Certainly, Glenn Miller found a special place in British hearts. Who can say what might have been the case had Miller gone to the Pacific and Artie Shaw visited Britain? Then there is Miller's disappearance after departing on a flight from Britain to France. Such an end, however tragic, has all the elements of high drama. All this, coupled to a post-war yearning for the past, turned Glenn Miller and his music into a symbol of a period when, despite all the adversity, the British came closer together as a nation than during any other period in modern times.

There is a curious irony that Glenn Miller should have become so inextricably intertwined with nostalgia. Even the most casual glance at Miller's attitude towards his music in the years before and during World War II suggests very strongly that he would find such nostalgic idolisation very strange indeed.

Origin of the Glenn Miller 'sound'—1: 'It arose in Pollack's band because we wouldn't have regular arrangements and he'd tell me and Matty [Matlock]to work out something on the last chorus. We'd do that octave thing. I think the Crosby band's use of clarinet-tenor unison influenced Glenn Miller.'

Eddie Miller

***

Top Ten records for January 1942:
'Chattanooga Choo Choo', Glenn Miller
'Blues in the Night', Woody Herman
'String of Pearls', Glenn Miller
'Elmer's Tune', Glenn Miller
'I said No', Alvino Rey
'This Love of Mine', Tommy Dorsey
'Remember Pearl Harbor', Sammy Kaye
'Everything I Love', Glenn Miller
'White Cliffs of Dover', Glenn Miller
'I Said No', Jimmy Dorsey

***

Origin of the Glenn Miller 'sound'—2: One night Glenn asked clarinetist Irving Fazola, whose job it was to play the solos on swing numbers, if he could see the tenor saxophone part from where he was sitting. Fazola could, and started playing and band and audience alike were transfixed.

Rolly Bundock

Four future swing era bandleaders were in the ranks of the 1934 Dorsey Brothers band: Tommy and Jimmy, of course, and Ray McKinley and Glenn Miller. Seen at Sands Point Bath Club, Long Island, NY, are (L to R) Bobby Van Eps, George Thow, Delmar Kaplan, Roc Hillman, Tommy, Don Mattison, Kay Weber, Skeets Herfurt, Jimmy, Miller, McKinley, Jack Stacey.

IN THE MOOD

Glenn Miller's early career found him working with a number of bands including Boyd Senter and Max Fischer. From 1925 he was with Ben Pollack for whom he also wrote numerous arrangements. A skilled musician, Glenn had an active, inquisitive musical mind. He was always interested in developing new ideas and trying them out on friends and colleagues, usually with success. As a trombone player he was efficient without ever displaying the qualities of his peers for some of whom he had the highest regard. Bobby Hackett, who played trumpet with Miller, remarked 'I think he would have traded in the whole thing to be able to play like Jack Teagarden or Tommy Dorsey.'

Before he formed his own first band Glenn Miller was hired by Ray Noble to act as contractor for a band Noble would lead at New York's Rainbow Room. Glenn's job entailed hiring the musicians and preparing arrangements. In so doing he continued with the experiments in style that had been a feature of his days with the Ben Pollack band. In some of the Noble band arrangements, Glenn required trumpeter Pee Wee Erwin to play with the reed section but an octave above the tenor saxophone lead. When Erwin quit his successor was less adept and Glenn rescored for clarinet in place of the trumpet. Ray Noble was not too enamoured with what he heard and many of the arrangements remained unused. Glenn was more perceptive than his temporary boss and when he formed his own band he tried the style out again to a public response that was quite remarkable. Needless to say, when Hollywood made a

'Glenn Miller had one of the best bands in the world at that time.'
Marty Paich

movie of Glenn Miller's life, his search for a 'new sound' became akin to the search for the Holy Grail although, given the number of versions extant of how the Miller sound came to pass, there is some excuse for the inaccuracy.

In 1937, two years after the Ray Noble job, Glenn Miller formed his own band, determined to achieve the highest possible standards of musicianship, something he pursued with unremitting zeal. A stern, square-jawed sometimes dour individual, Glenn could be a ruthless disciplinarian and was restlessly intent on smoothing out any bumps in the band. His ambition was to 'have a reputation as one of the best allround bands'. Although he had problems with his first band, which eventually folded during its first winter, Glenn persisted. Early in 1938 a new band was on the road and trying again. After a year, with the thought of packing it all in never far from his mind, he became aware that the band had acquired a following. A gig at Frank Dailey's prestigious Meadowbrook Ballroom in New Jersey was followed by a summer season at the Glen Island Casino. Thanks to extensive broadcasts, the band was riding high in 1939 and during this same period had three enormously successful records: 'Moonlight Serenade', 'Little Brown Jug' and 'In the Mood'.

Although the Miller band of this time did not have any truly outstanding musicians or jazz soloists, there were several solid, journeymen musicians who helped give the band a commendable consistency. The rhythm section of Chummy MacGregor, piano, Dick Fisher, guitar, Rolly Bundock, bass, and Maurice Purtill, drums, could swing when required to do so, even if they lacked the bite or bounce of many of their peers; the reeds included Wilbur Schwartz, whose clarinet played the one-octave-above lead for the rest of the section. As far as the fans were concerned the band could do no wrong. There were hit records,

Origin of the Glenn Miller 'sound'—3: 'One of Glenn's arrangements used trumpeter Pee Wee Erwin, playing an octave high, with four saxophones in unison beneath him. One day, Pee Wee didn't show for a rehearsal, so Glenn asked me to play the trumpet part on clarinet. That was it, the Glenn Miller sound was born.'

Johnny Mince

***

Origin of the Glenn Miller 'sound'—4: 'Glenn was experimenting constantly. One day he remembered a happy accident that had occurred in Ray Noble's band. Glenn had been voicing Pee Wee Erwin's trumpet as lead above the saxes. The musician who replaced Erwin had a more limited range and, so that the arrangements shouldn't be a total loss, Glenn reassigned Pee Wee's trumpet part to a clarinet. The new sound was pleasant.

'Glenn remembered the pleasant sound and, despite opposition from advisers, dropped the guitar from his band and added a fifth sax. That was the start of the now famous Miller style.'

George T. Simon

Glenn Miller with two of his long-serving sidemen, Al Mastren and Tex Beneke, at the Paramount Theatre, NYC, in 1939.

Sports jacket and two-tone shoes were not the only things that made Will Bradley stand out. His elegant trombone playing was always a delight and helped ensure that his 1941 band was always a pleasure to hear.

engagements at the best hotels and dance halls in the country, and appearance in movies, including *Sun Valley Serenade* (1941) and *Orchestra Wives* (1942).

Among the band's best-selling records of the early 1940s were 'Tuxedo Junction', 'Pennsylvania 6 5000', 'Frenesi', 'Chattanooga Choo Choo', 'Adios', 'String of Pearls' and 'American Patrol', all of which helped contribute to Miller's growing popularity, fame and wealth. The greater part of the Miller band's recorded output featured singer Ray Eberle whom Glenn had hired on the assumption that he could sing as well as his brother, Bob, then with Jimmy Dorsey. It was a mistaken assumption but neither Glenn nor the fans cared. As far as the general public was concerned, Glenn Miller's was now the sound of the swing era.

By this time America was involved in World War II and with several of his sidemen already drafted, Miller decided to call it a day. Although Miller's age, family commitments and impaired eyesight could have kept him out of the armed forces, he enlisted and was commissioned in the Army Air Force.

Immediately involved with the musical side of army life, Glenn helped organise a concert orchestra, a military band, and a dance band. Miller's approach to his work was as determined and thoroughly professional as had been his civilian work. Now, however, he could, and did, exercise his authority with even more weight than before. He was no longer merely a bandleader who hired and fired musicians, he was their superior officer. Like him or not, the boys in the band could do nothing about it; they couldn't even quit.

Glenn Miller's musicianship was just as it had always been: impeccable. And he was still experimenting. To the dismay of the top brass, and the great delight of the troops, he wrote new arrangements of traditional army marches and soon American soldiers were marching to Sousa with a swing.

In 1944 Miller took his musicians to England. For the American troops stationed there the band was, as the saying soon had it, 'better than a letter from home'. For British troops, and those civilians who managed to hear the band during London and Home Counties dance hall appearances, the band was a revelation. Of course they had heard Glenn Miller on record, but the AAF band was something else. With hundreds of

Standing room only for the Glenn Miller band at Great Lakes Naval Training Station in June 1942.

drafted big band musicians to choose from, the leaders of the service bands were all able to build ideal, if not necessarily all-star bands. Now, at last, Glenn had a sprightly rhythm section, something that had always been a problem area for him, with Trigger Alpert on bass and Ray McKinley, drums.

Glenn Miller's ambition to have one of the best all-round bands was more than fulfilled. Even if his civilian outfit had never reached the heights of Tommy Dorsey, his AAF band had no serious deficiencies anywhere in its ranks.

But, musically, Glenn was still not satisfied. As Ray McKinley later observed, 'He once said to me, "I've gone as far as I can go with the saxophone sound. I've got to have something new." ' Given Glenn's questing nature, and his determination to reach the top and stay there, it seems highly likely that he would have found 'something new' but he never had the chance. On 15 December 1944, Glenn Miller boarded a light aircraft to fly from England to Paris in order to prepare for the band's appearance there. The aircraft took off into dense fog and was never seen again.

Glenn Miller's awareness of the commercial requirements of the popular music business suggests that he would have moved with the times. Perhaps he would not have become a companion of the progressive faction but it is tempting to speculate that he might well have devoted some of his time to exploring the possibilities opened up by the new concepts of Stan Kenton and Boyd Raeburn. More likely, perhaps, Glenn would have found the style of the later Claude Thornhill band very much to his liking. One thing that seems certain is that he would not have stood still.

The persistence of Glenn Miller's music and the way in which it is loved by so many people is a curious legacy for a man who would never have rested on his laurels.

Crooners and Canaries:
During the swing era no big band was complete without its shiny-haired crooner and bouncy, party-dressed canary.

Bing Crosby's languid crooning came to national prominence thanks to his appearances with the Paul Whiteman band in the 1920s and his later great rival, Frank Sinatra, first clasped his thin arms around a microphone in front of Harry James's band before becoming a superstar with Tommy Dorsey. Sinatra changed perceptions of band singers by projecting his personality to staggering effect. Other personality singers who could also do much more than merely sing in tune included Dick Haymes (with Harry James), Perry Como (with Ted Weems) and Mel Tormé (with Artie Shaw). They, like Sinatra and Crosby, rose to prominence on a swell of popularity. Contrastingly, Jimmy Dorsey's Bob Eberly had personality and a fine voice but chose not to push himself forward, and settled instead of stardom for being one of the boys in the band.

Among the ladies were some good singers, like Jimmy Dorsey's Helen O'Connell, Goodman's Helen Ward and Martha Tilton, and Helen Forrest who sang with Goodman, Artie Shaw and Harry James. Mary Ann McCall grew from being an average singer with Tommy Dorsey and Charlie Barnet to become a fine stylist with Woody Herman. ▶

Placing a date for the beginning or end of the swing era is a hit-and-miss affair. Musically, it was under way from the early 1930s but as a social phenomenon it began during the return leg of Benny Goodman's 1935-7 cross-country tour. The end came late in 1946 when several big name bands folded, forced out as much by rising costs as by changes in the musical tastes of the public. September 1946 saw an across-the-board pay increase negotiated by the American Federation of Musicians in Chicago and New York of between 20% for gigs in small clubs and 33% for the classier jobs in hotels and theatres. By November one of the great symbols of the big band years, Frank Dailey's Meadowbrook Ballroom, was weighing the possibility of abandoning booking name bands. Those bands that clung on were obliged to cut wages by as much as 50%. Sidemen who needed $125 a week to break even were being offered $100.

Bandleaders watched the signs and acted accordingly. Charlie Barnet told *down beat*'s Bill Gottlieb, 'I'm breaking up my present organisation because I don't want to get caught in the middle when dance hall operators, theatres and clubs holler, "Uncle!" Operators can no longer stay in business for having to shell out the huge guarantees orchestras require to cover their monstrous payrolls.'

A band's share of a successful engagement could be high—too high to make sound financial sense. When the new Rainbo Ballroom opened in Chicago on 12 March 1946, 4,000 dancers packed in to welcome

Tommy Dorsey and his band. Tommy was on a $10,000 guarantee and 60% of the take. The high guarantee set precedents for other bands which followed, including Stan Kenton's and Les Brown's. Such high outgoings, coupled with the fact that in between the name bands the Rainbo used local semi-pro bands and, perhaps worst of all, the management had failed to obtain a liquor licence, led to a rapid decline in business. By August, the Rainbo had terminated its dances and the hall was being used to stage all-in wrestling.

Affecting Tommy Dorsey, and most other bandleaders, were high salary demands from young musicians. Tommy resisted fiercely, preferring to hire older men who were more experienced and who he believed were also more likely to compromise on salary negotiations.

Public tastes in entertainment were also changing. Dancing, the staple of the big bands, was no longer as popular and the dance halls were hard hit. People sought other forms of entertainment of which one, TV, did little to encourage any lingering interest in big bands.

The most obvious mark left by the big bands on American popular music was found in the work of such former band singers as Perry Como, Doris Day, Dick Haymes, Peggy Lee, Frank Sinatra, Jo Stafford, Kay Starr and Mel Tormé who carved hugely successful solo careers.

Less obvious, but of much long-term significance, was the change which had come over orchestral music and arranging. The strides taken during the 1930s and 1940s, and the relevance of the music of the era to what happened afterwards, can be discerned from the fact that the music brought to popular attention by the commercial successes of the swing era has become an integral part of the fabric of American popular music (and much of that of Europe, too). Music heard on radio and records backing singers, background music for movies and TV, the structure of scores being used, is very different thanks to the popularity of the swing bands.

If 1946 found the swing era at an end, the music most certainly was not. A few brave spirits optimistically continued or even formed new bands. Sam Donahue took a band into New York's Roseland Ballroom in the summer of 1946. Featuring a two-beat style *a la* Jimmie Lunceford, the band was a knock-out success with dancers. At the same time, Georgie Auld presented a new band with Al Porcino and Al Cohn in its ranks. The band was on a defiantly non-commercial kick and didn't last long. Buddy Rich was also featuring a new band in 1946 and despite Charlie Barnet's gloomy predictions Buddy insisted he was not about to cut 'personnel, salaries or guarantees. And we'll be playing as much jump music as we always have.'

Although now decidedly thin on the ground there were still enough big bands around to keep the fans fairly happy but 1947 brought realisation that the glory days were over.

As for the musicians who had gained fame (and sometimes notoriety) and had made and often lost fortunes, many played on. Some worked in radio and recording studios in New York, others in Hollywood. A lucky few stayed on in the surviving bands. Some of the younger musicans who had entered the big bands during the last few years of the era moved into small groups, often the bebop bands.

All these musicians, young and old, whether working in studios or in jazz, owed their new roles to the experience they had gained in the ranks of the big bands. For the most part, both groups retained an abiding affection for the music of the swing era.

▶ Doris Day started out with Bob Crosby before moving to Les Brown's Band of Renown and enormous success, and Jo Stafford brought her considerable vocal talents to the Tommy Dorsey orchestra.

Mildred Bailey's lilting voice was heard with various bands including husband Red Norvo's swinging outfit. The best jazz stylist among the white girl singers was Anita O'Day who sang with Gene Krupa's band in the early 1940s and who stamped her unique brand of outrageous hipness on the band's biggest hits.

Another latterday song stylist is Rosemary Clooney who sang with the Tony Pastor band before she, too, decided to go solo. Careers as singles were also possible for June Christy and Chris Connor who learned their trade competing with the mighty roar of the Stan Kenton band.

It is no coincidence that so many important song stylists, male and female, came up through the big bands. It was there, night after night, that they practiced and honed their basic skills often learning from the musicians all around them.

In time, when singers were 'in' and bands were 'out', the singers were the most tangible evidence of the musical qualities of the big band years. Those that made it did so because of their personality projection, which developed during their apprenticeship with the big bands.

RAY ANTHONY AND HIS ORCHESTRA

There are a number of parallels between Ray Anthony and Harry James: both were taught the trumpet by their bandleading fathers, both were child prodigies, there are distinct similarities in tone, phrasing and vibrato, and both were, at times, a touch too-florid. It is apparent that Ray modelled his playing on that of Harry who was his senior by six years. Those six years meant that despite turning pro at 16 Ray, born in 1922, missed the hey-day of the big bands.

Ray's first job was with Al Donahue where he was heard by Glenn Miller. After Miller, Ray was with Jimmy Dorsey for a while before being drafted into the Navy where he led a service band in the Pacific.

After the war he continued bandleading with a 19-piece outfit that appealed to dancers and also those who listened to radio remotes from such venues as the Chase Hotel in St Louis and Chicago's Rainbo Ballroom.

A stylish musician with an engaging personality, Anthony established a name for himself as a solid if rarely inspired music-maker. With a policy that was musically interesting yet was geared to commercial needs, Anthony managed to stay afloat despite the general decline in big band business. His 1946 band took on board the fact that audiences liked the Glenn Miller sound and he used a clarinet-led Miller-style reed section with tightly muted trumpets and a warm-toned trombone section.

In the 1950s, Anthony led an extremely popular dance band, gaining exceptional success and a number of citations in many major polls. His fine, swinging band was enjoyed by millions on TV and on numerous albums produced for Capitol Records.

Ray's bands always featured an array of top studio talent including such notable session men as the ever-dependable rhythm duo of Don Simpson, bass, and Alvin Stoller, drums, supporting lead trumpet Conrad Gozzo and trombonists Dick Nash and Ray Sims. The saxophone section was also well-stocked with fine players, including Leo Anthony, Georgie Auld, Med Flory, Bob Hardaway, Skeets Herfurt and Plas Johnson (who later achieved anonymous fame as the player of the theme on the soundtrack of *The Pink Panther*).

Ray Anthony's band was one of numerous post-swing era studio bands which developed the use of sweeping saxophone sections interspersed with punchy bursts of staccato brass on easy-swinging melodies, to which were added solos from tough-toned trombonists, an effusive saxophone, or a muted trumpet.

With studio, TV and recording work backing up occasional dance and concert tours, Ray Anthony continued working into the 1980s. Like a handful of other latterday bandleaders, Ray's early experience with the name bands of the swing era helped him survive through the rock 'n' roll years.

Ray Anthony, a fierce soloist, led an always swinging big band from the 1940s and remained a mover and shaker in the business into the 1980s.

Cashing in:
In the Spring of 1946 the Tex Beneke band, made up mostly of former Glenn Miller sidemen, broke the house record at the Mosque in Richmond, NY. The take was $9,999.60 of which the band took $4,999.60.

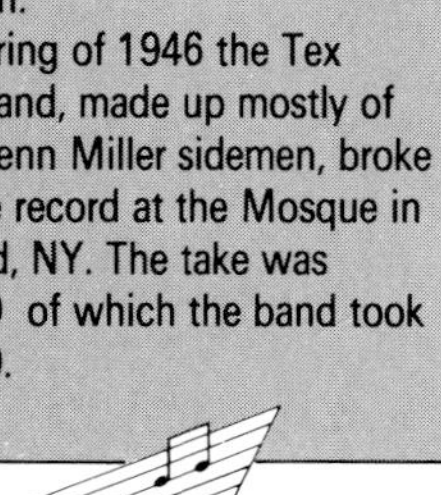

SYD LAWRENCE AND HIS ORCHESTRA

Syd Lawrence's musical career began in Chester, England, before World War II. It was here that his father ran a dance band but young Syd's own dance band experience did not really get under way until he was serving with the Royal Air Force in North Africa during the closing stages of the war. In the immediate post-war years he worked successively with the bands of Al Powell, Teddy Foster, Nat Temple, Geraldo, Sidney Lipton and Cyril Stapleton. With his dues paid, Syd then settled into a steady job with the BBC's Northern Dance Orchestra. In 1967, bored with the musical content of his daily routine, Syd formed a rehearsal band of like-minded souls and for the next two years built a good but limited reputation around Manchester. By the end of 1969 the band was receiving offers of work from farther afield and Syd decided to take the plunge into full-time bandleading.

An engagement to play at London's Royal Festival Hall on 17 November 1969, an occasion marking the 25th anniversary of the disappearance of Glenn Miller, proved to be a smashing success for Syd Lawrence and he has never looked back.

Although the band's book covers music made famous by most of the big band's of the swing era, his success is due primarily to his ability to recreate the music of Glenn Miller with affectionate and felicitous accuracy.

BILLY MAY AND HIS ORCHESTRA

Billy May's public acclaim came late in his career. He had already worked with top bands including those of Glenn Miller and Charlie Barnet (for whom he arranged 'Redskin Rhumba' and 'Pompton Turnpike' and co-scored 'Cherokee') but had become a staff arranger at NBC, later moving to Hollywood and studio work. On the coast he also worked with such stars as Phil Harris and Bing Crosby and in 1943 began working for Capitol Records, writing material for a wide range of projects.

In 1951 Billy was given the chance to produce a big band album. Searching for an identifiable sound he recalled his earlier love of Sy Oliver's arrangements for the Jimmie Lunceford band. With this in mind, he developed a simplified but truly individualistic use of the principles Oliver had expounded. The result: attacking brass, clean section work, and the unusual use of the saxophone section which produced a 'slurping' sound, gave Billy what he sought. His first album was so well received by public and critics alike that he was encouraged to form a working band for touring. The Lunceford connection was enhanced when Billy hired lead alto saxophonist Willie Smith to join the band.

Eventually, demands by the studios for his arranging and composing talents compelled Billy to hand over the touring band to Sam Donahue. This allowed him to concentrate on working with some of the best singers around, including Nat 'King' Cole, Sammy Davis Jr, and such big band alumni as Ella Fitzgerald, Anita O'Day, Frank Sinatra and Mel Tormé. Billy also continued producing record albums on which he employed a host of top session musicians.

Although Billy's arrangements majored on that distinctive slurred glissandi of the saxophone section, he also incorporated brief solos from such sidemen as trumpeter Don Fagerquist and saxophonists Justin Gordon and Joe Spang. The drumming of the dependable and dramatic Alvin Stoller was an essential part of the May band's drive, as was his pipping brass which employed such outstanding and experienced trumpeters as John Best, Pete Candoli, Maynard Ferguson, Conrad Gozzo and Mannie Klein. At various times the equally noteworthy trombone section included Murray McEachern, Tommy Pederson, Jim Priddy and Si Zentner.

Among the scores of tunes most readily associated with Billy May's sound and which gave him some of his biggest hits are 'Fat Man Boogie', 'Lean Baby' and 'In a Persian Market'.

CHAPTER EIGHT

KANSAS CITY COUNT

'SWINGIN' THE BLUES'

'Kansas City was something you can't speak about, you can't explain ... it was so bright and colourful.'

Count Basie

The mid-Western states of Kansas and Missouri have contributed much to American folk lore and popular culture. This was where Jesse James and his brother Frank became legends while they still lived and killed, where the Younger brothers roamed, where Charlie Quantrill led a band of murderous guerillas.

Kansas City, which lies partly in Kansas but mostly in Missouri, the two parts of the city separated by the Missouri River, grew apace in the post-Civil War years. Among the sharp-witted entrepreneurs who arrived in KC towards the end of the nineteenth century was Jim Pendergast, a gambling man who built up a small empire of hotels and saloons before turning a mercenary eye on the financial possibilities of politics. After Jim's death his brother Tom took over and by the 1930s nothing happened in Kansas City without the okay of Boss Pendergast and Tom okayed just about anything that made money: an endless stream of gambling dens, a widespread red-light district, and throughout Prohibition he turned a blind eye to illicit drinking joints.

Kansas City proved an irresistible lure to hot musicians drawn there by the brawling 'anything goes' atmosphere of Tom Pendergast's town and the freewheeling distinctive music it spawned.

To jazz musicians in the 1930s, and the lower levels of society with whom they were now inextricably bound: pimps, prostitutes, gamblers and anyone out for a good time in the old town every night, Kansas City was heaven. For sober-sided citizens of what was still, in spirit if not in fact, a wild and lawless frontier town, KC was hell on Missouri's once blood-soaked earth.

Among the countless nightspots offering music in KC were three clubs important in the development of jazz and, eventually, big band music: the Sunset, the Subway and the Reno Club. The first two of these employed good house musicians who provided the base for many excellent after-hours jam sessions; the Reno Club offered entertainment and dancing to blacks and whites (with separate dance floors), plenty to drink, and, thanks to the owners' links with Tom Pendergast, who controlled the police department, little risk of a raid.

Informal jam sessions continued well into the early hours. Pianist

'Back in the early thirties there was a band in Kansas City that more or less ruled the local jazz scene. It was that of the late Bennie Moten... I played "third piano" in that band. Bennie, of course, was the big man at the keys, and his brother Bus played piano-accordian.'

Count Basie

***

7 to 1:
One time, Fats Waller evolved a simple little theme and in 1929 Don Redman recorded it under the title 'Six Or Seven Times'. Buster Smith heard the record but when he wanted to use it at the Reno Club in Kansas City, where the Count Basie-Buster Smith Barons of Rhythm were playing, all he could remember was the fifteen note riff. 'We were fooling around at the club... I started playing that opening reed riff on alto. Lips Page jumped in with the trumpet part without any trouble and Dan Minor thought up the trombone part. That was it—a head.' Smith later wrote out some music, gave the tune a new title, 'Blue Balls', and it went into the band's book. A little while later, the band was broadcasting from a dance date in Little Rock and the announcer jibbed at giving out the unseemly title over the air. As it was about an hour after midnight, he suggested calling it 'One O'Clock Jump'. Only after the band's record was a hit and that simple riff had become Basie's theme tune did Buck Clayton sit down and copy the arrangement from the record.

***

'It was crazy. The whole band was *gone*.'

Lester Young

Sammy Price recalled one evening at the Subway Club when he came by a session at about ten o'clock, later went home to clean up and change his clothes, and when he returned, at one o'clock in the morning, they were still playing the same song.

Around 4am things would regularly hot up over at the Sunset with house pianist, Pete Johnson, digging into a blues groove. The Sunset's massive bartender was Joe Turner and when the spirit moved him he would lay down his towel and shout off soulful blues choruses that could be heard more than a block away.

Music was everywhere in the black section, while over on Twelfth and Eighteenth Streets, more than fifty cabarets swung out each evening.

Pianist Mary Lou Williams, remembering those free and easy happy days, recalled how out-of-town bands loved to play Kansas City. When the Ben Pollack band hit town she played piano for some of the boys in the band and Jack Teagarden sat in and sang the blues with her. Once, when Fletcher Henderson's band played KC, Coleman Hawkins became so involved at a jam session, where he was trying to outplay upcoming rivals Lester Young and Herschel Evans, that he lost track of time and was so late for the next day's gig that he burned out the engine of his brand-new Cadillac. Drummer Don Lamond confirmed that even as late as the end of the 1940s, when he was touring with Woody Herman's Second Herd, Kansas City was still a swinging town: 'That town just had a different atmosphere.'

Many of KC's finest musicians gained their early tuition through their

Sideman—June Clark:
Trumpet player Algeria Junius 'June' Clark worked with Fess Williams in New York where he was heard by Ed Smalls. Around 1924 he was invited to form a band to play at Ed's club, the Paradise. June hired a number of talented musicians including Jimmy Harrison, Benny Carter and a 20 year-old piano player newly-arrived in New York from Red Bank, New Jersey. Although he liked the pianist's playing June thought his reading was inadequate and because he showed no inclination to learn he fired him. The kid from Red Bank was named Bill Basie.

attendance at Lincoln High School where the music classes were supervised by Major N. Clark Smith. Major Smith had spent much of his early life as a drum major and leader of military bands. A well-travelled and experienced musician, Smith encouraged any latent talent he spotted and many of his pupils gained professional reputations in the ensuing years. The most important pupil of Al Lewis, who took over as instructor when Smith retired, was a young saxophonist named Charlie Parker.

Of seminal importance in the mid-West in KC's hey-day were some bands now only dimly recalled: Jesse Stone and his Blues Serenaders who worked out of St Joseph, George E. Lee and his Novelty Singing Orchestra, resident in KC, Walter Page's Blue Devils from Oklahoma City, and KC's finest, Bennie Moten and his Kansas City Orchestra. Further afield in the Southwest but also well known in Kansas City were the bands of Troy Floyd and Don Albert in San Antonio, Texas, Alphonso Trent in Dallas, Texas, and, later, the bands of Milt Larkins who was also famous in the Lone Star state, and Nat Towles who played around Omaha. All these and many more bands besides, were influential and contributed to the overall musical mode now associated with the Western territories.

The characteristics of KC jazz are easily recognised: a loosely swinging ensemble sound, the use of simple phrases and incessant brass riffs (the repetition of a single musical phrase), succinct piano interjections, frequent reliance upon the 12-bar blues, and the fresh innovative 4/4 rhythm. Instead of placing emphasis on the first and third beats, or on the second and fourth beats of a four-bar measure, Kansas City rhythm sections placed equal emphasis on all four beats. This created a smoothly flowing pulse which not only helped the band as a whole but inspired individual soloists through the greater freedom they now enjoyed.

At the peak of KC's creativity the bands which typified this peculiarly mid-Western sound were those of Andy Kirk and his Clouds of Joy, Harlan Leonard and his Rockets, Jay McShann and his Orchestra, and the glorious band of Count Basie.

But Basie's band, and the few others which briefly enjoyed national prominence, were far from being the only bands to project the spontaneous and flexible spirit which germinated in the exciting hothouse atmosphere of swirling nightclub life. In those hectic nights of the late 1920s and early 1930s, Kansas City was a melting pot of blues-drenched music.

One of the earliest Kansas City bands, led by Dave Lewis around 1920 and including trombonist DePriest Wheeler and drummer Leroy Maxey, regularly played for dancing in a ballroom situated at Fifteenth and Troost.

A few years later, Paul Banks led a band which included future Basie lead trumpeter Ed Lewis and Baby Lovett, a drummer originally from New Orleans who, in the mid-1940s, recorded with KC blues singer Julia Lee. Trumpeter Paul Webster who played in the Banks band later joined the great Jimmie Lunceford orchestra. Jap Allen, who played with Banks, eventually formed his own group which in turn featured the rising talents of pianist Clyde Hart and tenor saxophonist Ben Webster.

Jesse Stone, a native-born Kansas City pianist, was based in St Joseph and led one of the finest bands in the region. Unlike the majority of mid-West bands, which relied mainly upon 'head' and stock arrangements, the Stone band had a book filled with superior charts written by Stone himself. In Stone's band were future Basie baritonist Jack Washington

A date at Decca:
The full quality of the late 1930s Count Basie band can be appreciated simply by listing the personnel on, say, the recording sessions of 13 October 1937 through 6 June 1938: Buck Clayton, Harry Edison, Ed Lewis, trumpets; Eddie Durham, Dan Minor, Benny Morton, trombones; Earl Warren, Jack Washington, altos; Herschel Evans, Lester Young, tenors; the famed All-American Rhythm Section: Basie, piano, Freddie Green, guitar, Walter Page, bass and Jo Jones, drums, and the inimitable singing of Jimmy Rushing. These sessions produced such classics as 'Sent for You Yesterday', 'Swingin' the Blues', 'Blue and Sentimental', 'Doggin' Around' and 'Every Tub' (named for the cry that went up when an infrequent police raid occurred at a KC club and which derived from the expression, 'Every tub on its own bottom', a rather more colorful version of 'Every man for himself').

'Sent for You Yesterday' features Little Jimmy Rushing in fine vocal form, his high-pitched, slightly rasping tenor voice carrying easily over a shouting band. Other soloists include Harry Edison and Herschel Evans whose solo is particularly impressive. 'Swingin' the Blues' has a string of excellent solos including Evans, Lester Young and Buck Clayton while 'Blue and Sentimental' is a showcase for Evans. If he proves less adventurous on the song than might, say, his section mate, Lester Young, it is a glorious demonstration of an immense talent that was stilled abruptly eighteen months later with his death at the age of 29. Evans is also well in evidence on 'Doggin' Around' as is Lester Young, the man who did more than any other musician to change the role of the tenor saxophone in jazz.

***

'There was a variety of styles... all the way from... Texas up to Minnesota.'
Andy Kirk

Members of the Les Hite band pose for a publicity shot of film actress Ursula Jeans, star of *Cavalcade* in 1933. (L to R) Sonny Craven, George Orendorff, Charlie Jones, Joe 'King' Porter, Marvin Johnson, Marshal Royal, Lionel Hampton.

and future Lunceford lead trumpet Eddie Tompkins. Both were reliable section men as well as being good 'get off' performers.

Stone was a major influence on KC music and his band was one of the recognised top territory bands. When Stone was eventually defeated in a musical battle with the Blue Devils the band broke up acrimoniously. Stone began supplying arrangements for many other territory bands, including those led by Terrence Holder (which was later to become Andy Kirk's Clouds of Joy) and Thamon Hayes (whose band eventually evolved into Harlan Leonard's Rockets). Stone later joined Earl Hines's organisation in Chicago, contributing many fine arrangements and performing as substitute pianist.

During its best period, Stone's band was the musical equal of the more prestigious Bennie Moten band and its book could be compared favourably with that of Alphonso Trent's band. Both the Trent and Stone bands relied heavily on their stylish arrangements, perhaps to the detriment of sidemen who could otherwise have expanded their solo abilities. The majority of territory bands generally relied upon stock charts and heads,

The envy of many for their sartorial elegance and their superb musicianship, the Alphonso Trent band stayed in the territories and thus were kept out of the national limelight. In Memphis, Tennessee in 1932 were (L to R) Chester Clark, Hayes Pillars, John Fielding, A. G. Godley, George Hudson, Dan Minor, Peanuts Holland, Anderson Lacy, Eugene Crook, Trent, James Jeter, Leo 'Snub' Mosley, Louis Pitts, Brent Sparks, Robert Jackson.

> Dancers dictate:
> 'There was a group that used to come right around the band and they'd say, "Play so-and-so", so I'd ask them, "What way do you want it, man?" So they'd pat off the tempo they wanted, and that knocked me out.'
>
> *Andy Kirk*

or standards such as 'Tiger Rag', building their success on the ability of soloists to produce a favourable response with the public.

The band which sealed the Stone band's fate, Walter Page's Blue Devils, worked out of Oklahoma City, 300 or so miles south west of Kansas City.

The Blue Devils had neither the prestige of the Moten band nor the novelty appeal of George E. Lee's band and arrangements of the quality of Jesse Stone's were beyond the as-yet undeveloped skills of trombonist-arranger Eddie Durham. Where the Blue Devils excelled was in their enthusiasm and relish for band battles.

The Devils were a rough blues playing unit, with a proclivity for 'head' arrangements amply endowed with unison riffs to emphasise the improvised solos of sidemen who were more than simply proficient.

Within the Blue Devils' personnel lay the seeds of the emerging Kansas City style, which later spread across the nation, changing the sound of jazz and big band music.

According to drummer Jo Jones, trumpeter Hot Lips Page would begin a background riff after a soloist had blown maybe nine or ten choruses, the other horns picking up on his phrases. 'Not many arrangers could improve on Lips when it came to backing up a soloist,' Jones remarked. Hot Lips was Walter Page's half-brother and joined the band in 1928, later recalling, 'King Oliver, of course, was the chief influence on the Blue Devils, then Jelly Roll Morton, and then Duke Ellington, in that order.'

Walter Page was a fine bass player and anchor man, while in Buster Smith the Devils had an alto player of considerable talent. Other Blue Devils were Bill Basie on piano and the innovatory tenor saxophonist Lester Young.

Walter Page's incomparable Blue Devils, the band which paved the way for the Kansas City giants. Seen here at the Ritz Ballroom, Oklahoma City, in 1931 are (L to R) Hot Lips Page, Leroy 'Snake' White, Walter Page, James Simpson, Druie Bess, A. G. Godley, Reuben Lynch, Charlie Washington, Reuben Roddy, Ernie Williams, Theodore Ross, Buster Smith.

In contrast with the businesslike Moten organisation, the Blue Devils had not the remotest chance of landing a meaningful recording contract although they did record two titles: 'Blue Devil Blues' and 'There's a Squabblin' ' which feature searing Lips Page trumpet and the clarinet and alto of Buster Smith, plus blues shouter Jimmy Rushing's first known recording.

Like the bands in New York and elsewhere, Kansas City groups had been growing in size through the 1920s. In 1927 the leading band in the city, that of Bennie Moten, had three brass, four reeds and four rhythm. With the addition of extra brass and reeds in the early 1930s, the instrumental format approached that which was to become a standard for the big bands. Not that Moten had yet adapted to the new musical style. In his early years as a bandleader he owed much to the style of King Oliver's New Orleans-based music.

Born into a musical family in Kansas City in 1894, pianist Moten was a gifted musician, composer and arranger and by the early 1920s had his own popular dance band which grew in authority and size as the decade progressed.

Moten's principal rivals in the region were George E. Lee and Walter Page's Blue Devils, and it was the Devils which suffered most when Moten tempted away key personnel.

The changes in personnel of Moten's band resulting from his raid on the Devils were even more important than the band's increase in size and its growing confidence for among the musicians brought in were Bill Basie (whose arrival allowed Moten to lead and concentrate on arranging), Hot Lips Page and Jimmy Rushing.

When a few more changes were made, including the addition of saxophonists Herschel Evans, Ben Webster and Lester Young, and the

'But, Jesus, Jimmy Rushing could sing the blues, couldn't he? He was a comedian, a hell of a guy, but he could really sing the blues.'
Dicky Wells

recruitment of Walter Page himself, Bennie Moten's band was now supreme.

By 1935, despite some hard times, the Bennie Moten band had begun to develop a reputation outside the mid-West and was clearly poised to become a major force in the growing big band scene. Tragically, Moten underwent a tonsillectomy conducted with only a local anaesthetic. He moved during the operation and the surgeon accidentally severed the jugular vein.

Shaken by Moten's sudden death, and after spending some time playing solo at the Reno Club, Bill Basie eventually formed a band which drew substantially upon the old Bennie Moten crew. A gifted piano player who hailed originally from Red Bank, New Jersey, but had settled in the mid-West in the mid-1920s, Basie always acknowledged how much he had learned with Moten. It was, he observed, 'a great tempo band'.

Basie's first band at the Reno Club was known as the Barons of Rhythm and he shared leadership with alto saxophonist Buster Smith. It was during a broadcast from the Reno Club over a new local radio station that the amiably rotund, sleek-haired Bill Basie was named 'Count' by the announcer.

It was another Reno Club broadcast John Hammond heard while sitting in his car in Chicago outside the Congress Hotel where Benny Goodman was appearing. 'I couldn't believe my ears', Hammond later wrote, and he was so enthusiastic he insisted Benny should listen too. Benny was less than impressed, although as Hammond wryly acknow-

Before Basie, the most famous Kansas City band of them all was Bennie Moten's seen here in 1931 at the Fairyland Park, KC. (L to R, front row) Vernon Page, Basie, Hot Lips Page, Ed Lewis, Thamon Hayes, Eddie Durham, Woody Walder, Buster Berry, Harlan Leonard, Booker Washington, Willie 'Mack' Washington, Jack Washington. At rear (L to R) stand Bennie Moten, Ira 'Bus' Moten, Jimmy Rushing.

ledged, he hadn't been too diplomatic in his conversation with the King of Swing. 'There I was in the parking lot of the Congress, telling him that a nine-piece group in Kansas City was the best I had ever heard, while across the street he was enjoying a triumph with one of the smash bands of the country.'

During the following months the personnel gradually changed and was enlarged but this gathering of remarkable individual talents not only provided highly-charged music, it also led to a sometimes ragged ensemble sound which counted against the band when it first tried breaking into the New York big-time. Few of the band were skilled readers and many of the arrangements were not written but were 'heads', pulled out of the smoky atmosphere of the Reno Club by musicians revelling in their music. Their enthusiasm was enormous, as Basie recalled, 'we just wanted to get to work and play'.

This enthusiasm carried the band over the hurdles of sometimes scrappy performances in Chicago but, thanks to hard work, and the loan by Fletcher Henderson of some of his arrangements, they survived to open at New York's Roseland Ballroom in November 1936. While the band received a mixed reception from critics, the white dancers loved the flowing beat. Perhaps even more important for the band was its enthusiastic reception by the notoriously hard to please black audience at Harlem's Apollo Theatre. In February 1937 the band became the first black outfit to play the William Penn Hotel in Pittsburgh. This engagement was important to the band's continuing success as it was broadcast and thus helped bring its refreshing sound and spirit to a growingly appreciative audience.

The Jeter-Pillars Orchestra

Bands with dual leadership have been relatively rare. These few include the Dorsey Brothers and Hudson-DeLange, both of which came to grief over disagreements between the leaders. One dual-led band which managed to retain harmony for many years was the black territory band led by James Jeter and Hayes Pillars. They were boyhood friends who played together in the Alphonso Trent band and after Trent disbanded decided to form their own group. Successful throughout the 1930s and the war years, when they toured the South Pacific, the band folded in 1947.

The Jeter-Pillars band was highly versatile, producing popular dance music of most kinds and, when called upon, could swing mightily. Their finest jazz soloist was trumpeter Harry Edison who went on to fame and the nickname 'Sweets' with Count Basie. In the 1950s Sweets Edison graced countless studio sessions and was a favourite of Nelson Riddle who used his muted horn to great, decorative effect on the Frank Sinatra albums which helped underwrite the singer's comeback.

THE KID FROM RED BANK

The remarkable collective sound and individual solo talents of the early Basie band was never to be repeated. Basie's later bands followed different paths, appealing to different sections of the public. Thus arises one of the curiosities of the big band years, the fact that while the jazz fan tends to prefer the early Basie band, the big band enthusiast inclines more towards the bands Basie led in the late 1950s and onwards.

The early Basie band was the epitome of swinging simplicity. The band's arrangements were mostly 'heads' conceived by the band collectively, discussed and perfected without the necessity for too many dots on paper. Indeed, the reading ability of many members of the band of the late 1930s was decidedly suspect. The band included many musicians who were distinctive jazz soloists of the very highest order plus 'the All-American Rhythm Section': Count Basie on piano, Freddie Green, guitar, Walter Page, bass and Jo Jones on drums.

Jo Jones's use of the high hat cymbal and his shifting of the emphasis away from the bass drum was highly original (although he always insisted on crediting Walter Johnson with the innovation); Walter Page and Freddie Green had rock-steady rhythmic sense and Basie himself was a master of elegant understatement. Basie's tempo-setting frequently took the form of an exploratory few bars on piano until he found what he wanted at which point he would 'nod in' the rest of the rhythm section before bringing in the full band. Collectively, this rhythm section played with a light, even swing with an unflagging four beats to the bar. The result of this combination of striking individual rhythmic talents was a crisp section that was unique for its time and in its context has never since been surpassed.

The individual brilliance of the Basie soloists became the envy of all other bandleaders with pretensions towards playing hot, jazz-based big band music. Rarely could be found such immense jazz talent as that displayed by Buck Clayton, Harry Edison, Benny Morton, Dicky Wells, Herschel Evans and Lester Young.

For all their occasional raggedness, the brass and reed sections showed astonishing rapport with the soloists, offering them imaginative backing and an understanding of dynamics that the most sophisticated of arrangers found hard to match.

While other bands might have chosen to concentrate upon sophisticated tone colouring or counterpoint, the Basie band concentrated above all else on swinging.

As with almost all the mid-West and Southwest bands, Basie's crew majored on the blues, brilliantly employing the form's sighing lines, its repetitions and its climactic use of the preacher's exultant refrain.

Following a set of remarkable recording sessions in 1937–8 a few changes in personnel occurred but these did not weaken the band, indeed, some strengthened it. Dicky Wells replaced Durham, Shad Collins was added to the trumpet section, Chu Berry came in for Evans (and was in turn later replaced by Buddy Tate), while Jimmy Rushing shared his vocal duties first, briefly, with Billie Holiday and then with the effervescent Helen Humes.

Records made during 1939 and on into the early 1940s included many striking performances which helped rewrite big band style: 'Taxi War Dance', 'Miss Thing', 'Pound Cake', 'Clap Hands Here Comes Charlie', 'Tickle Toe', 'Moten Swing'.

Fine soloists abounded in the early 1940s band, some old hands, others new, but the ensemble passages show that the freewheeling head arrangements on the strength of which the band had charged out of Kansas City in the mid-1930s has given way to a similarly freewheeling sound but one which is now being read off Fletcher Henderson-inspired charts by Jimmy Mundy and Buster Harding. Other soloists continued to add strength to the band: Lucky Thompson, Emmett Berry, Illinois Jacquet among them. It is in the ensembles that change is most readily heard; it begins to sound crisper while still retaining an enviable looseness.

By the end of World War II the band was still in good shape. The recording ban of 1948 affected Basie, as it did other surviving big bands, although air shots which have emerged show the band to be in enthusiastic good form but, by the end of the decade, Basie was finding the going tough.

Forced to regroup as a sextet throughout 1950, Basie reformed his big band in 1951 for an engagement at the Apollo and also made records featuring arrangements by Neal Hefti. These records indicated the way the future Basie bands would sound with much tighter ensembles than hitherto. Intermittent gigs for a big band kept interest alive and at the end of 1951 he managed to hang on and never again reduced to the small group.

The new band played with a well-drilled precision that would have been foreign to the Reno Club gang but thanks to an impeccable rhythm section, which included Freddie Green and drummer Gus Johnson, the band swung furiously. The solo talent, while lacking the skills of Buck Clayton, Dicky Wells and Lester Young was still impressive and the saxophone section, under the leadership of Marshal Royal, was remark-

Nat Towles And Milt Larkins

In the mid-1930s, two good but overlooked bands originated in Texas. One was led by Nat Towles, the other by Milt Larkins. Towles began his career in New Orleans playing with Punch Miller and Henry 'Red' Allen. Moving to Austin, Texas, Towles formed a band which quickly proved to be an extremely popular outfit. Among the band's personnel were a number of talented sidemen who later made a mark in jazz. Fred Beckett became featured trombonist with Harlan Leonard and much later Henry Coker was a cornerstone of Count Basie's trombone section. Buddy Tate and C. Q. Price respectively held down the tenor and alto chairs in Towles' band, and Sir Charles Thompson was the pianist. In later years Buddy Tate, perhaps a trifle over-enthusiastically, claimed that the Nat Towles band was superior to Basie's. 'We would have torn them apart.'

Among Towles' major competitors in Texas was a Houston-based band led by trumpeter Milt Larkins. Inspired by veteran New Orleans trumpet star Bunk Johnson, Larkins formed his first band in 1936. Members of the band in its early years included tenor saxophonist Arnett Cobb and alto saxophonist and blues singer Eddie Vinson. Later, Larkins employed another earthy tenor player, Illinois Jacquet, and singer T-Bone Walker. An exuberant band, the Larkins crew had a high reputation among musicians who met and battled with them, and often lost. Eddie 'Cleanhead' Vinson remembers the Milt Larkins band with affection: 'We didn't know how good we were until we played against some of the name bands.'

Lester Young's unmistakably angled saxophone dominates the Count Basie band at Treasure Island, San Francisco, in 1939. (L to R) Basie, Walter Page, Buddy Tate, Freddie Green, Jo Jones, Earl Warren, Buck Clayton, Benny Morton, Ed Lewis, Jack Washington, Young, Dan Minor, Harry Edison.

The tiny bandstand at the Famous Door on 52nd Street had barely enough room for Count Basie's wonderful band on their breakthrough visit in 1938. Herschel Evans solos under the watchful eye of section mate Lester Young. (L to R) Walter Page, Jo Jones, Freddie Green, Basie, Benny Morton, Evans, Dicky Wells, Ed Lewis, Earl Warren, Harry Edison, Jack Washington, Young.

able. This section: Royal and Ernie Wilkins, altos, Candy Johnson, Paul Quinichette, tenors, Charlie Fowlkes, baritone, made every other big band saxophone section, past, present and future look to its laurels. Playing such Hefti charts as 'Fawncy Meeting You' and 'Sure Thing' alongside Nat Pierce's exemplary 'New Basie Blues', the band's records had a dramatic effect on the big band scene. New standards had been set.

Improvisation *v.* arrangements—3: The loose, swinging Basie style originated from the use of head arrangements based largely on the blues and created by members of the band. Their success relied heavily upon the superb improvisational skills of Lester Young, Herschel Evans, Buck Clayton, Harry Edison, Dicky Wells, Benny Morton and their fellows. As the band progressed so the need for written arrangements increased and arrangers such as Eddie Durham and Buster Harding, sympathetic to the free-wheeling spirit of the band, were commissioned to write simple but effective orchestrations. With the new Basie band of the 1950s the arrangements remained relatively simple and writers like Ernie Wilkins and Neal Hefti, along with Johnny Mandel and Manny Albam, were able to give continuity to the Basie sound. Wilkins also managed to transpose something of the Basie quality to the Harry James band. Aided by a saxophone section well-drilled by ex-Lunceford lead alto Willie Smith, Wilkins combined the qualities of the Lunceford ensemble with the Basie sound while the presence of Buddy Rich on drums added further crackling dynamics.

***

'We've got to keep this in mind, dancing was about the only pleasure.'

Andy Kirk

Despite Count Basie's supremacy on the national, and eventually on the international, scene he did not have it all his own way in and around Kansas City in the early days where he was up against some great musical talents.

One of the most musicianly bands from the Southwest and mid-West territories to gain national prominence was that led by Andy Kirk. A multi-instrumentalist, Kirk joined Terrence Holder's Dark Clouds of Joy in Dallas, Texas in the late 1920s. When Holder quit, Kirk took over leadership of the band and by the early 1930s Andy Kirk and his Clouds of Joy had become one of the most popular bands of the region. Thanks to the efforts of George E. Lee who heard and admired the band, Kirk obtained an engagement at Kansas City's Pla-Mor Restaurant. During this gig the band auditioned for a recording contract, using a deputy pianist. The deputy was Mary Lou Williams who came up with a batch of arrangements, several of which were of her own compositions. The records were successful and some time later Mary Lou joined as a regular member of the band.

The Clouds of Joy was a subtly swinging outfit, with an ensemble sound which, while not achieving the full-throated roar of many of the bigger bands, never drifted into tinniness. Mary Lou Williams's arranging talents grew apace and the consistency of performance the band achieved owed much to her skills. On such numbers as Ellington's 'Ring Dem Bells' the band plays with great zest over a rhythm section which, for fluidity and its subtle beat, is very nearly as distinguished as Basie's. Indeed, on some tunes, 'Twinklin' ' for example, Mary Lou sets the tempo and mood as might Basie.

The band's outstanding soloist was tenor saxophonist Dick Wilson whose light tone and favouring of the upper register brought him closer to Lester Young than most other players of the instrument of the time. Wilson's contribution to the band's success was important and he is featured on numerous titles including 'Ring Dem Bells', '47th Street Jive'. 'Moten Swing' and is in exceptionally fine form on 'Lotta Sax Appeal'. Wilson's death in 1941 at the age of 30 was a major loss.

During the early 1940s the band's success continued despite the death of Wilson and the departure of Mary Lou Williams but the consistency of performance and the lithely swinging elegance which had distinguished the Clouds of Joy had begun to fade.

One of the longest lasting black bands and certainly one of the very few territory bands to achieve success nationally, Andy Kirk and his Clouds of Joy was an outstanding musical organisation. The band's tuneful work from the period between 1936 and the start of the AF of M recording ban in 1942 remains a pleasant reminder of the high standards set by bands from the territories.

Another outstanding territory band from the mid-West, but which earned much less fame than the Clouds of Joy was Harlan Leonard's Rockets.

Although a highly trained musician and a former member of the

Harlan Leonard's Rockets strike a pose in 1938. (L to R) Edward 'Peeny' Johnson, Richmond Henderson, Sidney Miller, Ben 'Snake' Curtis, James Ross, Roselle Claxton, Edward Phillips, Harlan Leonard, Jimmy Keith, Burnie Cobb, Darwin Jones, Freddie Culliver.

Bennie Moten band and, later, the band led by Thamon Hayes, Leonard never considered himself to be a soloist. His forte was as an accurate and dependable section man. 'You could divide jazz musicians into two classes, the trained men, like myself, and the people I call "naturals"... those with the great *natural* ability, who were usually self-taught and used unorthodox fingering, embouchure, reeds and so on. You needed both kinds in a strong band ... A band's intonation and sound quality depended a great deal on accurate section leadership...

The Rockets originated out of the Thamon Hayes band which folded during a trip to Chicago. With the Pendergast political machine in a state of collapse in KC, many leaders were either disbanding or moving on and Leonard was able to capitalise on the disarray and become the leading band in the city. A well-drilled unit playing in the customary KC idiom, the band had two major soloists in tenor saxophonist Henry Bridges and trombonist Fred Beckett, cited by J. J. Johnson as a major influence on modern trombone playing. A great contribution to the band's success was the modern arranging skills of Tadd Dameron, backed with arrangements by Roselle Claxton, Eddie Durham, James Ross and Buster Smith.

The band's arrival in New York City coincided with the opening of the Golden Gate Ballroom in Harlem which planned to rival the Savoy. In a burst of publicity, the ballroom's management booked the Leonard band along with the bands of Coleman Hawkins, Les Hite, Claude Hopkins and the Milt Herth Trio. Although an extremely slick unit, the Rockets never had the breaks.

After Basie's departure from Kansas City for bigger and more distinguished pastures, one of the city's top bands was Jay McShann's.

Pianist McShann became a Kansas City bandleader almost by chance. Changing buses in Kansas City en route between his home in Muskogee, Oklahoma, and Omaha, Nebraska, he decided to spend a little time in KC, mainly for the opportunity of hearing the Count Basie band. This

'When I joined Count Basie I was only 19 years old and I was having too much fun to be serious and appreciate how important jazz was to American art and culture... Everyone in that band had a distinctive style. When you heard a Basie record you knew who was taking a solo... I dearly loved Count Basie because had it not been for him there wouldn't be any Buck Claytons or Lester Youngs or Jo Jones's, none of us, because he exploited us to our advantage. He would let us play as long as we wanted to play, as long as it was interesting. It was a great school.'

Harry Edison

Walter Brown singing with the jumping Jay McShann band in 1942 but the real star is reed section member, Charlie Parker. (L to R) McShann, Leonard Enois, Gene Ramey, Brown, Bob Mabane, Gus Johnson, Parker, Buddy Anderson, John Jackson, Bob Merrill, Freddie Culliver, Orville Minor, Lawrence Anderson, Joe 'Taswell' Baird.

was in 1937 and Basie had left town but McShann ran into some old friends and was persuaded to stay. In Basie's absence the big band in town was Harlan Leonard's Rockets and when they too left McShann decided to form his own band. He had built up a reputation as a good piano player, and was able to secure work for a five-piece band at Martin's on the Plaza, one of the best clubs in town. Eventually, on a trip to Omaha, he poached a batch of good sidemen from the Nat Towles band and so became leader of a big band.

McShann's hiring of singer Walter Brown proved important to the band's success when Brown had a number of hit records. From its early days the band had the loose, freewheeling sound associated with the Kansas City bands, thanks to the fine rhythm section of McShann, Lucky Enois, guitar, Gene Ramey, bass, and Gus Johnson, drums, with extremely good soloists in trumpeter Buddy Anderson and tenor saxophonist Bob Mabane. The young, Kansas City-born Charlie Parker was also an early inspiration to the band. Parker's alto saxophone solos on 'Swingmatism', 'Hootie Blues' and 'The Jumping Blues' all contain hints of the dramatic changes which would evolve in jazz in the next few years.

On a visit to New York, McShann's band was a huge success at the Savoy and at the Apollo Theatre and might well have gone on to greater things but the draft whisked away the band's promising young men and in 1942 McShann had difficulty finding replacements. Late the following year McShann himself was drafted.

SIXTEEN MEN SWINGING

The later Basie bands not only came as something of a shock to the jazz audience, they were a revelation to big band fans and musicians alike. The sound of big bands, especially in Britain, began to take on a distinctly Basie-inspired sound from the mid-1950s onwards. The new band was a tight, cohesive unit with sixteen men swinging and at times sounding like one. The rhythm section settled down for a while with the excellent Gus Johnson on drums but he was dislodged to make way for Sonny Payne, a flashy performer whose antics were enjoyed by audiences even though his timing was such that Freddie Green briefly kept a stick to poke at Sonny when he rushed the tempo. Yet, the extrovert and hard-driving Payne proved complementary to a band which enthused over its ability to play with well-drilled perfection. The brass was a select group and while there were still several soloists of note to be found it was in the ensembles that they had most impact ripping into phrases with great precision and panache. The saxophone section was similarly scattered with good soloists and bit hard on fine unison parts written with understanding by arrangers like Nat Pierce, Neal Hefti and Frank Foster. Superbly executed, these arrangements ably drew upon the qualities of the musicians for whom they were written. But technical perfection eventually led to a certain predictability whereas the early band had always been capable of surprising the listener.

Ernie Wilkins had been hired at Clark Terry's urging when Basie needed a replacement alto. But the real talent of Wilkins, initially hidden, was his skill as an arranger.

By the late 1950s, the band was at its most powerful with a book choc-ful of striking arrangements by Foster, Hefti, Quincy Jones, Thad Jones, Pierce and Wilkins. The band proved to be a massive success with audiences both for its concert appearances and on records.

Concerts were now the setting for the band, unlike the dance halls of

The Milt Larkins band at the Rhumboogie Club, Chicago, in 1942. (L to R) Cedric Haywood, Lawrence Cato, Milt Larkins, Alvin Burroughs, Moses Gant, Calvin Ladnier, Tom Archia, Clarence Trice, Frank Dominguez, Arnett Sparrow, Jesse Miller, Sam Player, John 'Stringline' Ewing.

old. This brought changes in presentation and style. The album, 'The Atomic Mr Basie', shows this band off to superb and impressive effect and helped exercise Basie's enormous influence on numerous other bands.

The undoubted merits of the Basie band's section work and their well-rehearsed precision changed perceptions among musicians. After the band's 1957 visit to Britain there was a noticeable shift in the work of British arrangers and big band performances generally. After a decade or so of following the patterns of Glenn Miller and Tommy Dorsey, the new exemplar for British bands was Basie. When set against, say, the music of Stan Kenton, who also appeared in Europe during the mid-1950s, Basie's precise swing proved enormously attractive particularly in its deceptive simplicity.

Through the 1960s and 1970s and on into the early 1980s, the Basie band toured and recorded. Later arrangers included Sammy Nestico, Johnny Mandel and Bill Holman but for all their originality, they did not turn the band in any new direction. The sections played with precision, soloists went through their paces, but moments of creative tension lessened.

'In the old band we had great soloists. This band... is just more rehearsed.'

Harry Edison

***

Quotes from the Count:
'I can't play in a small group because you have to play too much. And, then, I guess I'm too simple—I just like the sound [of a big band],that's all.'

'... the guys will say, "Well, look, Basie, what are you gonna play?" and I say, "The same old beef stew".'

'Eating must go on, and rent must be paid...'

In the 1950s and 1960s bands, a considerable amount of solo work fell on the shoulders of trumpeter Joe Newman who, at his best, played with piercing attack. Another trumpet player of note, and a significant contributor to the band's book, was Thad Jones. Veteran trumpeter Snooky Young also worked effectively with Basie. The trombones included the authoritative Henry Coker, the smoothly elegant Benny Powell and the always exciting Al Grey.

Marshal Royal in the lead alto chair rehearsed the band meticulously while tenor saxophonist Eddie 'Lockjaw' Davis gave many dynamic performances.

Two changes boosted the band's overall qualities in the 1970s: the young drummer Butch Miles gave the rhythm section a dramatic spark while tenor saxophonist Jimmy Forrest proved a popular soloist.

For all the Basie band's popularity, only the Count and Freddie Green retained a link between this band and that other, extraordinary unit which had crowded onto the tiny stage at New York's Famous Door back in 1938.

Count Basie, the Kid from Red Bank, died in April 1984 and with his passing the strongest and longest-lasting link with the raw, wild, but intensely musical days of Kansas City was finally severed.

The thoughtfully oblique solo skills of Lester Young and others in the early Basie band and the massive international success of the Count's later bands have understandably clouded the qualities of the many other fine groups which had jostled for audiences back in Kansas City in the 1930s.

Unquestionably, Basie's band became the best but even if many of these other bands played to only localised success in KC and the Southwest, their value as training grounds for individual musicians who later went on to carve successful careers with big-name bands should not be overlooked.

It says much for the music of Kansas City that in addition to producing such significant musical revolutionaries as Lester Young and Charlie Parker, it also generated a unique concept for big band music, a concept played around the world and exemplified by the inimitable Count Basie.

ALPHONSO TRENT AND HIS ORCHESTRA

Next to the Moten-Page-Basie triumvirate, the band of the Southwest with the greatest reputation was undoubtedly Alphonso Trent's. Musicians' reminiscences and historical researches by Franklin S. Driggs, Ross Russell and others have built a compelling and impressive picture of the band which, sadly, cannot be complemented by recordings. Quite clearly, the handful of records the band made give an inadequate picture of its abilities.

Trent, who was born in Arkansas, had the benefit of formal tuition and worked extensively as a pianist before forming his first band. His success began when he inherited Eugene Crooke's Synco Six and took this small band into the Adolphus Hotel in Dallas, Texas, in 1925. The band was expanded to ten pieces including trombonist Snub Mosley (who later became highly proficient on the slide saxophone, an instrument he devised himself), James Jeter, alto, and A. G. Godley, generally acclaimed by drummers as the father of Kansas City style drumming. Later additions to the band included the combative violinist Stuff Smith, Charles Pillars, alto, Hayes Pillars, tenor (who later joined forces with his section mate to form the Jeter-Pillars Orchestra), and trumpeters Peanuts Holland and Sy Oliver.

The band's personnel was remarkably consistent, a result of high wages and exceptionally good conditions for a territory band: smart uniforms, expensive instruments, limousines. The settled personnel doubtless helped the band maintain its high standards although the high regard in which they were held by other musicians might well result from mild envy at such unusually congenial working conditions.

On the strength of the tiny handful of records the band made it was obviously a well-rehearsed, swinging outfit and featured excellent soloists in Holland, Hayes Pillars and, especially, Mosley, a master-technician. The band also enjoyed the services of an exceptional arranging talent in Gus Wilson (brother of pianist Teddy) whose score for 'Clementine' is highly regarded. It was in respect of its book that the Alphoso Trent band differed most from other territory bands. Largely eschewing 'heads' the band played written arrangements with great skill and verve although this concentration upon arranged music proved detrimental to soloists.

Due to inept management, the band fell on hard times before the swing era was under way and folded in 1933. Alphonso Trent continued playing with small groups throughout the decade (for one of which he unearthed the extraordinary genius of the electric guitar, Charlie Christian) and on into the 1940s although by then music was only a part-time occupation. He died in 1959 at the age of 54.

THE ARRANGER'S TOUCH—3

Early big band arrangements were subject to much controversy. In the 1920s the bands of Paul Whiteman and Fletcher Henderson led the way in showing how 'special arrangements' could be applied. Whiteman, through his pseudo-symphonic style wherein solo improvisation was quashed; Henderson, whose arranger, Don Redman, left ample space for the hot soloist. It was bands such as Whiteman's and Art Hickman's which first established the use of saxophone sections although these were rigid units not far removed from the earlier syncopated band sounds. Initially, Redman incorporated the same call-and-response patterns used by Whiteman, content simply to duplicate the extremely popular Whiteman sound. Later, however, Redman was to say, 'That thirty-piece band could read the notes, but they couldn't seem to get the real feeling.' Neither, in the first instance, could Redman but when Louis Armstrong blew into New York from Chicago to take a seat in the Henderson trumpet section things began to change. Louis's solos were a revelation, standing out in striking contrast to the rest of the band and forcing Redman to rethink his approach. Eventually, he laid down the foundations of swing orchestration as we know it today. Clarinetist Tony Scott has observed that, 'it all starts with the soloist. What he plays today, the arranger writes tomorrow.' This is just how it was with Redman. After considering the implications inherent in Louis's solo improvisations, Redman was able to formulate his approach by transposing some of the excitement of New Orleans collective 'faking' to the larger unit and translating the few crude lines of music from King Oliver's repertoire which Louis Armstrong was able to show him into section work. In much the same way, Bill Challis, arranger with the Jean Goldkette band, acted as catalyst for the talents of Bix Beiderbecke and Frankie Trumbauer, writing excellent arrangements prompted by the playing of these two great jazzmen.

CHAPTER NINE

SWING OUT: BLACK BANDS

'RUFF SCUFFLIN' '

'We were all happy and all in the same groove.'

Trummy Young

'When you talk about bands that could swing, don't forget the Lunceford band! I was with them for three or four years, and I'm telling you that that was one swinging band!'

Ferdinand Arbelo

During the heady days of the swing era the white bands of Benny Goodman, Jimmy and Tommy Dorsey, Harry James, Glenn Miller and Artie Shaw captured the imagination of dancers, the teenage bobby-soxers and their hep cat boyfriends. Yet for all these success stories there were countless white bands that didn't make it, which faded during the uphill struggle or burned-out spectacularly after brief moments at the top. The great majority simply got by, making a living and touring endlessly, eating slop and drinking cheap whisky and hoping, always hoping, for the big break.

How much worse it was for black bands that didn't make it to the very top. Even those that did: Basie, Calloway, Ellington, Lunceford and a few others, failed to achieve the same degree of financial success or public acclaim as their white cousins. The black bands that failed, or spent their years scuffling, had practically nothing going for them, except an unquenchable desire to make music.

A combination of circumstances and attitudes determined the course taken by black big band music. At its root was the educational system in America in the first half of this century. Educational opportunities were separate and, whatever reformers might aver to the contrary, still unequal. Young black musicians often had to make do with only rudimentary musical education, if they were lucky enough to get any at all.

With only rare exceptions the musical policy adopted by black bands concentrated their repertoires on hot music. Many black bands relied upon stock arrangements which allowed little opportunity for development of a distinctive musical style. However, generally blessed with better rhythm sections capable of setting ideal tempos, most could outswing their white counterparts and were thus popular with dancers of both races. But, musically, that lack of formal education often meant that they were rougher and less well-rehearsed than white bands. However striking their hot soloists might be, they needed much more to gain a foothold on the ladder of commercial success.

It is a mark of the quality and durability of some black bands that while a few, Basie and Ellington for example, were numbered among the long-running successes of the big band years, others, notably Earl Hines, Billy Eckstine and Dizzy Gillespie, were among the great movers and shakers who helped drag big bands into the bebop era.

Of the earlier successes, that of Cab Calloway was perhaps the most

Lucky Millinder's Blue Rhythm Band in 1937. (L to R) Billy Kyle, Millinder, Tab Smith, Danny Barker, Oneill Spencer, Harry Edison, Benny Williams, Eli Robinson, Charlie Shavers, Ronald Haynes, Al Cobbs, Eddie Williams, Carl 'Bama' Warwick, Johnny Williams.

Like it or not, the musicians in Cab Calloway's band sometimes had to join in the whoopin' and hollerin'. Here, the band is seen on stage at the Cotton Club, January, 1935. (L to R) Lamar Wright, DePriest Wheeler, Ed Swayzee, Keg Johnson, Doc Cheatham, Claude Jones, Benny Payne, Leroy Maxey, Calloway, Eddie Barefield, Morris White, Arville Harris, Al Morgan, Andy Brown, Walter 'Foots' Thomas.

COLUMBIA
CBS

'Jubilee is highly honoured to have as its guest the International Sweethearts of Rhythm, an 18-carat aggregation consisting of nothing but gals—so without further popping-off at the gums, gal-vanize us, gals, galvanize us.'

Ernie Whitman
(AFRS announcer)

***

Sideman—Hilton Jefferson: Respected by his peers, alto saxophonist Hilton Jefferson is an example of a musician of stature being overshadowed throughout his career by the extraordinary talents of others; in his case by Johnny Hodges and Benny Carter.

Jefferson's credentials could hardly be bettered. He spent his long career in such top-ranking bands as those led by Claude Hopkins, Chick Webb, King Oliver, Fletcher Henderson, Duke Ellington and Don Redman.

The band with which Jefferson is generally associated is Cab Calloway's. Although allotted few solos, his performance on 'Willow Weep for Me' makes this one of Calloway's best-remembered recordings. Cushioned by an Andy Gibson arrangement, the ease with which Jefferson executes his solo is a perfect example of big band solo craftsmanship.

***

'You know, I loved that band and most of the guys in it are big names now. Ben Webster, Cozy Cole, Dizzy, J. C. Heard.'

Cab Calloway

spectacular. Indeed, it was difficult to overlook such a flamboyant individual. An unfortunate side effect of Cab's flamboyance is that the band he led for many years is often undervalued.

Visually, Cab offered far more to the general public than did any other bandleader. Dressed in white or yellow or powder blue 'Zoot' suits—baggy, narrow-bottomed trousers, long drape jackets—with a huge, wide-brimmed hat and floor-trailing watch chain, he gyrated in front of the band to such good effect that he would probably have achieved just as much success if his musicians had been second-rate. As one disgruntled musician remarked, 'whenever we got going, and this was a band that could really swing, there he was up to all that hollerin' and yellin'!'

Cab Calloway began working with The Missourians in the late 1920s and was so successful that the band's name was changed to Cab Calloway and his Orchestra. An engagement at the Cotton Club confirmed the early promise and by the mid-1930s, as the swing era got under way, it was immensely popular with both black and white audiences. From the mid-1930s onwards the band's personnel become progressively stronger with Calloway showing his appreciation of jazz talent by hiring exceptional musicians. But, unlike the Basie and Ellington bands, its members had fewer opportunities to shine. When those opportunities arose, however, the soloists eagerly grabbed them with often extraordinary results as recordings show.

Although the band's recordings continued to feature Cab's vocals there was now more solo space. Chu Berry plays exquisitely on 'Ghost of a

Sabby Lewis Band at Club Zanzibar, NYC, 1944.
(L to R) Joe Booker, George Nicholas, George Fauntleroy, Irving Randolph, George James, Freddy Webster, Jerry Heffron, Leonard Graham, Maceo Bryant, Howard Scott.

Chance' and 'Lonesome Nights', while his swinging urgency on uptempo numbers is demonstrated on 'Take the A Train' and 'Tappin' Off'. Hilton Jefferson's solo opportunities were drastically limited with the band, and elsewhere, during his career, thanks to his consummate skills as a section leader. When he was let off the leash, as on 'Willow Weep for Me' he plays with effortless charm.

Although several members of the trumpet section were capable of fine solos, the star was undoubtedly Jonah Jones who projects well on such tunes as 'Jonah Joins the Cab', 'Special Delivery' and 'Take the A Train'.

The rhythm section's drive was outstanding and both Milt Hinton, bass, and Cozy Cole, drums, were allowed commendable solo excursions, the bass player on 'Pluckin' the Bass' and 'Ebony Silhouette', the drummer on several features, which he executes cleanly and with considerable precision and a commendable absence of flash, among them 'Ratamacue' and 'Crescendo in Drums'.

Such an eccentric performer as Calloway was bound to have his copyists. Two of the better ones were Willie Bryant and Tiny Bradshaw.

Willie Bryant, a singer-dancer, picked up many members of the disbanded Benny Carter band in 1934. Although some of the band's recordings suffered the fate of Calloway's, that of being hidden behind the leader's questionable vocal abilities, there was simply too much talent to disappear completely. Among the outstanding musicians with Bryant at one time or another were Edgar 'Puddenhead' Battle, Benny Carter, Cozy Cole, Eddie Durham, Taft Jordan, George Matthews, Ben Webster and Teddy Wilson. Bryant relied on too many 'occasional' arrangers to allow the band to develop a distinctive style and while these arrangers included such top-rankers as Battle, Carter and Teddy Hill the band's identity revolved around Bryant's Calloway-influenced vocalising.

Like Calloway before him, Tiny Bradshaw worked for a time with Marion Hardy's Alabamians. Tiny's own band, formed in 1934, included some exciting soloists, including trumpeter Shad Collins, trombonist George Matthews, and the dependable Happy Caldwell on tenor

Calling the Cab:
'It's so difficult to keep a big band together these days [1958].Bands nowadays are more or less concentrating in the ensemble sound in playing, because soloists don't stay in a band too long before they become stars in their own right, and it's pretty hard to keep a man who can take a good jazz chorus in an orchestra. He wants to be on his own, and the result is that most of the bands have to depend on ensemble work to develop a consistent style of their own.'

Cab Calloway

Odds-on favourite for many in 1934 was Don Redman and his Orchestra. (L to R) Don Kirkpatrick, Shirley Clay, Reunald Jones, Talcott Reeves, Sidney De Paris, Rupert Cole, Manzie Johnson, Bob Carroll, Don Redman, Ed Inge, Gene Simon, Harlan Lattimore, Benny Morton, Quentin Jackson, Bob Ysaguirre.

Above: Blues shouter Jimmy Witherspoon made his name with the Jay McShann band. (*Courtesy: Bob Charlesworth*) *Below:* Basie trumpet star Joe Newman still playing tastefully in the 1980s. (*Courtesy: Bob Charlesworth*)

saxophone. Billed as the 'Super Cab Calloway', Tiny recorded a number of fine sides including the swinging 'Shout, Sister, Shout' with its exhilarating ride-out chorus. Tiny eventually found success with a honking rhythm and blues band in the 1940s.

Among numerous black bands which played a role in the development of swing while remaining firmly locked on the outside was the Blue Rhythm Band. Although existing for almost a decade the band rarely receives credit for the part it played in propelling jazz along the swing path. The band was for years third string in the Irving Mills stable and as a result was popularly regarded as inferior to Calloway and Ellington. Its chief flaw was a lack of identity. Trombonist Harry White, who often composed and arranged for the band, displayed his personal high regard for the work of Duke Ellington, while other arrangers caused the band to suggest the driving beat of the Luis Russell band or the moody magnificence of Don Redman.

The band's true value lay in the work of the many fine soloists who graced its ranks. Early members included the fine trumpet players Ed Anderson and Shelton Hemphill, tenor saxophonist Castor McCord, baritone saxophonist Crawford Wetherington and pianist Edgar Hayes. Later jazz soloists were two talented extroverts, trumpeter Henry 'Red'

Louis Armstrong and his Orchestra in 1931 at the Suburban Gardens, New Orleans. Louis' first trip back to New Orleans since leaving to join King Oliver in 1922, in Chicago.
(L to R) Lester Boone, Al Washington, Tubby Hall, George James, Charlie Alexander, Louis Armstrong, Mike McKendrick, John Lindsey, Zilner Randolph, Preston Jackson.

Allen and trombonist J. C. Higginbotham, the always excellent clarinetist Buster Bailey, and the distinctive alto saxophonist Tab Smith.

The band's biggest hit on record was 'Ride, Red, Ride', which features Red Allen's powerful and dramatic trumpet playing. Many other records include excellent jazz solos unfortunately nullified by instantly forgettable vocals.

During the band's lifespan it was fronted by various musical directors including Edgar Hayes, Baron Lee (Jimmy Ferguson), drummer Willie Lynch, trumpeter Eddie Mallory and Lucky Millinder. Irving Mills, having added his name to so many of Duke Ellington's compositions, now added it to an entire band. The Mills Blue Rhythm Band, billed as the 'Instrumental Gentlemen from Harlem', recorded, toured and played engagements at prestigious black venues, and was used to back Louis Armstrong. Despite all this activity and the fact that it survived for several years the band achieved some recognition but no lasting fame.

After the Blue Rhythm Band folded, director Lucky Millinder formed his own big band which he led throughout the 1940s. A rowdy but rhythmically exciting crew, the Millinder band tended to use its powerful, unremitting drive to overcome the fact that it had a somewhat anonymous sound with only fleeting solo spots despite having some strong individuals on hand. Among these were trumpeter Freddie Webster and several booting tenors, who later honked their way to fame on the rhythm and blues circuit, including Sam 'The Man' Taylor and Pazuza Simon and Bullmoose Jackson. Veteran alto saxophonist Tab Smith also went on to record some rhythm and blues hits.

Millinder's band often played at the Apollo Theatre in Harlem where they backed many top-line acts during the 1940s. The band was also a regular at the Savoy during this same period and became especially popular as they moved towards the r & b market which the dancers there increasingly favoured.

Above: Illinois Jacquet tenor star of Lionel Hampton band in the 1940s, still exciting audiences in the 1980s. Seen here accompanied by ex-Basie, drummer, Gus Johnson. (*Courtesy: Bob Charlesworth*)
Below: Farmer on flugel. Art Farmer began his career in the 1940s playing trumpet with the Horace Henderson Orchestra. Seen here in the 1980s playing flugelhorn. (*Courtesy: Bob Charlesworth*)

Walter Barnes And His Royal Creolians

On 23 April 1940 the Walter Barnes band arrived in Natchez, Mississippi, to play an engagement at the town's leading black dance hall, the Rhythm Club.

The Rhythm Club in Natchez was an old building which had seen several lives, including a spell as a church. Outside, like many buildings of its kind and locale, it was constructed from iron sheeting; inside the walls were decorated with dried Spanish moss. Plagued with people trying to sneak in without paying, the Rhythm Club's management kept the rear exit doors locked and bolted and there were bars at all windows. The only way in—or out—was through the front door; the only ventilation was a powerful exhaust fan. On the night of 23 April a fire started, perhaps the result of a carelessly dropped cigarette or match. Within minutes, the inside of the walls were sheets of flame and heavy, asphyxiating smoke filled the hall. The fast-running fan helped spread the flames but failed hopelessly to clear the smoke. Reports stated that Walter Barnes urged his men to keep playing, perhaps in the hope that this action would quell panic. In the event, his action, however brave and selfless, did not avert the inevitable tragedy.

More than 200 people died at the Rhythm Club that night. Numbered among the dead were most of the Walter Barnes band, with only the bass player and drummer surviving. Apart from the immediate tragedy of so many deaths, it is sad to note that if Walter Barnes and His Royal Creolians are remembered at all today, it is because of their fate rather than their music.

Much of the credit for the Millinder band's drive rests with drummer Dave 'Panama' Francis who, in the 1970s, rejuvenated the concept of another Harlem band, that of Al Cooper's Savoy Sultans. Panama Francis and his Savoy Sultans played to great acclaim at many European jazz festivals and made several records which echoed the old days and were played with bouncing swing by a team of veterans of the black bands of the 1930s and 1940s.

Another alumnus of the Blue Rhythm Band who formed his own band was Edgar Hayes whose highly proficient band had the benefit of the talented and much underrated Henry Goodwin on trumpet who gave the band's performances a dynamic edge. Hayes's band also enjoyed the services of the young drummer Kenny Clarke, who later fathered bebop drumming and would, in time, become co-leader of an important big band. Both Goodwin and Clarke are heard to advantage on 'Edgar Steps Out'.

One of the most distinguished of jazzmen, highly regarded within the profession as an elder statesman, Benny Carter's involvement in jazz began around 1923. Two years later, aged 18, he joined a dance band led by Billy Fowler at New York's Strand Roof. During the remaining years of the 1920s, Benny continued his apprenticeship with the bands of Elmer Snowden and Charlie Johnson and, for a few weeks, with an augmented Duke Ellington orchestra in a Broadway show. In 1928, by now an accomplished alto saxophonist and a budding, and self-taught, arranger, Benny joined Fletcher Henderson's band undertaking some of the arranging chores necessitated by the departure of Don Redman. By the beginning of the next decade Carter had also played with McKinney's Cotton Pickers, Chick Webb and others, and had briefly led a band of his own. He also found time to take up the trumpet on which he became a skilled performer. Although the alto saxophone remained Benny's first instrument he continued doubling on trumpet throughout his career and also, occasionally, played tenor saxophone, clarinet, trombone and piano. In 1935 Carter visited Europe as a member of the Willie Lewis band and in 1936 became staff arranger to Henry Hall's dance band at the BBC in London. During his sojourn in Europe he recorded and briefly led an international band in Holland.

Returning to America in 1938, Carter formed a series of bands which, if they never attained the heights of popularity accorded to others, were always superbly schooled, musicianly outfits. His skill and sensitivity as a performer and arranger continued to add to his reputation among musicians while his writing for the reed section can be regarded as visionary.

In the 1940s, although still only in his thirties, Benny Carter had become a father-figure in the profession and his bands were open to the changing fashion in jazz and while they never became bebop bands nevertheless offered scope for experimentation in new musical forms.

Into the late 1980s Benny Carter continued playing, touring America, Europe and Japan with a small band. Jazz has known a number of 'Kings', some of them accorded the title by the public, some thanks to media hype. Returning to a tradition as old as jazz itself, it is his fellow musicians who dub Benny Carter 'the King'.

Another highly respected musician is Teddy Wilson who formed a big band in 1939 following his popularity as a member of the Benny Goodman entourage. Unlike other Goodman alumni who formed bands (Hampton, James, Krupa), Wilson was not the kind of musician to

Teddy Hill Orchestra at the Apollo Theatre, Harlem, 1937.
(L to R) Bill Beason, Wilbur DeParis, Russell Procope, Dicky Wells, Sam Allen, Cecil Scott, Frankie Newton, John Smith, Shad Collins, Howard Johnson, Richard Fulbright, Bill Dillard.

Coleman Hawkins fronting his big band at Kelly's Stables, NY, 1939.

There was never any need to gamble on the musicianship of the impeccable Benny Carter, seen here at the Moulin Rouge, Las Vegas, Nevada, in 1955. (L to R) Carter, Jewel Grant, Teddy Edwards, George Washington, unk, unk, unk, Jack McVea, Harry Edison, Joe Felix, John Simmons, Frank Murray.

Musicians on Lunceford:
'Lunceford was much more of a showman than Duke. With Ellington you took what you got and you never knew whether it was going to be absolutely brilliant or not. Lunceford's band with their white suits and showmanship was impeccable and swung so hard I remember the floor of the old Casa Manana literally shaking with it.'

Bill Perkins

engage in musical pyrotechnics. Instead of flamboyance he offered elegant musicianship. While dancers approved the rock-steady tempos and other bands admired their skills, what the Teddy Wilson band offered was not what the public at large wanted. The band, which lasted only a year, included Shorty Baker, Doc Cheatham and Ben Webster.

What audiences wanted, especially in theatres and clubs, was a mixture of music and spectacle. Too often, they were given flash along with indifferent musicianship. Occasionally, as with Cab Calloway, the bands gave them good music dressed up in the glitter of showbiz. One band gave the audiences the best of both worlds: masterly showmanship blended with music of the very highest order. The band was Jimmie Lunceford's.

THE HARLEM EXPRESS

Of the four outstanding and most influential leaders of black big bands, Fletcher Henderson, Duke Ellington, Count Basie and Jimmie Lunceford, it is Lunceford whom time has treated least fairly.

Henderson is remembered for his band's initial breakthrough in terms of arranged jazz and for his association with Benny Goodman. Ellington will forever be a hallowed name in the annals of twentieth-century music, while the much-loved Basie epitomises swing at its forthright best.

Contrastingly, little remains today of Lunceford's popular appeal although his band was once considered to be the most exciting big band of all time and the distinctive elements which made up the band were the envy of many top bandleaders.

Andy Kirk's elegantly swinging Clouds of Joy at the Trianon Ballroom, Cleveland, in 1937. (L to R) Kirk, Ted Brinson, Booker Collins, Pha Terrell, Ben Thigpen, Mary Lou Williams, Dick Wilson, Ted Donnelly, John Williams, Paul King, John Harrington, Earl Thompson, Harry Lawson, Buddy Miller.

In some respects, the Lunceford band may be considered as one of the first college bands, originating as it did as the Manassa High School band in Memphis where Lunceford taught music. Lunceford himself was taught music in Denver, Colorado, by Wilberforce J. Whiteman, Paul Whiteman's father, and later took a degree in music at Fisk University.

Between graduating and taking up his teaching post, Lunceford gained experience as a sideman with the bands of Elmer Snowden, Wilbur Sweatman, John and Mary Lou Williams and George Morrison. Interestingly, Andy Kirk, another future bandleader whose work was eminently tasteful, worked alongside Lunceford in Morrison's band.

The high school band Lunceford formed with his students at Manassa High included Moses Allen and Jimmy Crawford, later bass player and drummer for the pro band. When Lunceford decided to take his school band on tour he took along Willie Smith and Eddie Wilcox who at that time shared arranging responsibilities. Like their leader, Smith and Wilcox had studied at Fisk University. Of their work for the early band, Wilcox later recalled, 'We didn't really hear bands that gave us ideas. It was what we wanted to do. The melodic quality I had, came from studying classical piano. That was how I wanted it to sound... Willie was influential in the way the reed section phrased from the beginning, because he was so positive in what he wanted to do, and so dominating in tone and quality.'

To a great extent, the shape and sound of the Jimmie Lunceford band was built around the arranging talents of two men, trumpeter Sy Oliver and pianist Ed Wilcox (although Eddie Durham also exerted considerable

'[The Lunceford band would] start to rock and they'd just rock all night long.'

Count Basie

***

'Because so many people wanted to book our big band and couldn't afford it, I decided to offer a small unit for club locations.'

Cab Calloway

Star soloists with Andy Kirk's band were tenor saxophonists Don Byas and Dick Wilson.

'Joe [Thomas]had a lot of personality, and a whole lot of tricks on the horn. He had a way of slopping over notes in a run. Willie Smith wouldn't settle for that kind of stuff. He would turn his back on you, refuse to listen if you played that way. "Play all the notes in the run, man." ... Willie was a perfectionist.'

Ed Wilcox

***

Louis Armstrong and his Orchestra: In the late 1920s, Louis Armstrong began working with big bands. Used simply as a backcloth for Louis's sensational playing, they were never allowed to develop a personality. That was Louis's department and although he toured with various big bands for the next 15 years they rarely showed any flair. Louis, however, endlessly created marvellous solos which his band supported with the utmost discretion.

influence with fine charts including 'Harlem Shout', 'Lunceford Special' and 'Pigeon Walk').

The significance of Oliver's work can be determined from the extent to which the Tommy Dorsey band took on a dusting of the Lunceford magic when Oliver switched camps in 1939. (Many bands used such Lunceford visual effects as unison movements of the sections although no one matched the elan with which Lunceford's entire trumpet section tossed their instruments in the air and caught them on the beat.) Such later leaders as Sam Donahue, Billy May and innumerable studio groups were greatly influenced by Sy Oliver's stylings for the Lunceford band. Indeed, many of today's standard big band arranging practices derive from Oliver's use of sections and ensemble.

Sy had started writing during his stint with Zack Whyte's Chocolate Beau Brummells when, to avoid arguments with older self-taught sidemen, he sought to prove that what he preached about harmony was correct. Oliver joined Lunceford in 1933 and immediately stamped his own identity on the band. His use of two-beat rhythm punctuated by stop-time breaks with shattering brass and brilliantly intricate saxophone choruses became a strikingly distinctive contribution to the rich sounds of the swing era, and were later developed by many studio arrangers.

Oliver's arrangements lent themselves to the popular, more commercial aspects of swing far more than did those of, say, Duke Ellington. So many bands have since assimilated the Lunceford sound as styled by Sy Oliver that his work tends to be devalued. Maybe today thousands do it, but Lunceford-Oliver did it first—and usually better.

The move away from head and stock arrangements and reliance upon soloists towards precision section work and ensemble unity can be directly linked with the Lunceford sound as created by Oliver and Wilcox, and on the rehearsal duties of lead alto saxophonist Willie Smith, one of the most exacting taskmasters in the big bands. Smith was certainly a major band asset as a section leader. He worked with a number of bands, bringing quality and identity to every section he graced including those of bands led by Charlie Barnet, Harry James, Billy May and Buddy Rich. During the Lunceford band's successful years it became a standing joke among fellow musicians that the section went to bed at night and dreamed of playing a particularly difficult passage; yet the precision and careful attention to detail insisted upon by Smith never resulted in any mechanical feeling. Indeed, the reeds always sounded lighthearted and fresh.

Black irony:
An incident in Erskine Hawkins's career demonstrates one of the repeated ironies and injustices of the racial divide in big band music, jazz and pop. This is the manner in which white cover versions of records by black artists have been heavily promoted by record companies and radio stations. A striking example among the big bands is 'Tuxedo Junction', a tune collectively composed by members of the Erskine Hawkins band, which was more successfully recorded by the white bands of Gene Krupa, Jan Savitt and, especially, Glenn Miller.

Jimmy Lunceford's Harlem Express had a number of popular successes, including a nifty Oliver arrangement of a tune written and sung by trombonist Trummy Young. More than half a century later, ''Tain't What You Do (It's the Way That You Do It)' retains all of its engaging charm.

No band during the swing era could swing so spectacularly and with quite the precision of the Lunceford unit. The band's biting section work on everything they played, has rarely been surpassed. The relentless swing of the band came despite Oliver's arranging habit of emphasising two beats to each measure rather than four, a seemingly retrograde step. This method worked amazingly well in his imaginative and complex arrangements. Important in delivering this effect was another of the band's superb assets, Jimmy Crawford, one of the greatest, and most neglected, of big band drummers.

The Erskine Hawkins band at the Apollo Theatre in Harlem, NYC, in 1943. (L to R) Dud Bascomb, Ida James, Dickie Harris, Sammy Lowe, Gene Rodgers, Matthew Gee, Cap Sims, Ed McConney, Paul Bascomb, Bill Johnson, William McLemore, Jimmie Mitchelle, Lee Stanfield, Julian Dash, Hawkins, Haywood Henry.

The trumpet section demonstrates the Jimmie Lunceford flash in Detroit in 1940. (L to R) Paul Webster, Snooky Young, Gerald Wilson, Ted Buckner, Joe Thomas, Lunceford.

The Lunceford band was a highly disciplined unit which excelled at flamboyant showmanship. The joyous, swinging beat from Jimmy Crawford's drums was visually enhanced by the attitude and actions of the musicians, each man urging on his fellows with unrestrained and genuine enthusiasm.

Like the band of Duke Ellington (and it was these two which dominated the early and mid-1930s black big band scene), the Lunceford band played jazz that was simultaneously complex in structure yet subtle in its harmonies and was the envy of the business.

Lunceford himself had what Leonard Feather described as a nonchalant personality and, indeed, the band was owned not by Lunceford but by Harold Oxley. Lunceford was himself a salaried employee but was well paid and happily spent his considerable earnings on his great hobby—flying. In spite of their enthusiasm and the great feeling of togetherness in the band, Lunceford's sidemen eventually began to complain at the punishing slog of one-nighters and a level of pay which did not compare favourably with the amount Jimmie spent on the aeroplanes he wrecked with alarming regularity. In 1942, after an unresolved hassle over pay, several key players quit.

'I never realised what a great band [Lunceford's] was until it was all over.'
Joe Thomas

Jimmie continued with a much-changed band but the old flair and zest had gone; also missing were the irreplaceable talents of Willie Smith and Sy Oliver. The new Lunceford band never managed to attain the heights of its predecessor.

In 1947, at the age of 45, Jimmie Lunceford collapsed and died from a heart attack.

THE INTERNATIONAL SWEETHEARTS OF RHYTHM

One of the most dynamic and exciting bands of the late 1930s and 1940s was an all-girl band known as The International Sweethearts of Rhythm. The equal of the hot, intensely swinging style of, say, the Lucky Millinder band, the Sweethearts were blessed with a number of superb soloists, especially trumpeter Ernestine 'Tiny' Davis and tenor saxophonist Vi Burnside.

Formed in 1937 by Laurence Clifton Jones, who ran a school for poor and orphaned children at Piney Woods, Mississippi, the band at first achieved only limited success. By the end of the 1930s, thanks to having several long-serving members, the band had achieved a splendid ensemble sound but after some disagreements with Jones, most of the band quit but hung onto their name.

In 1941, under new management and dedicated to playing hot, hard-swinging music, the Sweethearts' fame spread. The band's musical director was Eddie Durham, formerly arranger with Count Basie, but this association was also doomed. Durham formed his own all-girl band, taking with him some of the original Sweethearts. The replacement for Durham was Jesse Stone, the noted Kansas City bandleader and arranger. With the band now fronted by Ann Mae Winburn, the International Sweethearts of Rhythm entered their greatest phase.

The arrival of Davis and Burnside, and trumpeter Ray Carter, gave the band soloists of real stature. Indeed, were it not for the built-in prejudice against women in jazz who are not singers or piano players, any of these musicians would have been revered by fans. Burnside, especially, was a strong jazz soloist whose breathy sound can be favourably likened to Ben Webster's. Of great importance to the band's swing was drummer Pauline Braddy, with the band from its inception, who numbered among her admirers and advisors such drumming stars as Big Sid Catlett and Jo Jones. It is Braddy's attack, as much as the ensemble sound, which does most to place the band on a par with its male counterparts. Indeed, the result of any blindfold test of the band's recordings could not help but deflate any sexist big band fan.

In the early 1940s a few white women, among them trumpeter Toby Butler, joined the band and were obliged to wear dark make up in some states in the South.

At the end of World War II the Sweethearts toured American military bases in Europe, played the Olympia Theatre in Paris, and broadcast to servicemen on the Jubilee show on AFRS.

After the war some members of the band moved on and in 1949 the International Sweethearts of Rhythm folded. Anna Mae Winburn formed a new band the following year but by the mid-1950s the Sweethearts had become a thing of the past. Sadly, they have also been largely overlooked by fans although the sterling efforts of Rosetta Reitz has resulted not only in an important record album but also in a TV docmentary being screened in America and Britain.

THE MISSOURIANS

If the Missourians are remembered at all, it is as a forerunner of the Cab Calloway band. In fact, before Cab came on the scene, this neglected band had a considerable reputation. Based originally in St Louis, where they were known as Wilson Robinson's Syncopaters, the band toured extensively before testing their prowess in New York City in 1924. It was a timely move and, under the direction of violinist Andy Preer, they soon landed a plum job—house band at the Cotton Club. They held this job for more than two years until Preer's death.

The band had changed its name to the Cotton Club Orchestra and it was under this name that they continued to work, touring with singer Ethel Waters. Back in New York in 1928 and renamed The Missourians they worked extensively at all the major black venues including the Savoy and Alhambra ballrooms.

The band had several fine soloists including trumpeters Roger Quincy Dickerson and Lamar Wright and a powerful, swinging trombonist in De Priest Wheeler. Among the reeds were William Blue, Andrew Brown, George Scott and Walter 'Foots' Thomas. The rhythm section was quietly effective, urged along by drummer Leroy Maxey.

In 1930, Cab Calloway joined as singer and front man and soon the band changed its name again, becoming the Cab Calloway Orchestra. So successful was this later version of the band that today the name of the Missourians, once a highly regarded band, is usually relegated to a minor footnote in big band history.

CHAPTER TEN

SWING TO BOP: MORE BLACK BANDS

'THINGS TO COME'

'So the arranging, the chord progressions and things in progressive music, Dizzy is responsible for.'

Billy Eckstine

If Jimmie Lunceford offered the rare combination of flamboyance and musical polish, Lionel Hampton took the powerhouse route to the top. Strikingly different from the suavely sophisticated Jimmie Lunceford band, Hampton led his raw, shouting and often unruly band from 1941 with barely a break for the next forty-plus years. While many bands enjoyed commercial success by pandering to the public, Hampton built his success by developing his own highly personal musical instincts.

HAMP THE CHAMP

Lionel Hampton started out as a child prodigy and by his late teens had clocked up many miles and much musical experience as drummer and occasional pianist with several territory big bands including, most notably, Paul Howard's Quality Serenaders and he was a member of the Les Hite band at Frank Sebastian's Los Angeles Cotton Club. This band provided the backing for Louis Armstrong both at the club and at a number of important record sessions in the early 1930s, at one of which Hamp first tinkled cautiously on the vibraphone, a new-fangled and little known electrically powered form of xylophone.

'It was a very hot band. That's why the people were all so happy in those days. Nobody slept at the Grand Terrace.'
Earl Hines

Initially, Lionel played vibraphone as a member of the Benny Goodman Quartet, and later with the Sextet. Once in a while he would play piano and even sit in on drums with the big band when Benny was having his recurring drummer problems. As a result of his records and his live appearances with Benny all across America, Lionel's startling musical personality became well known. On ballads he played the vibraphone with an emotional intensity made all the more remarkable by the fact that he achieved this on a percussive instrument; on flagwavers he rampaged through an astonishing display of technical accomplishment which invariably built up a hypnotically compelling beat.

No other musician in jazz ever had such a split personality or could slip so easily from one extreme to another, often in the space of a bar of music. When such changes occur, the effect is dramatic.

The big band Lionel formed followed the pattern of his personality. Primarily playing vibraphone, he led the band through moments of extreme sensitivity and almost ethereal beauty before plunging headlong into performances of astonishing extravagance. Yet, even at its most outrageous, the band swung mightily and could build up an almost frightening dynamic charge.

Tenor saxophonist Dexter Gordon steps out for a duet with 'Mr B' who is here playing valve trombone in front of his 1945 orchestra.

When the music was as hot as Lionel Hampton could make it, the boys in the band had to find unconventional ways of keeping cool. Lionel drums as trumpeter Art Farmer solos at the Bandbox, NYC, in 1953.

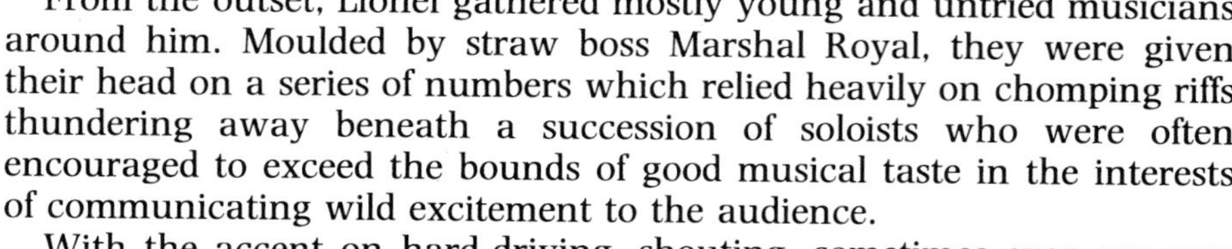

From the outset, Lionel gathered mostly young and untried musicians around him. Moulded by straw boss Marshal Royal, they were given their head on a series of numbers which relied heavily on chomping riffs thundering away beneath a succession of soloists who were often encouraged to exceed the bounds of good musical taste in the interests of communicating wild excitement to the audience.

With the accent on hard-driving, shouting, sometimes even raucous but always exciting music, the band was a sure-fire hit with the younger element.

Jump Jim Crow:
One night at Boston's Rio Casino, bandleader Billy Eckstine told off a white girl who had racially insulted him. Her boyfriend kicked Billy who promptly flattened him and a full-scale fight broke out between Eckstine's band and some of the customers. The band's engagement was cancelled halfway through its two week run. Apparently unaware of the implications of his remarks, the Rio Casino's lawyer explained: 'They kept using the front entrances after we explained that all employees had to come in through the rear.'

Hamp's rhythm sections laid down a heavy, but never turgid, back beat over which the ensemble passages built up solid walls of sound. There were occasional chinks, however, and through these gleamed a succession of brilliant solos by a parade of precocious talent including volatile tenor saxophonists Illinois Jacquet and Arnett Cobb.

The brass section was exceptionally powerful and the trumpets alone could have reduced Jericho to rubble. Among the trumpeters who played in the mid-1940s band were Benny Bailey, Al Killian, Joe Wilder, Lamar Wright, Snooky Young and high note specialist Cat Anderson. Hamp also employed the services of another high note man, the erratic Leo Sheppard. With appropriate hyperbole, Leo's section mate Benny Bailey described this high note wizard in a *down beat* interview: 'He played higher than anybody, Cat Anderson included... So high that it defied the human ear. You've never heard anything like it. There wasn't even a *note* anymore. It just disappeared into outer space. He wasn't always accurate, but sometimes you could see *smoke* coming out of his horn. No kidding.'

Although the rhythm section of the band was called upon more for its endurance than its subtlety, it did at one time include the still emerging talent of Charles Mingus on bass while guitarist Billy Mackel kept his chair for almost 40 years.

Hampton's alertness to the talents of young musicians brought about an especially fine band in the 1950s. As Quincy Jones, who joined the band in 1951 at the age of 18, remarked, Lionel was 'curious, interested in everything new.'

The band Lionel took to Europe in 1953 was filled with a most amazing array of young talent. The trumpets included Clifford Brown, Art Farmer and Quincy Jones, Jimmy Cleveland, a brilliant technician, was in the trombone section, alto saxophonist-arranger Gigi Gryce was along, too, as was Alan Dawson, a gifted young drummer.

This band never recorded with Lionel although, in direct contravention of Hamp's rules, the band did record in Paris under the nominal leadership of Brown. On the band's return to America Lionel discovered the deception and, ever mercurial, fired all the young adventurers and started again.

In the late 1970s, and on into the 1980s, Hamp made occasional concert and festival appearances with all-star big bands that fully lived up to their billing. The performances of these bands retained all the vigour and excitement of the earlier years and the music they produced lacked none of the old fire.

Lionel played on with a seemingly inexhaustible fund of energy and spirit, never failing to retain a high level of invention in his solos despite the relatively limited range of numbers his band performed. Invariably, he succeeded in whipping up the sweating enthusiasm of his musicians, to say nothing of his often delirious audiences.

In 1988, as the only surviving working bandleader with connections traceable back to the swing era, Lionel Hampton has kept the flame burning longer than most and has energetically pursued musical ideals which have always placed excitement at the top of his priorities.

Another black bandleader with more than a touch of musical flamboyance was Erskine Hawkins, 'The Twentieth Century Gabriel'.

A highly variable soloist, Hawkins had a tendency to show off, thus gaining for himself the derogatory nickname, 'Irksome' Hawkins.

The first formal appearance of Erskine Hawkins and his Orchestra was in 1938, the year the band won a recording contract with RCA Victor, but the band's inception dates from two years earlier when it was known as The 'Bama State Collegians. The Hawkins band was particularly popular with dancers, and enjoyed great success at the Savoy. It was while playing there that 'Tuxedo Junction', the band's biggest hit, evolved out of a little tune the band played as they made way for the evening's second band.

Although Hawkins allocated himself a substantial amount of solo space, his band included several other soloists of distinction including trumpeter Wilbur 'Dud' Bascomb, tenor saxophonist Julian Dash, and Haywood Henry who doubled on baritone and clarinet.

The Hawkins band was one of many black bands which succeeded among the black section of America, notably in the South, but failed to compete in the more rewarding white-dominated end of the market. The band did have its moments however, including a band battle with Glenn Miller who recorded 'Tuxedo Junction' to great commercial benefit. As Dud Bascomb recalled, 'We were poorer looking than Glenn Miller's band and maybe even hungrier but our band was *mean* that night—we all but killed Glenn!'

Whether out of genuine feeling for the financial benefits Miller's recording of 'Tuxedo Junction' brought him as one of the listed composers, or out of deliberate irony, Erskine Hawkins later wrote a tune he dedicated to Glenn, entitling it, 'Miller Junction'.

In contrast to the wide-ranging success of the Erskine Hawkins band, Sabby Lewis's success was concentrated around Boston, Massachusetts, where they worked at the Savoy Café for three years from 1939. Many visiting musicians, including Woody Herman and Stan Kenton would sit in. One night Benny Goodman sat in when the band started out on 'One O'Clock Jump'. After about three-quarters of an hour on this one tune the manager of the club was growing restless. As Sabby recalled, 'he walked over to the bar and said to the bartender, "Who's that bum sitting in? Nobody is drinking, we got to get rid of him!" '

The Lewis band provided work for a number of top line musicians including trumpeters Cat Anderson and Joe Gordon, saxophonists Paul Gonsalves and Sonny Stitt, bass player Al Morgan and drummers Jimmy Crawford, Alan Dawson and Roy Haynes.

Despite one big hit, 'Bottoms Up', a reworking of Illinois Jacquet's version of 'Flying Home' which sold more records than the original, the Sabby Lewis band never clicked in the national bigtime but continued to work well into the 1950s, a feat many of its better known counterparts failed to accomplish.

Many black musicians, wanting to continue in music in the mid-

Claude Hopkins and his Orchestra: Claude Hopkins led a relaxed and attractive-sounding band for a decade or more. A lightly swinging unit, the Hopkins band never went in for powerhouse tactics. The band featured a number of excellent sidemen including trumpeter Cladys 'Jabbo'.

1940s, were obliged to move into the jumping, squealing rhythm and blues field, backing a new crop of blues shouters.

Among the bands which edged in this direction were those of Cab Calloway, Lionel Hampton, Erskine Hawkins and Lucky Millinder. Yet at the same time, within these same nurseries, lay the seeds of bebop.

A sequence of three important big bands helped nurture radical changes in jazz form—first was the band led by Earl 'Fatha' Hines.

A consummate pianist who played with Louis Armstrong on a series of groundbreaking record dates in 1928, Hines had early big band experience in Pittsburgh and Chicago. Deeply involved in the bustling Chicago jazz scene of the 1920s, he worked with the bands of Erskine Tate and Carroll Dickerson, of which he was, for a while, musical director. In 1928 Hines was offered the chance of forming a big band to play the newly opened Grand Terrace in Chicago.

The engagement called for a measure of flamboyance, something Earl's piano work has never been short of. The band, wearing white suits, played on a raised stand above a dance floor where the showgirls performed their routines. The whole place was set off with mirrored walls and imaginative lighting. The band's repertoire included a big production number of 'Piano Man' with Hines at a white grand and the girls plinking out notes on miniature pianos.

Although enormously popular at the Grand Terrace, Hines's long residency had an adverse effect upon his standing in big band history. Just as failure to stay long enough in one place adversely affected some bands, so the opposite, failure to move location, kept Hines from centre stage.

By the early 1930s Earl's band was in fine form thanks to the presence of several important musicians and the work of an outstanding arranger, tenor saxophonist Jimmy Mundy. Soloists included trombonist Trummy Young, who later became a mainstay of the Jimmie Lunceford band, the reed section included Darnell Howard and Omer Simeon. Among other fine instrumentalists were tenor saxophonist Cecil Irwin, trumpeters George Dixon and Walter Fuller, Lawrence Dixon, guitar, and Quinn Wilson, bass, all of whom provided arrangements for the band.

A few years later, in 1937, another important saxophonist-arranger joined Hines. This was Budd Johnson whose contributions to the band's book extended its range and gave it a sound and style that was at least the equal of many better known big bands of the swing era.

Recordings by this band demonstrate superb musicianship, unremitting swing and performances sparked by fine solos. The comparative calm and deliberation of the recording studio, so often anathema to jazz musicians of earlier years, seems in Hines's case to have brought out the best in the band.

The fact that the Grand Terrace was owned and frequented by mobsters led Jo Jones to remark, 'Earl had to play with a knife at his throat and a gun at his back the whole time he was in Chicago.' With customers like gang overlord Al Capone out front the musicians might be excused if they were not always able to concentrate on the music.

Nevertheless, recordings from the late 1930s display an outstanding band. The personnel had been relatively stable and this continuity helped towards an integrated sound. The band's rhythmic pulse was aided by the arrival, in 1938, of Alvin Burroughs, an excellent drummer, who had earlier worked in the Southwest with the bands of Walter Page and Alphonso Trent.

Improvisation *v.* arrangements—4: In the 1940s, when jazz music was being split asunder by the innovations of such musicians as Charlie Parker and Dizzy Gillepsie, arrangers had to learn all over again how to incorporate new musical thinking into big band terms. Essentially a product of the big bands and a master of the new forms, Gillespie needed an arranger who could take the manner of his playing and construct from it a score much in the same way as Don Redman had done with Louis Armstrong in the 1920s. He found such a man in Gil Fuller. As Dizzy explained, 'I'd sit down at the piano and play it, and he'd write it down and score it.' Fuller did not advance arranging in the same manner that Redman had done. He still used the same basic patterns and in doing so made the section sound at times lumbering and rather ponderous. Conversely, Tadd Dameron, writing for the same band, had a light and relaxed quality reminiscent of the sounds of Kansas City picked up while he was working with the Harlan Leonard band. Dameron, an extremely creative arranger, had only a fleeting influence on big band arranging due mainly to his failure to keep a regular band of his own or to become identified with any particular band.

During Fuller's time with Gillespie he organised a big band session under his own name for the Discovery label. He managed to select a compatible group of musicians, all of whom were sympathetic to his complex writing style and they produced an excellent set of originals and standards. These sides had a considerable impact, thanks in part to a driving rhythm section which included Art Blakey, drums, and Percy Heath, bass. In particular, 'Blues to a Debutante', 'The Scene Changes', 'Mean to Me' and 'Tropicana' show big band bebop at its best.

Of all the piano leaders, Earl Hines is the most striking soloist in the context of a big band. Ellington mostly contented himself with a supporting role, while Basie reduced his contribution with the dedication of an inspired minimalist. Hines is always a key figure in his band's work, whether as a discreet member of the rhythm section or flamboyantly in the spotlight.

A major problem for many critics of the band is its failure to establish a distinctive personality. In conversation with Russ Wilson in 1963, Hines stated, 'It never was a typed organisation because I didn't want it to become such. That's why I used a variety of arrangers from all over the country—so there'd be no one certain style ... the only time the listeners knew it was my band was when they heard my piano.' Although commendable in its intention, this deliberate policy proved detrimental to the band's status.

Among new talents who joined Hines were vocalist Billy Eckstine in 1938 and in the early 1940s trumpeter Dizzy Gillespie, tenor saxophonist Wardell Gray and alto saxophonist Charlie Parker.

More readily identifiable than Earl Hines as the first of the bebop big bandleaders was singer Billy Eckstine. Encouraged by Budd Johnson to form his own band, Eckstine left Hines in 1943. Although the original

Singer Billy Eckstine learned to play trumpet while with the Earl Hines band to overcome a union registration difficulty. Backstage at the Royal Theatre, Baltimore, in 1942 are (L to R) Scoops Carry, Hines, Shorty McConnell, Eckstine, Budd Johnson.

Teddy Hill and his Orchestra: Teddy Hill holds a special place in jazz thanks to his association with Minton's Playhouse during the evolution of bebop. Yet, Hill's big bandleading days in the 1930s were also of interest. Hill began his career as a trumpet player but decided to change to a reed instrument after his spirits had been dampened listening to and receiving lessons from Fess Whatley. (Other big band graduates of Whatley's School Band in Alabama were Paul Bascomb and Shelton Hemphill.) After a spell with Luis Russell's band, Hill formed his own band in 1932 and worked extensively in the New York area featuring such top flight sidemen as Roy Eldridge and Dicky Wells. In 1937 Hill toured Europe playing engagements in Paris and London. He disbanded in 1940, turning his efforts into running Minton's, a career decision which, indirectly, helped bring about radical changes in jazz and the fortunes of the big bands.

•••

Buddy Johnson and his Orchestra: A band which became tremendously popular with black audiences but remained relatively unknown to whites, was that led by pianist Buddy Johnson. Along with his wife, singer Ella Johnson, Buddy had a number of hits in the rhythm and blues field, including 'Please, Mr Johnson'.

•••

'I joined Dizzy Gillespie's great band which was one of the greatest experiences of my life... It was just a really tremendous band.'

Slide Hampton

Dizzy Gillespie—bop superstar

intention was for the new band to act merely as support for Eckstine's singing, what resulted was a band which over the four years of its existence featured most of the important names of bebop. Among Eckstine's Hell Raisers at one time or another were Charlie Parker and Wardell Gray, both of whom he knew from the Hines band, tenor saxophonists Gene Ammons and Dexter Gordon, baritone saxophonist Cecil Payne, while the trumpet section saw a veritable who's who of bop: Miles Davis, McKinley 'Kinney' Dorham, Dizzy Gillespie and Theodore 'Fats' Navarro. The band's rhythm section included bass player Tommy Potter and drummer Art Blakey, whose 'bomb-dropping' style encouraged the boppers but dismayed many dancers.

With such musicians on hand, the band clearly needed arrangers of considerable skill and advanced ideas and they were found in the persons of Gillespie, Tadd Dameron, Gil Fuller, Budd Johnson and Jerry Valentine, who played trombone in the band. Much of the band's book was based on blues arrangements and broad chorded accompaniments for Eckstine's popular vocalising and that of the band's other singer, Sarah Vaughan, who had also been with Earl Hines. There were straightahead swingers, too, but when the band had a chance to blow their *tour de force* ensemble sound, with Blakey's bombs, created an exciting full-bodied backcloth against which the solos of Navarro, Dorham, Stitt and the others directly reflected the bebop innovations currently being explored.

'Cool Breeze', charted by Dameron, 'Oo Bop Sh'Bam', 'Second Balcony Jump' and 'I Love the Rhythm In a Riff' are among a number of recordings which illustrate the exciting sound of the Eckstine band at its peak.

The band's fortunes were mixed. Charlie Parker recalled that, 'Out West, nobody liked us; in the Middle West, the Negroes liked us; but in New York, everybody loved us.'

The Eckstine band survived until January 1947 when a combination of rising costs and changing public tastes forced the leader's decision to fold. Looked at simply through the personnel involved, this band formed a logical bridge between the swing era-rooted Earl Hines band and the wholly bebop-oriented Dizzy Gillespie band. During its short life, Billy Eckstine's was one of the very few bands, and possibly the only black band, which gave the new generation of jazz musicians an opportunity to learn their trade in the ranks of a big band.

Dizzy Gillespie's experience with Eckstine persuaded him of the viability of a big band with boppish overtones. He duly formed a band, ignoring the vital commercial factor that his old boss's singing had drawn in most of the paying customers.

Gillespie hired Gil Fuller as his arranger and employed drummer Max Roach but found audiences apathetic to what the band was trying to achieve. Indeed, in the South, blighted as always by the colour line, apathy was sometimes replaced with downright antagonism. The band folded but Dizzy reformed in 1946, with Fuller again arranging abetted now by Tadd Dameron. This band included John Lewis on piano and Kenny Clarke on drums. Recordings by this band demonstrate for the first time how the new conceptions in jazz could be made to work in the setting of a big band.

Thanks to the skills of the arrangers and the outstanding musicianship of Dizzy and his sidemen, the band was a musical success although still failed to become a financial stayer. Records by the band display rugged strength rather than the immaculate polish of, say, Jimmie Lunceford

The outstanding bebop big band was Dizzy Gillespie's, seen here at a 1947 RCA Victor recording session in New York. (L to R) Raymond Orr, Cecil Payne, Elmon Wright, Bill Shepheard, James Moody, Dave Burns, Howard Johnson, Taswell Baird, Matthew McKay, John Brown, Joe Gayles, Ray Brown, Gillespie.

but the undoubted fire and excitement the band communicated made it a major force in big band music, however brief its existence.

Among the best numbers recorded by the band were the portentously titled 'Things to Come', 'Stay On It', featuring Cecil Payne on baritone saxophone, 'Two Bass Hit', a feature for Al McKibbon, and 'Ow!' which features the leader's fantastic technique, echoed in the lip-splitting trumpet section work. 'Algo Bueno (Woody 'n' You)', 'Cool Breeze', 'Cubana Be-Cubana Bop' and 'Manteca' have a strong Latin flavour, something that would become a feature of much of Dizzy's later work with small groups. On 'Algo Bueno', the leader is again in dominating form, riding over Chano Pozo Gonzales's conga drumming and brassy explosions by the band. In the final ensemble passages the band turn up the heat in a formidable manner. Similarly, the hot wind blowing through 'Cool Breeze' makes nonsense of the tune's title.

This particular series of records made by Dizzy Gillespie's big band raises the question why Stan Kenton could stay on a Latin American kick for so many years with great success while Gillespie's band was doomed to such a short life. Only rarely did Kenton achieve comparable fire and drive, and his band certainly did not swing as fiercely as Dizzy's. One answer, perhaps facile, raises the matter of the colour line.

For all his commercial failure, Dizzy's big band was typified by an irrepressible spirit and although often lacking precision, that spirit helped make it one of the best bands of the bebop era.

By 1949 commercial considerations had taken their toll on the band

Above: One of 'Four Brothers'. Tenor star Al Cohn touring as a single in the 1980s. (*Courtesy: Bob Charlesworth*) *Below:* Teddy Edwards tenor star with the Bill Berry LA Big Band in the 1970s. (*Courtesy: Bob Charlesworth*)

and Dizzy plumbed unsuspected depths of banality in some of his recordings for Capitol and the following year Dizzy called it a day, reducing the list of nationally known working black big bands to just three: Basie, Ellington and Hampton.

But now, at least, there was one sign of progress on another front. Integrated bands were fast becoming commonplace. Ellington had Louie Bellson on drums in the early 1950s and if one white face did not a revolution make, there was a steady increase of black musicians in white bands.

Van Alexander, arranger:
When still only 21, arranger Van Alexander was asked by Ella Fitzgerald to write an arrangement for a nursery rhyme. With Ella collaborating on the lyric, Alexander produced 'A-Tisket A-Tasket' which became an instant hit for the Chick Webb band. After a brief bandleading career Alexander first joined Larry Clinton, then Kay Kyser. After World War Two Alexander wrote for Abe Lyman and Tommy Tucker before entering the Hollywood studios where he wrote extensively for the movies and TV.

These changes were not without their problems; black musicians who made the transition had differing views on the move into 'white time'. To Roy Eldridge, featured trumpet soloist with Gene Krupa in 1941–2, it was a traumatic and humiliating experience; for Sy Oliver, arranger for Tommy Dorsey in the mid-1940s, it was a considerable artistic and financial success.

Black bandleader Lucky Millinder viewed the moves, particularly of arrangers, with considerable bitterness. In a long article in the *Amsterdam News*, 21 December 1940, he resentfully protested at the imitation of black swing bands, blaming such black arrangers as Sy Oliver, Eddie Durham, Andy Gibson and Don Redman for aiding white bands in their quest for commercial success. As Millinder saw it, this was to the detriment of black bands. Contrastingly, others viewed it as a racial breakthrough and applauded those white leaders who included blacks in their organisations.

In fact, those black musicians who did work with white bands are among the few, outside the top eight or nine black bands, to gain any fame with the white audience. For the thousands of good to excellent black sidemen who remained with lower ranking black bands, their fame barely reached beyond the limited circle of their fellow musicians.

Of the many excellent black bands of the 1920s, 1930s and 1940s, some of which were startlingly innovative, only a handful are remembered today—and these only by a dedicated few.

QUINCY JONES

Having studied composition and arranging in Paris, Quincy Jones played an important role in the musical success of a number of bands including Dizzy Gillespie's superb 1950s band which was formed for a State Department sponsored tour of Greece, Turkey, the Middle East and Pakistan. Jones regarded the orchestra as his personal instrument on which he liked to improvise. 'I like to describe my feeling, my moods and my thoughts so that writing becomes the same as improvising a solo for me.' He never lost sight of form or the individual personalities of the musicians. 'The only way to write this feeling into a score is to let the head and the heart work together.'

Unfortunately for big band music, Jones moved into the world of pop music where he exercises considerable musical influence; fortunately, he left a handful of albums of beautifully voiced, loping big band music. These albums, produced throughout the 1950s and early 1960s, include 'The Birth of a Band', 'The Quintessence', 'This Is How I Feel About Jazz' and 'Go West, Man'. In the bands he assembled for these sessions were trumpeters Pete and Conte Candoli, Harry Edison, Joe Newman and Clark Terry, trombonist Jimmy Cleveland, saxophonists Benny Carter, Art Pepper, Zoot Sims and Phil Woods and drummer Sam Woodyard. With such skilled performers the resulting music remains outstanding.

In assembling his albums Jones did not rely solely on his own arrangements, using scores by Jimmy Giuffre and Melba Liston which allowed plenty of space for solo statements within a tastefully swinging showcase.

CHAPTER ELEVEN

WOODY HERMAN AND THE THUNDERING HERDS

'BLOWIN' UP A STORM'

'Nobody does what Woody does as well as he does. If we could only figure out what it is he does.'

Phil Wilson

In the Spring of 1987 Hollywood bestowed one of its commendably well meant if slightly bizarre favours on Woody Herman. A gold star bearing Woody's name was unveiled on Hollywood Boulevard, at the corner of Highland Boulevard. This gesture hardly compensated for the fact that at the time, even though he was desperately sick, Woody was being hounded by the US Internal Revenue Service. In the event, before 1987 was out, the award and the activities of the IRS ceased to have any real meaning because Woody Herman was dead.

But far more evidence remained of Woody's life than a gold star on a Los Angeles sidewalk and a still-open file on a tax collector's desk. What remained was an overflowing cornucopia of recorded music, a wealth of talented musicians who made their way to the top through Woody's band, and endless happy memories, for friends, musicians, and fans, of big band music at its very best.

Woody Herman had a band for half a century and through it expressed his musical philosophy although he rarely wrote for the band. Woody's musicians came and went with startling speed and through the ranks of his bands passed some of the brightest names of contemporary music although, in many instances, they achieved their greatness only after serving part of their apprenticeship with Woody. More than most bandleaders, Woody Herman moved with the times. His restless interest in what was new found him comfortably enveloping swing in one decade, then bebop, and rock in another.

Woody Herman proved that survival was not a matter merely of endurance but could be achieved through adjustment and accommodation. He had a phenomenal ear for upcoming talent and the courage to give that talent its head.

Over the years, Woody Herman's bands offered the best of hard-swinging, exciting music that was filled with good humour and delight, and, perhaps above all else, sheer enthusiasm. He also had countless strikingly original soloists and arrangers with enormous depths of skill.

Perhaps surprisingly, given his later enthusiasm for staying abreast of the musical times, when Woody was himself young and fronting his first

'It was marvellous, too, to work with Bill and Chubby and Flip, Ralph, Pete, and, of course, Sonny and Davey, too. That was an exciting group to be with. Ideas and whole new tunes sprang out of that group like sparks. Flip would blow something, Pete would grab it, and the first thing you knew we had a new number.'

Woody Herman

band, formed from the ashes of the Isham Jones band, it was anything but modernistic.

For all the absence of an adventurous approach, the new band Woody led was very good and gradually developed a penchant for playing the blues. Somewhat surprisingly for a white band, this was taken up as a creditable quality and used in the band's billing. Although the Band That Plays the Blues had a rough ride during its first few years, by the end of the 1930s it had financial stability thanks to a couple of hit records, a Jiggs Noble re-arrangement of 'La Cinquantaine' entitled 'Golden Wedding' and a Joe Bishop blues, 'At the Woodchoppers Ball', which was a smash. Another Bishop blues arrangement, 'Blue Flame' became, and remained, Herman's theme tune.

A number of other successful records were made but, gradually, as the 1940s unrolled, the band's arrangements became more complex and the Herman band moved on from being simply blues performers.

Newcomers to Woody's band found life very different from that in most other big bands. With, say, Benny Goodman a newcomer was just another sideman, with Woody he was allowed a 'voice', perhaps for the first time in his career.

Among the new arrivals were Chubby Jackson, bass, Cliff Leeman, drums, and Ray Wetzel, trumpet, whose talents allowed more adventurous arrangements to be used. Although unknown before their sojourn with Herman, Jackson, Leeman and Wetzel are typical of the sidemen who gained admiration and success within the Herman band.

This was an exciting, explorative time for the Herman band as it

'Well, just about now we ought to tell you, not that you don't know, we're sending your way the rollicking rhythms of Woody Herman and his Orchestra from the Café Rouge at the Hotel Pennsylvania in New York City. And now it's time to flock around the bandstand all you alligators while Woody beats out the tale of 'Goosey Goosey Gander'.

Radio announcer, 1945

***

Sideman —Sonny Berman:
Sonny Berman was a brilliant star of the first Woody Herman Herd. His wide range and seemingly effortless control allowed his lyrical conception full scope and his few recorded solos with the band remain models for consideration by today's big band trumpeters.

Sonny's typically forceful solo on 'Your Father's Mustache' is filled with humour while his most famous recorded solo of all, on 'Sidewalks of Cuba', rips through the ensembles with savage intensity leaving an indelible impression in the listener's memory. But Sonny was also capable of gently evocative lyricism, as can be heard on 'Billy Bauer's Tune' (later retitled 'Pam'). Sonny's emotional outpourings were a unique part of the Herman magic, an often savage excess of sound which typified the exuberant approach of the First Herd.

Sonny's death from a heart attack in 1947, at the age of 22, was a tragic loss to big band music.

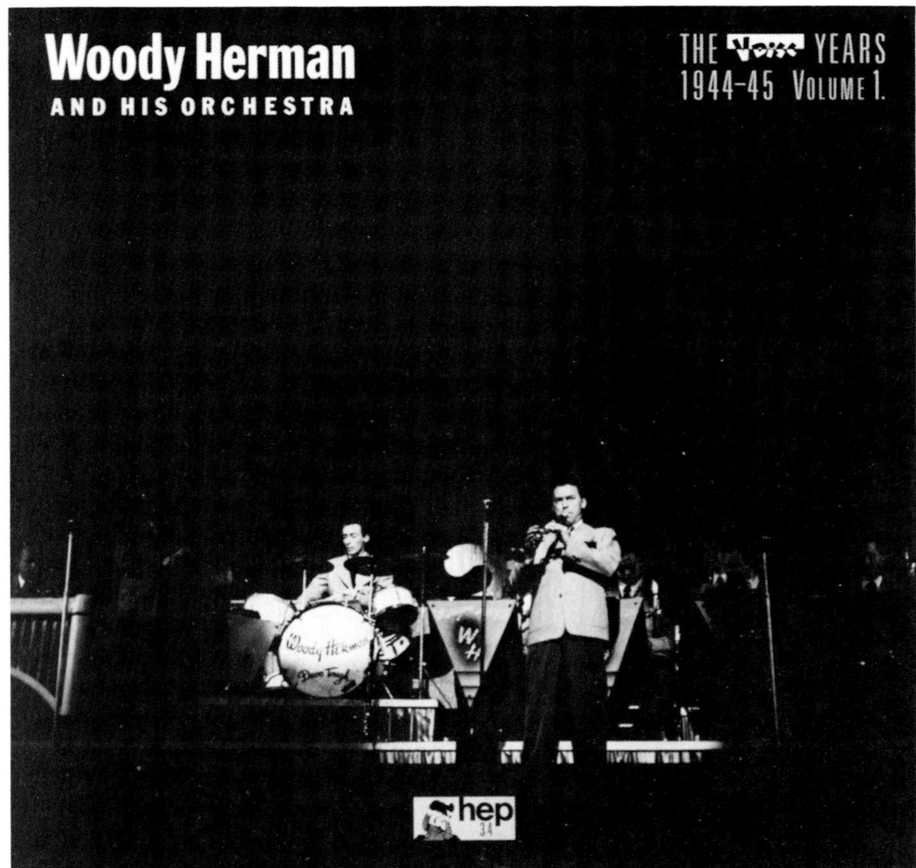

moved inexorably towards a new majesty of sound which eventually exploded onto the big band scene in 1944 with the arrival of new boys Ralph Burns, piano, Bill Harris, trombone, trumpeter Neal Hefti and drummer Dave Tough.

The band's rhythm section of Burns, Billy Bauer, guitar, Jackson and Tough, was among the finest in big band jazz and brought a new potency to an already exciting band which, thanks to a George T. Simon piece in *Metronome*, became known as the Herman Herd.

Burns, a gifted arranger as well as an excellent pianist, must be credited with much of the band's success. The full, rich sound of his arrangements gave the band a new image, bringing sophistication as well as excitement to the Herman roar. Neal Hefti also showed his writing talents with such exceptional pieces as 'The Good Earth' and he and Burns joined forces to score an imperishable version of 'Caldonia'.

Sam Marowitz played lead alto in the band and Flip Phillips brought authority and a lusher but still virile sound to the tenor chair vacated by Vido Musso. The band also had the exultant trombone of Bill Harris, the stratospheric trumpets of Pete Candoli and, especially, the brilliant Sonny Berman, who joined in 1945 giving the section a soloist of rare skill and imagination. Tragically, Berman died in 1947 but in that short span managed to add a glitter to the First Herd sound that lives on in recordings.

Further interesting acquisitions were made to the trumpet section with the arrival of Pete Candoli's young brother Conte and Shorty Rogers. Not least of Shorty's contributions were his arrangements, one of them entitled 'Igor' in appreciation of Igor Stravinsky who wrote 'Ebony Concerto' for the Herd.

Inevitably, personnel changes were made but somehow Woody managed to find substitutes even for the seemingly irreplaceable. One example of the impossible being achieved was when Don Lamond replaced Dave Tough at the drums.

The band's great popular success culminated in a Carnegie Hall concert performance in 1946. The ripping, roaring First Herd, with its numerous star performers, soared on a great wave of success. Never before had there been such a declamatory sound in big band music.

Although the Herman band always enjoyed the services of highly talented arrangers, there was still room in the First Herd days for head arrangements and some of the band's greatest hits originated in this way. 'Apple Honey' is an outstanding example and its informal origins mean that the several recorded versions are all different, some subtly, others dramatically so. The original Columbia recording from 1945 starts with a blaze of brass before the saxophone section sets in with a driving riff just long enough to allow the trumpets to mute up for a catchy phrase. Solos by Flip Phillips, Bill Harris, Margie Hyams on vibraphone and Woody follow before Pete Candoli blasts out a short solo in a register high enough to imperil the sonar system of any bats in the vicinity of the recording studios. The whole thing is booted along by Jackson's plangent bass and the shimmering cymbals of Dave Tough, ably demonstrating his qualifications as the best white big band drummer of his generation (and, maybe, several succeeding generations, too). Dave's bass drum tags became a feature of the First Herd, even after his departure, and long before such things were the commonplace they later became. Unlike the copies, here they aptly fit the loose-lidded approach of the band and its music.

Sideman—Bill Harris:
Bill Harris was one of the great 'naturals' of jazz. It is difficult to conceive of Harris ever making a success of playing any other instrument. His sound on trombone was so personal that no one has ever attempted to model himself on Bill's violently carousing style which fully utilised the instrument's powerhouse properties. Even in quieter moments, his solos have about them a menacing air of impending mayhem. Harris typified the great jazz individualists of old whose truly personal styles were built as much upon their musical inadequacies as upon technical facility and finesse.

***

Sideman—Serge Chaloff:
When baritone saxophonist Serge Chaloff joined the Woody Herman band in 1947 he had already absorbed the new bop idiom. Chaloff owed to the innovative styles of such earlier champions of the bulky instrument as Harry Carney. What he added was his own variation on lessons learned from bebop innovators Dizzy Gillespie and Bennie Harris during their time together in the Boyd Raeburn band.

Chaloff's tumbling phrases maintained a fullness of tone on even the most intricate uptempo arrangements. While his ballad playing was performed with tender assurance. His full use of dynamics has rarely been equalled by any other baritone saxophonist and he achieved a subtle yet intense lyricism.

Unfortunately, Chaloff's influence on the Herman band did not end with his musical ideas and the narcotics problems which bedevilled the lives of a number of Second Herdsmen were ostensibly a direct result of Chaloff's ultimately fatal habit.

The 1949 Herman Herd was featured at one of Gene Norman's Just Jazz concerts in Los Angeles. (L to R) Earl Swope, Bill Harris, Ollie Wilson, Terry Gibbs, Buddy Savitt, Sam Marowitz, Woody, Gene Ammons.

Good humour and simple *joie-de-vivre* were features of most of Herman's output and this is amply demonstrated on several tunes including 'Caldonia' with Woody's infectious singing and the band's vocal howls. The band, meanwhile, roars on with the trumpets in wailing form. Excellent solos by Woody, Phillips and Harris retain the strong jazz feel.

'Northwest Passage' is another head arrangement, opening with a trombone figure which is picked up by the reeds and by Margie Hyams' vibes before she lays into a short, swinging solo. Woody's clarinet, Flip's tenor and Harris's ripe trombone are set against a screaming brass section. Then the whole band roars out before a quiet coda from the rhythm section; a final brass shout with Candoli's ear-splitting horn ends it, apart from, of course, Dave Tough's tag.

Woody disbanded in December 1946 but was back in business again in 1947 with the Second Herd.

The 'Four Brothers' band of 1947–8 represented a particularly modern approach to big band music with its new-sounding reed section, of three tenors and one baritone, shooting through bebop-phrased Jimmy Giuffre arrangements and igniting them with searing excitement. If they hit a musical high, financially the band sank to a new low, an effect of the combination of the band's modern approach and the 1948 recording ban. It was a far cry from the tremendously popular appeal of Herman's First Herd.

For all its lack of immediate popularity with the public, in retrospect the Second Herd can be seen as an important departure in big band music. Unlike other contemporary attempts to incorporate bebop phrasing into a big band setting (Gene Krupa's 1947 band and Charlie Barnet's in 1949, for example) Herman succeeded in creating a subtle yet convincing amalgam of musical idealogies.

The Second Herd's most striking feature was, of course, the reed section. Although there were two alto saxophones (Sam Marowitz and Herbie Steward) it was the work of their deeper-toned section mates which caused the stir. These were Stan Getz and Zoot Sims on tenors and Serge Chaloff on baritone (with Steward doubling on tenor). None of these can be rightfully termed 'new boys' to the big band business but if their teeth were cut elsewhere each certainly took his biggest bite into subsequent fame with Woody. As it transpired, only Getz and Sims parlayed their success into long careers as solo performers of the first rank. Steward's later career was as a session man while Chaloff, one of the first musicians on baritone to make an impression after Ellington's Harry Carney, died young.

The idea of a tenor-dominated team had originated with Gene Roland who ran a band in New York in 1946 but which barely got beyond the rehearsal stage. Roland's four tenor saxophones included Getz but it was Roland himself who hung onto the notion of this particular musical effect and he tried it again with a Vido Musso band for which he was arranging, also in 1946. The saxophones here included Getz, Sims, Steward and Jimmy Giuffre. This band was heard by Ralph Burns and Woody who promptly hired the three tenors for the band while Giuffre was invited to produce a piece which would effectively showcase the new sound. The result, 'Four Brothers', was a huge success and, like so much of Herman's music, remains strikingly undated.

Bandstand broadside—3:
'These days it seems that all the cats want to be on! Sidemen used to worry about two things, whether they were playing the kind of music they liked to play, and whether the leader was laying sufficient loot on them at the end of the week. Today many of them worry about their *billing*, their spot in the show and, so help me, the colour of the spotlight that hits them when they take that solo!'

Woody Herman

The Second Herd's brass included Bernie Glow, Marky Markowitz, Shorty Rogers and Ernie Royal on trumpets, while the trombones featured a striking bebopper named Earl Swope. Don Lamond, who had replaced Dave Tough in the First Herd, was still on hand and the band cooked superbly, never allowing the bebop influence to interfere with straightahead swinging. Vibraphonist Terry Gibbs remarked of this band, 'That was a swinging, fun-loving band of don't-care-what's-gonna-happen-tomorrow wailers.'

One of the problems for the Second Herd was its timing. 'We were a little premature with the music,' Woody observed, 'a little too early for the public to appreciate it.' This was highlighted by the irony of the band achieving first place in *down beat*'s Readers' Poll *after* folding.

Luckily for later generations of big band fans, the 1948 recording ban was circumvented by the appearance over the years of a number of air shots. They show an authoritative band, sparking the fine arrangements of Giuffre and Rogers. Pride of place, however, went to the saxophone section (in which, in time, Herbie Steward was succeeded by Al Cohn).

Woody's insistence on staying in the forefront of changes in the big band scene did not blind him to the dangers of uncritical acceptance of everything that was being done in the name of 'progressive jazz' in the late 1940s. In a long article in *down beat* in 1948, Woody expounded on the problems.

Some leaders and arrangers, he averred, had allowed themselves to be blinded by their own brilliance and had moulded 'progressive jazz through an abtruse pattern of mystic formulae into an ethereal incantation only they are subtle enough to comprehend and adore'.

Woody was particularly concerned at the way in which such leaders had lost touch with 'the possible beauty of the natural jazz form' and had become bogged-down in technicalities. 'Jazz cannot be that tightly patterned, it is loose, fluid and cannot be attacked mathematically.'

In a comment obviously directed at Stan Kenton, Woody went on to say how the sheer volume offered by some bands overlooked the importance of the flexibility of dynamics. He was also most insistent upon the importance of the freedom a band could enjoy when not strait-jacketed by a too-precise chart. Yet this led to frequent criticism that the band used too many heads. 'What the critics don't understand is that jazz can't be an arranger's paradise with every note for every instrument scored from the first to the final bar... Soloists are the only true interpreters of jazz... To use the ideas of one arranger over and over every time a number is played is like serving up baled hay. It gets awfully dry.'

'I don't think I ever was a good jazz player.'
Woody Herman

***

Sideman—Stan Getz:
The Woody Herman sideman who gained most personal success and fame in later years is undoubtedly Stan Getz. Before joining Woody, Getz had already worked with numerous big bands including those of Jack Teagarden, Stan Kenton, Jimmy Dorsey, Benny Goodman and Gene Roland, to say nothing of working with several small groups in the period between 1942 and 1947.

While retaining his totally personal and highly recognisable style, Getz has never ceased to develop and is always moving with the times, ready to take on new challenges.

In his days with the Second Herd his languidly lyrical playing will be forever associated with the Ralph Burns composition, 'Early Autumn'. In Getz's playing of this period can be heard the pattern for an entire generation of coolly elegant tenor saxophone stylists.

Woody ended the impassioned article by nailing his colours firmly to the mast of progress, declaring that 'true jazz won't stop progressing for it's in the heart of each musician handed down from oldster to youngster. The kids of today are the soloists of tomorrow and through them flow the course of jazz.'

With considerable justification, critics have measured 'Summer Sequence', an extended work by Ralph Burns, against Duke Ellington's longer works and not found it wanting. The melodies used in this composition, which effectively bridged the First and Second Herds, have a limpid beauty enhanced by fine solos. In the studio recorded version by the First Herd the solos on the first three parts of the suite are by Woody, on clarinet and alto, Phillips, Harris, Sam Rubinowich, baritone, and Chuck Wayne, guitar. When the time came for release of the original recordings, the record company asked for a fourth part to the suite so that the whole work could be issued on two 78s. Burns obliged and despite the fact that it was some time since he had written the first sections he succeeded admirably. Adding an elegant quality to this fourth part of 'Summer Sequence', recorded by the Second Herd, is Burns's own piano playing, with good interplay between him and guitarist Gene Sargent. The highlight, however, is a superb solo from Stan Getz.

'Four Brothers' is much more tightly written than any of the earlier flagwavers and the deft precision of the saxophones, whether in ensemble or solo, is the strongest feature. Although Woody's clarinet solo is of a different idiom, he fits in well and the rest of the band still has its chance to shout.

'Keen and Peachy', a Burns-Rogers re-working of 'Fine and Dandy', is another performance in the 'Four Brothers' mould. In fact, this was recorded a few days earlier and for a while enjoyed greater popularity, perhaps because it has a more immediate appeal to fans of the earlier Herd with the band stretching out while the saxophone soloists have a looser role to play.

Al Cohn's 'The Goof and I' is a strong blues-based number featuring Chaloff and Swope, and Woody himself.

Towards the end of 1948 personnel changes and a heavier reliance on charts by out-and-out swinger Shorty Rogers shifted the sound of the band again. Many of Shorty's big band scores have much of the straightahead fire of earlier Herds with an occasional nod towards Basie.

Precise numbering of Herman Herds was never too easy, some writers categorising the Band That Plays the Blues as the first, while the transitional bands which came between distinctive Herds also caused confusion. It was Woody who, in the early 1950s, tagged his current band the Third Herd. If the new band lacked the precision of the Second 'Four Brothers' Herd, and missed the stampeding roar of the First Herd,

The Four Brothers band at the Commodore in 1948. Woody joins the front line of (L to R) Stan Getz, Al Cohn, Sam Marowitz, Zoot Sims, Serge Chaloff. Background support comes from, among others, Fred Otis, Mary Ann McCall, Harry Babasin, Ernie Royal, Bernie Glow, Shorty Rogers.

it more than made up for such deficiencies with its unbuttoned swing.

Newcomers during the early 1950s included trumpeters Dick Collins and Red Rodney, Cy Touff, bass trumpet, trombonists Urbie Green and Kai Winding, while the reed section employed Arno Marsh, Bill Perkins and the wonderfully talented Richie Kamuca. The Herd's rhythm section had a succession of bass players including Monty Budwig and the drum chair was taken by Chuck Flores and the fleet Jake Hanna. An important addition was pianist Nat Pierce whose Basie-inspired charts were a great asset to the band.

During the mid- to late 1950s the Herman band worked extensively but largely in obscurity. Members of one of the bands Woody led at this time wryly referred to themselves as the 'un-Herd' but it was still a fine group featuring such musicians as Bill Berry in the trumpet section, British-born Bobby Lamb was alongside old-hand Bill Harris in the trombone section, and there were also the aforementioned Marsh, Kamuca and Budwig.

Record dates produced a mixed bag. An album entitled 'The Fourth Herd', although rich in personnel: Al Cohn, Zoot Sims and Don Lanphere on tenors, Bob Brookmeyer, valve trombone, Nat Pierce, piano, was a disappointment with everyone seemingly having simultaneous off days but the band recorded at the 1959 Monterey Jazz Festival featured an array of musical talent well up to the best standards of the past. The saxophone team of Sims, Lanphere, Med Flory, Kamuca and Perkins all showed their paces.

'It took me about 200 musicians to find the [1947 Four Brothers]band I was looking for, but now I am happy at last.'

Woody Herman

During the 1960s and 1970s Woody Herman's band was variously labelled: sometimes it was the Swinging Herd, alternatively, the Thundering Herd. These later bands of Woody's had enviable qualities and, in some instances surpassed, however momentarily, all that had gone before.

The 1962 band was put together for Woody by Nat Pierce who drew upon many former colleagues from his days with the Herb Pomeroy band in Boston. This 'Swinging Herd' did exactly that thanks to Nat and his fellow rhythm section members, Chuck Andrus, bass, and Jake Hanna, drums. They provided the coiled spring needed to drive a fierce five-man trumpet section, which included Paul Fontaine and the iron-lipped Bill Chase, and the bucketing trombone team of Phil Wilson, Henry Southall and Kenny Wenzel, from one swirling climax to another. Nick Brignola's baritone saxophone gave the reeds a sonorous depth while Sal Nistico and Carmen Leggio produced an effusion of tumbling tenor chases.

Woody was not the only bandleader bringing young musicians out of the universities and colleges but there were differences in the way he used such newcomers to the manner in which they might be employed by, say, Maynard Ferguson or Buddy Rich. There, a young musician would find himself in a band largely made up of youngsters like himself with just one or two sidemen, and the leader, of course, as veterans. Woody mixed tyros with veterans in proportions more suited to drawing the best from them. To some extent this was the way in which Stan Kenton, too, used younger men in his later bands but there was a marked difference in the end product. With Kenton, the individual tended to fade into the brasswork; oft-times it could have been almost any highly competent musician sitting there. With Woody, while it was all Herman-style music, individual musicians, regardless of age and experience were allowed—indeed, they were expected—to contribute.

The 1967 Herman band, which appeared in Europe, included bass player Carl Pruitt and drummer John Von Ohlen alongside veteran-veterans Carl Fontana, trombone, Joe Romano, tenor saxophone, Cecil Payne, baritone and Al Dailey, piano, and new-veterans Bill Chase, trumpet, and Sal Nistico, tenor-arranger.

As record album succeeded record album, the personnel shifted. More than ever there were new-veterans, young musicians whose talents had been honed from their exposure to the hard facts of life in a big band where night after night, on form or not, they had to project their music and play with commitment and energy. It could not be any other way because the man in front of the band, whatever the date on his birth certificate, was always eager, exuberant, enthusiastic and imparted all of these characteristics with committed zeal.

1963 and 1964 albums, entitled, a bit unimaginatively, 'Woody Herman—1963', followed by 'Encore' and 'Woody Herman—1964', showed off a band that featured fine soloists, ripping ensembles and a rhythm section ranking with the best of the early Herds. Trumpeter Bill Chase and trombonist Phil Wilson are standouts among the soloists, both playing with great spirit and, like the best of their predecessors, confidently demonstrating an ability to walk the tightrope between unbridled enthusiasm and sheer exhibitionism. Breathtaking solos by Wilson and Nistico are matched by trombonist Henry Southall while the rhythm section really burns.

Big band societies in Britain: Big bands live on through the music and the musicians, but the fans also play their part.

Just as jazz record appreciation societies blossomed in Britain, so too the country has become an important centre for big band societies, associations and conventions.

Most often formed while the musicians so lauded was still alive and active, there are groups in Britain dedicated to preserving interest in the work of Count Basie, Les Brown, Duke Ellington, Harry James, Stan Kenton, Glenn Miller and Artie Shaw. Britain is also home to Big Band International and several localised organisations up and down the country among which the Huddersfield Big Band Society (Honorary President Les Brown) is prominent in keeping big band music alive.

Corresponding organisations operate throughout America, and fans can keep in touch with events and developments through the pages of *The Big Bands*, a magazine emanating from North Hollywood, which provides an endless fund of information on the whereabouts of names from the past. But the ▶

The personnel changed again in the mid-1960s for an album introducing outstanding newcomers, tenor saxophonists Gary Klein, Andy McGhee and Raoul Romero and Yugoslavian-born trumpeter Dusko Goykovich, who brought to the band his own highly distinctive, dry-toned melange of Central European and North American musical heritages. Among the Nat Pierce charts recorded by this band are 'The Good Life', featuring Klein, and 'Dr Wong's Bag' which spotlights McGhee. There is also 'Wa-Wa Blues', a rollicking trombone feature for Wilson and Joe Carroll.

On 'Light My Fire', from 1968, the band plays contemporary pop music. Just as many university bands have found the inclusion of pop music a means of keeping their young musicians in touch with the music they were called upon to play, so several commercial big bands followed a similar route but for different reasons as record company executives mistakenly thought that this was one way to improve sales, viz: Basie's unfortunate 'Beatle's Bag'. Newcomers to the Herman band include saxophonists Frank Vicari, Steve Lederer and Thomas Baras alongside Sal Nistico who was fast becoming a veteran-veteran at the ripe age of 28. Trumpeters include Gary Grant and Henry Hall while the rock-oriented rhythm section is joined by guitarist Phil Upchurch.

The inclination towards contemporary pop music meant an inevitable move towards rock rhythms which, by and large, do not mix too well with jazz-oriented bands. The necessarily heavier beat and the overstatement of the drummer, contrasting wildly with the delicate understatement of, say, Dave Tough and Jake Hanna with various Herman bands, inhibits fluid swing. As attempts to perform jazz-rock go, Herman's version of the hybrid on albums such as 'Children of Lima' is not inadequate. But it becomes wholly satisfying only fleetingly, particularly when Greg Herbert or Woody himself is soloing.

A 1976 '40th Anniversary: Carnegie Hall Concert' album is a grand reunion of many early Herd veterans. Fortunately, the set generally manages to avoid the tendency of such occasions to be good only in parts. Most of the set is special and if some of the old-timers who came along for the festivities do not quite repeat the glories of the past it is still a creditable all-round effort. Indeed, some moments, as when Stan Getz makes a welcome return for an exquisite 'Blue Getz Blues' and an equally fine version of 'Blue Serge', the present outweighs even the golden glow of nostalgia for the past.

At an age when most men would be happily retired to carpet slippers and nostalgic day-dreaming, if not actually long-dead and buried, Woody Herman continued playing. To some extent this was not entirely of his own free will. Illness which should have brought retirement, or at least a substantial period of rest, coincided with Woody's discovery that mismanagement of his affairs during the 1960s had resulted in a financial catastrophe. His manager at the time, Abe Turchen, had gambled away money set aside for tax. Now, in 1985, Woody was not only broke, but he also owed the US Internal Revenue Service millions of dollars in unpaid taxes.

Forced to play on, Woody put illness behind him and even though dreadfully sick he survived, continuing to bring delight to audiences and

▶ magazine is not merely backward looking; latterday performers who keep the big band flame burning through concert and dance date tours can also be found here.

The Stan Kenton Convention was begun in Britain in 1987 and visitors to the first gathering heard music from Ernie Eyes's British band, Shades of Kenton, and guests who included ex-Kentonians Rolf Ericson, Shorty Rogers, Bud Shank, Jiggs Whigham, and John Worcester, while the guest of honour was Vic Lewis.

Already well into its stride and fast becoming a major jazz event is the Duke Ellington Convention, which is devoted to perpetuating the memory of a great musician by keeping his music alive. Begun in America in 1983, the convention is now an established part of the musical calender and the venue alternates between America and Britain with other countries expressing interest in hosting this important celebration of Duke's music.

Here again, visiting musicians of the calibre of Bob Wilber, Alice Babs, Bill Berry, Willie Cook, Buster Cooper, Herb Jeffries and Jimmy Woode meet and socialise with, and perform for, enthusiasts who gather from all over the world.

Such organisations which exist today help keep alive interest in the music, and this in turn helps keep the music alive.

Gone but not forgotten; friends at Woody Herman's funeral:
'One of the joys of my life was to make an album with Woody.'
Rosemary Clooney
***
'He would have stayed on the road without all his financial problems. He just loved it.'
Les Brown
***
'... the greatest Pied Piper of modern American music.'
Jack Siefert
***
'Herman is the epitome of the big band era.'
Saul Levine
***
'It was easy to be his friend.'
Msgr. George J. Parnassus
***
'That tax problem should be forgotten. The IRS should make an exception.'
Tony Bennett
***
'People who've met him will never say a bad word about him.'
Nat Pierce

to impart his enthusiasm and knowledge to a new generation of young jazzmen.

In 1986 Woody celebrated his 50th anniversary as a bandleader by touring with a 16-piece band which included such stalwarts as tenor saxophonist Frank Tiberi and trumpeter Bill Byrne alongside yet another batch of new men any one of whom might well prove to be a jazz star of the future.

A celebratory album, '50th Anniversary Tour', recorded live at The Great American Music Hall, San Francisco, in March 1986, opens, unusually enough for Woody, with a Duke Ellington tune, 'It Don't Mean a Thing If It Ain't Got That Swing' on which baritone saxophonist Mike Brignola solos well. On the old Bob Crosby band's classic, 'What's New', trombonist John Fedchock proves that what is new can also remain happily rooted in the past.

If the final Herman Herds do not approach the untouchable glories of the past, they display moments of excitement and solo skills of the highest order. What always comes through, however, and always did, throughout half a century of music-making, is Woody's boundless enthusiasm.

More than most bandleaders Woody Herman made it part of his vocation to see that young musicians had a place to grow; in so doing he ensured that he remained forever young.

Woody's death, in October 1987, closed a door not only on a major chapter in the story of the big bands, but also, sadly, on one of the few remaining opportunities for young jazz stars of tomorrow to learn their trade alongside veterans and under the tutelage of a lively-minded leader who, even at the end, bore his troubles with fortitude.

Woodrow Charles 'Woody' Herman did not start out to become an institution, nor did he plan to make his orchestra a university for big band musicians, but this is what happened and three generations of musicians and fans have cause to give thanks.

EDDIE SAUTER

Eddie Sauter, one of the swing era's finest arrangers, was first noticed when he wrote and played with the Red Norvo band. After working with Benny Goodman he wrote for Artie Shaw's band with considerable success. After Shaw, Sauter helped to build a library for the Ray McKinley band to such telling effect that the band's billing included the words 'playing arrangements by Eddie Sauter' in letters 40% as large as Ray's own name. This recognition, an undeservedly rare event, caused fellow arranger George Handy to seek a similar deal for his work with Boyd Raeburn, a demand which resulted in a brawl between Handy's manager and Raeburn.

When Eddie Sauter was hospitalised with tuberculosis, he began corresponding with Bill Finegan who had arranged for Tommy Dorsey and Glenn Miller but was then studying at the Paris Conservatoire. The end result was the formation in 1952 of the Sauter-Finegan band, a 21-piece outfit, which had so many musicians doubling that it gave the joint arrangers an almost endless range of colours from which to work. The Sauter-Finegan partnership reached a peak of inspiration with their descriptive writing on such pieces as the whimsical 'The Doodletown Fifers' and the evocative 'Midnight Sleigh Ride'. Finegan smilingly remembered the latter as his 'best work on record—a chest solo... I beat my chest to simulate the sound of a sleigh horse running on hard packed snow; this is probably my finest effort on wax—or snow.' Although conceived as a studio group, Sauter and Finegan did take the band on the road but it effectively folded in 1957 when Sauter took up the post of musical director with the South-West German Radio Big Band in Baden-Baden.

Fellow arranger Mel Powell said of Sauter, 'Eddie was one of the most skilful arrangers around... He was an innovator...'

CHAPTER TWELVE

NEW CONCEPTS

'PROGRESSIVE GAVOTTE'

'Each era has had its "modern" musicians, but they have always had to resort to new means in order to create a music different from their predecessors.'

Stan Kenton

A fortune-teller seeking to predict the future for the 22-year-old piano player who joined Everett Hoagland's California-based band in 1933 would have had little help from Stan Kenton's music at the time. Hoagland's band was one of the better local dance bands, but neither Kenton's playing nor his arranging were in any way exceptional and in no way prepared audiences for the tumult that was to follow.

Among the earliest of the post-swing era big bands, which were tagged with the label 'progressive', were those of Woody Herman, Kenton, Boyd Raeburn and Claude Thornhill all of whom were active as either leaders, sidemen or arrangers in the swing era itself. Of these four, Woody Herman remained closest to the precepts of the swing era. Contrastingly, the bands of Raeburn and Thornhill explored aspects of music which at best puzzled their audiences, at worst alienated them entirely although both, and especially Thornhill, retained a high level of musicality.

The member of the quartet of bandleaders who became most readily associated with the term 'progressive' and raised most hackles in the jazz establishment is Stan Kenton. He also became and remained the most commercially successful of all the progressive bandleaders.

'This is the first band I've ever worked on where I've felt like a gentleman and a human being and have been treated that way.'
Unnamed member of the 1960 Stan Kenton band.

***

'Jazz is being differentiated from pop music as well as classical music. The modernists deserve the credit for proving that jazz doesn't have to be danced to.'
Stan Kenton

***

'Stan's writers generally don't write things that swing.'
Lennie Tristano

ARTISTRY IN KENTON

All Stan Kenton's bands were labelled with a term which sought to be descriptive but most often missed the mark. His first band was described as the 'Artistry in Rhythm' orchestra. Aimed at the dance hall trade, the band was a good, tight, reasonably swinging aggregation. A high proportion of Kenton's arrangements called for powerful brass section work and offered strong and interesting saxophone voicings. These had a slightly abrasive but by no means unpleasant sound and helped make the Kenton band instantly identifiable from the outset.

Thanks due in part to regular broadcasts, the band quickly built a highly vociferous following among younger fans. The music sounded modern, different and LOUD. It may be that the local attraction of the Kenton band lay in the fact that it originated in California at a time when practically every name band of note was east coast-based. The lift given by the West Coast crowd undoubtedly helped the band on its way. But that alone was not enough and certainly did not account for Kenton's popularity as he toured America during 1942 and 1943. Not that it was flowers all the way; gigs at New York's Roseland Ballroom and at Frank Dailey's Meadowbrook in New Jersey were little short of disastrous as dancers discovered that not much of what was happening on the stand could be danced to.

Then, Capitol Records, a relatively new company, bowed the knee to the American Federation of Musicians, agreed to the terms which had brought about a recording ban, and signed Kenton up for a date in November 1943. He quickly became Capitol's top-selling star, his tall, lean frame and toothy grin occupying a high proportion of the company's advertising space.

Bob Graettinger—eccentric genius:
During his stay with Stan Kenton, the controversial arranger Bob Graettinger used the Ellington principal of writing for each individual musician rather than for each section. The result was music not only difficult to play but each part was independent of the other. To get to know the musicians, Graettinger took to travelling with the band on their circuit of one night stands. The musicians would look out into the crowd from the bandstand and see the gaunt, haunted-eyed figure of Graettinger first in one spot, then another. Kenton's fine alto saxophonist Art Pepper recalled that Graettinger 'would block out everything if he could and listen to just one particular person and get that person's sound; the way that person played. He spent months doing that, just standing and listening to the band.'

Graettinger's unusual approach to his work extended to the manner in which he laid out his scores, using symbols and colouring to indicate what he wanted played. His major works for Kenton, the suites 'City of Glass' and 'This Modern World', were far ahead of their time, anticipating much of the atonality of the later 'free' jazz musicians. Graettinger, who died in 1957, crossed the borders of jazz and big band music; indeed, he spent more time outside than in and as a consequence his work is today sadly neglected.

Stan quickly cottoned onto the fact that he had a potential following for the all-stops-out style of much of his band's book: 'Artistry Jumps', 'Intermission Riff', 'Machito', 'Unison Riff' and 'Peanut Vendor'. Here, screaming brass ruled. The trumpets scrambled over one another as each strove to cap his colleagues, a barrel-chested trombone section sent out blaring tidal waves of sound, and if the saxophones sometimes struggled to be heard, they refused to be overcome. Under it all was a rhythm section which, as time went by, was obliged to sacrifice subtlety and swing in favour of sheer volume.

It was apparent that Stan loved volume just as much as did the fans. Many stories have been told to verify this. Guitarist Sal Salvador told Stan Woolley how, during the playing of 'Artistry in Rhythm', the sound sometimes disappeared. 'I turned around and looked at the guys and their cheeks were all out and they were blowing like crazy but my ears had just cut-out at a certain point.' Another tale told of Stan demanding more and yet more volume in rehearsal until he was finally assured that the band could not possibly play any louder. He was advised to have his ears syringed. He did, and next day was almost deafened by the thunderous roar of the band.

Nevertheless, there was always room in his 1940s bands for easy-going numbers: 'Eager Beaver', 'Tampico' and 'Painted Rhythm', and such mildly elegaic pieces as 'Opus in Pastels', which were arranged by Kenton and Gene Roland, and Pete Rugulo's 'Interlude' and 'Laura'.

Kenton's energies were phenomenal and he flung himself into everything with enormous zest. Fortunately, he was able to delegate much of his arranging chores to others. A long string of fine arrangers worked for the band, including Pete Rugulo, whose work could be so similar to Stan's that, like Billy Strayhorn and Duke Ellington, it was hard to discern where one left off and the other started.

In 1950 Stan Kenton unveiled his 'Innovations in Modern Music' band which included French horns, violins, violas, cellos and a tuba in addition to his regular five trumpets, five trombones, five saxophones and a five-piece rhythm section. This 43 piece band caused further dissension, this time within the ranks of the Kenton fans themselves. There were some who simply did not understand what he was trying to accomplish. Without doubt, he had left the orthodoxy of the big band scene far behind but the jazz-oriented fans were occasionally encouraged by some of the offerings of the Innovations band, especially those numbers featuring soloists whose names were enshrined in the titles of the tunes: 'Art Pepper', 'Maynard Ferguson', 'Shelly Manne', 'June Christy'. Fans of less adventurous music were tossed such occasional titbits as 'Take the A Train', 'Laura', and 'September Song'.

But if the early appearances by and recordings of the Innovations band caused problems for some fans, further discord was yet to come. In 1951 the band performed and recorded Bob Graettinger's 'City of Glass' suite, a work of uncompromising complexity and neo-classical leanings.

Stan Kenton at the piano with bass player Eddie Safranski in 1945.

Although in later years members of the band confirmed their respect for the music and clearly admired the sheer difficulty of what they had to play, many of the band's fans saw this work as evidence that Stan Kenton had left the path of jazz and big band music.

The Innovations band did not last long, due mainly to the enormous cost of its upkeep. Although Kenton was never overtly commercial he was always aware that if he was to continue, he had to give the public at least a measure of what it wanted. The next band dropped down in size to a more manageable but still large 19-piece unit. This was the 'New Concepts in Artistry in Rhythm' band which played new arrangements of some of the old hits, in many cases improving upon the originals. There were also interesting new charts by Gerry Mulligan whose preference for writing tight arrangements which condensed the sound of a big band conflicted with Stan's view that a big band should sound like a big band. Nevertheless, Mulligan left a legacy of good music,

Concert at the Hollywood Bowl: July 1950 saw the final concert in Stan Kenton's 'Innovations in Modern Music' series at the Hollywood Bowl where his 38-piece band played to an audience of more than 14,000 paying customers. Featured soloists included singer June Christy and high-note trumpet specialist Maynard Ferguson. The audience, on what was a chilly night, stayed to the end, not even joining in the usual scramble to escape post-concert traffic jams.

***

Improvisation *v.* arrangers—5: 'Kenton's perspective is that of a composer throughout and my feeling is that all great jazz will come from improvising not writing.'

Lennie Tristano

including 'Young Blood', a tune which sparkled with originality of thought and was played with verve by the band.

Throughout his career, Kenton and his fellow arrangers for the band, displayed a liking for Latin American rhythms. Always eager to try something new, Stan commissioned Johnny Richards to write the 'Cuban Fire' suite and the result was one of the band's most successful longer works.

Kenton's international reputation had been built upon records but in 1953 a European tour included a stopover in Dublin which was attended by some 3,000 fans shipped over from England on a trip organised by *Melody Maker* magazine. The enthusiasm which greeted the band both on and off-stage was astonishing to Stan and his men who ever afterwards spoke with awe of their reception. In 1956, with the ban on American musicians playing in Britain finally lifted, the way was open for a visit and this and subsequent tours were always highly successful.

Bandstand broadside—4:
'Working with a group of musicians over a period of time presents many problems that are emotional and psychological rather than simply musical... 'There are some musicians who are immature emotionally, regardless of how wonderfully they may play. Most of all, it seems to me, a musician needs affection.'
Stan Kenton

In the early 1960s Stan's ceaseless quest for new sounds led him to form his 23 piece 'New Era in Modern Music' orchestra which, thanks to having in its ranks an instrument not associated with jazz and big bands, was more usually known as the 'Mellophonium' band.

Stan had wanted a new voice for the brass section. He had tried French horns and even alto trumpets before turning to mellophoniums. The results were mixed but the sound certainly was different.

The mid-1960s saw yet another label: the 'Neophonic' orchestra, a 28 piece band whose library flirted uncomfortably with neo-classical music. From the late 1960s onwards, Kenton's music continued to fluctuate between experimentation and updated and renewed versions of older styles.

Gene Roland's arrangements for Kenton's 'Adventures in Blues' album blend brass and reeds successfully on such numbers as 'The Gold Nugget' and 'Aphrodisiac' and the flagwaving 'The Blues Story' on which the 15 strong brass section is used most effectively. Trumpeter Marvin Stamm and lead alto Gabe Baltazar are outstanding soloists while the whole band swings enthusiastically.

Not surprisingly, given his penchant for experimentation, Kenton also tried his hand at fusions but with varying levels of success. On one particularly well-received album, '7.5 On the Richter Scale', Kenton looses his band on such numbers as the themes from the movies, *Live and Let Die* and *The Godfather*, and Dale Devoe's '2002 Zarathustrevisited'. The use of rock rhythms breathes fresh life into compositions which had already been somewhat overexposed. Also on the album are excellent charts by Marty Paich, 'Body and Soul', Hank Levy, 'Down and Dirty', and Ken Hanna, 'It's Not Easy Being Green'. As always, it is the Kenton brass which strikes sparks throughout, often at the expense of the reed section.

In 1977 Stan fell, fracturing his skull and was subsequently operated on for the removal of a blood clot. During his absence the band played on, led for a while by clarinetist Buddy De Franco and when Stan returned to the band he was as enthusiastic as ever but his gruelling schedule was beginning to tell. The band played its final concert on 20 August 1978. Although plans were afoot for re-forming the following year, Stan's health deteriorated rapidly and he died on 25 August 1979.

In his will Stan Kenton stipulated that his band would never follow in the footsteps of Glenn Miller or Tommy Dorsey; there was to be no Stan Kenton Orchestra after his death.

The Misty Miss Christy cools it in front of the tartan-clad Stan Kenton band at the Hollywood Palladium in 1951. Included are Shelly Manne, Maynard Ferguson, Shorty Rogers, Ray Wetzel, Bob Cooper, Art Pepper, Milt Bernhart.

A waiter at the Commodore Hotel listens to the Kenton saxophone section backing trombone soloist Eddie Bert during a 1947 engagement in New York. (L to R) Stan Kenton, Jack Costanzo, Laurindo Almeida, June Christy, Shelly Manne, Bob Cooper, Al Porcino, Bert, Art Pepper, Harry Forbes, George Weidler, Harry Betts, Ken Hanna, Walt Weidler, Milt Bernhart, Bob Gioga.

HOLLYWOOD

Boyd Raeburn's Wild Bunch in 1945. (L to R) David Allyn, Margie Wood, Joe Burdeice, Stuart Anderson, Leonard Green, Irv Kluger, Jackie Carman, Hal McKusick, Johnny Mandel, Tommy Allison, unk., Frank Socolow, unk., unk., Hy Mandel, unk., Raeburn.

It was a wise decision; no one else could have brought to a re-created band the same drive, dedication and unbridled enthusiasm Stan Kenton always displayed for his highly individual brand of big band music.

Loved or hated, and neither term is too strong for the emotions his music generated, Stan Kenton made an impressive mark on the post-war years.

Among other adventurously-inclined musicians were several tagged, like Kenton, as 'progressive', a term which quickly took on a faintly patronising if not downright insulting air. Not for the first time in jazz, a label had come between the musician and his potential audience.

The effects of this labelling on the bands of Boyd Raeburn and Claude Thornhill were very different. Of the two, Raeburn and his wild bunch undoubtedly didn't give a damn.

Boyd Raeburn's early attempts at bandleading were insubstantial although he did enjoy a measure of success as a society-bandleader. It was not until 1944, more than a decade after he had formed his first band, that Boyd made an impact. Aided by several fine musicians, some of whom were drop-outs from the recently disbanded Sonny Dunham band, and the considerable arranging talents of Johnny Mandel and Eddie Finckel, the Raeburn band had some of the direct, swinging fire of the current Woody Herman band, allied to material that was as complex and intellectually demanding as Stan Kenton's later works.

Like Kenton, Raeburn used unorthodox instruments: French horns, woodwinds and even a harp. The arrival in 1945 of the eccentric George Handy simultaneously strengthened the arrangers on hand and placed the band even further outside the accepted norm for dance hall gigs of the period. Whatever people might think of the music, it was for listening not dancing. By 1946 arranger Johnny Richards had come aboard and the band included many ex-Kentonians, refugees from one or another of Herman's Herds, and several noted figures from the emerging bebop movement: Red Callender, Pete Candoli, Conrad Gozzo, Bill Harris, Irv Kluger, Dodo Marmarosa, Earl Swope, Lucky Thompson, Britt Woodman and singer David Allyn. However, a tour of one-nighters in the Southwest brought about certain temporary changes in the spring of 1946 when two black musicians, Thompson and Woodman, were dropped as the leader commented bitterly upon the futility of fighting racial prejudice.

The band's music in the mid-1940s was dominated by Handy whose arranging of standards and many of his own compositions showed a highly original talent untrammelled by the preconceptions of dance band arranging all around him. (Handy's contributions to the band have been challenged, notably by Eddie Finckel who claimed sole authorship of several major Raeburn successes, including 'Boyd Meets Stravinsky' and 'March of the Boyds', which were attributed to Handy and Raeburn.) Handy's personal eccentricities tended to obscure the enormous skills with which he approached his work.

The assertiveness of the young musicians with whom Boyd Raeburn surrounded himself, matched as it was to the leader's inclination to make his point physically when necessary, resulted in several fist fights and mass walk-outs by players, arrangers and singers. Boyd wasn't too worried; as he told *down beat*, 'A few ... were frantic kids that I'm just as happy without.' His view of Handy was that he was very talented but immature as a man. '[He]has some amazing ideas, and a rare talent—but he's listened to too many wrong people and become so impressed with his own importance that it's affecting his music.' At this time, the end of 1946, Raeburn was more than happy with Handy's replacement, Johnny Richards, who extended the band's range with great flair.

Shorty's Giants:
Ex-Kenton trumpeter-arranger Shorty Rogers, who had also worked with Woody Herman, made some highly successful big band records in the early and mid-1950s. A co-founder of the West Coast 'cool' school, yet another strikingly inappropriate label, Rogers worked extensively in small groups in and around Los Angeles when he wasn't otherwise engaged with Kenton or Herman. His exciting if sometimes raw big band drew heavily upon fellow-Kentonians and this influenced the solos and the shouting ensemble passages. The Rogers band, however, swings much more than Kenton's, as befits a man who compiled one of his record albums from his own Basie-style work. Shorty was an important influence in the rising popularity of modern jazz. He convinced record companies to use music and musicians unknown to them, insisting that he knew best. He also taught endlessly, leading John Graas to ask, 'Is there anyone on the Coast who *didn't* study with Shorty?'

In the late 1980s, Shorty Rogers plays on, still fiery, still teaching, working with young musicians at home and abroad, still an important influence on big band music everywhere.

Serge Chaloff, baritone sax, 1952.

Sailing into summer with the Claude Thornhill band at Balboa Beach, Los Angeles, in 1940. (L to R) Bob Sprentall, Ralph Harden, Tasso Harris, Joe Aguanno, Bob Jenney, Jane Essex (Dover), Thornhill, Dale Brown, George Paulsen, Hal Tennyson, Bill Motley, Hammond Russum, John Nelson, Don Whittaker, Ray Hagan.

Boyd finally ran out of enthusiasm in 1957, by which time his backers had also run out of money. He retired to the Bahamas to run a furniture business with his wife, Ginnie Powell, formerly the singer with the band. Boyd Raeburn died in 1976.

The effect of the 'progressive' label on Claude Thornhill's elegant band might deter listeners who would find it very difficult from that of either Kenton or Raeburn.

In the 1930s Claude Thornhill had worked as pianist or arranger, or both, for numerous bands including those led by Benny Goodman, Andre Kostelanetz, Ray Noble and Paul Whiteman. Hankering still for the pleasure he had gained from this earlier experience, and aware that several of the musicians he had worked alongside: Will Bradley, Glenn Miller, Artie Shaw, Charlie Spivak, were now making names for themselves, Claude decided to form his own band.

In his 1940 band Thornhill sought perfection in balance and intonation, rehearsing his musicians endlessly through the 60 or so scores he had written while planning the band. He was especially careful in removing vibrato, except where he wanted to create a special effect. He was aided in this by the addition, in 1941, of two French horns, essentially vibratoless instruments. Thornhill liked to use the orchestra to provide a background of slowly shifting pastel patterns against which he could play his distinctive, delicate piano. Gil Evans, then a young aspiring arranger, was hired by Thornhill in 1941 and has repeatedly asserted how much this experience influenced his own later work.

Claude's first post-war band also used French horns, an unusual instrumentation which allowed for striking colourings and a romanticism which set the band apart from most of its contemporaries. The 17-piece band gradually increased until it reached 22 pieces but was then folded before Thornhill started up again in 1947 (this time adding the slightly archaic-sounding tuba). Gil Evans was again writing arrangements, many of them slow and moody ballads.

Among the rising young musicians who played in the band were Lee Konitz, Red Rodney and Gerry Mulligan. Rodney recalled the band as 'an excellent vehicle for good music'. Interviewed by *down beat* in 1964, Gerry Mulligan remarked on the band's sound and how amazingly softly it played. Yet, despite this quality, the end result was highly effective. As Mulligan observed, 'The sound of that band, starting out from this soft quality, would swell and you could almost see it spreading into the hall...'

Gil Evans was responsible for bringing modern jazz into the band as he sought to score for multiple instruments what Charlie Parker was currently doing alone. Thornhill did not at first object, accepting that the time was right for experimentation. But dissent was brewing between Thornhill and Evans over how the band would develop. Claude was happy to have the band simply playing sustained chords against which he could weave his trickling piano but Evans considered that the band's sound was becoming too sombre, too bleak. They parted company but Evans never lost his admiration for Thornhill as a musician and as a man: 'My influence, such as it has been, was really through him.'

To a great extent Claude Thornhill pioneered the use of instruments which were then unusual in big bands, flutes and piccolos for example, and his ideas were followed by Elliot Lawrence (not to good effect), Boyd Raeburn, Johnny Richards, Stan Kenton, who added more horns and created a brassier effect, and, not surprisingly, Gil Evans himself in his 1950s band.

Dogged by ill-health, Claude disbanded in mid-1948 but then reformed late in the same year with a more commercially oriented band. Now, the tendency to play smoothly was intensified until, as John S. Wilson observed, 'The music flows out at you like rich, creamy fudge, with Claude's piano meandering through it, dropping cool spots of peppermint to brighten the heavy mixture.'

Claude Thornhill continued playing through the 1950s and thereafter occasionally until his death on 1 July 1965 at the age of 55.

Musicians thought highly of him, not least Duke Ellington who mused, 'I wonder if the world will ever know how much it had in this beautiful man...'

The immensely wide range of music offered by Stan Kenton, Boyd Raeburn and Claude Thornhill underlines the flaw of labelling any facet of jazz and big band music. Perhaps the term 'progressive' helps differentiate between what had happened in the field in earlier years but it is a flawed definition. The music of some later big bands was so advanced as to make all but the most experimental works of Kenton, Raeburn and Thornhill seem positively traditional.

But in their day, they were anything but traditional and they brought sparks of originality, great vitality, enthusiasm and, in Kenton's case at least, thunderous excitement for a new generation of big band fans.

Shades of Kenton:
High on the list of excellent British rehearsal bands is the Shades of Kenton band. Directed by Ernie Eyes, from a base in Salford, Manchester, the band's name denotes the source of its inspiration. Playing original and recreated Kenton charts with great zest, the band has provided backing for visiting Kenton alumni including Bill Perkins, Shorty Rogers, Bud Shank and Jiggs Whigham and was the 'house band' at the first international Stan Kenton convention held in Britain in 1987.

***

'... I would like to say one thing about Kenton. Who is offering to the young American composer anything near what Kenton is offering in terms of freedom to his arrangers? For that he deserves great credit.'

Dave Brubeck

***

Hiring and firing—2:
'Stan [Kenton] pulls Ken [Hanna] aside and says: "I need a baritone sax player. Do you know any?" Ken turned around and pointed at me. Now I was a tenor sax player, but that night I went down and auditioned for Stan and he said, "Let's go on the road!" I did, but I didn't like it. We were just running for six months.'

Hank Levy

FORTY YEARS OF BRITISH BIG BANDS

In the years following World War II and before American bands began touring Britain in the mid-1950s, by far the greatest impact on the British scene was made by Ted Heath.

In the hard days of the Depression, while still a young teenager, Ted was his family's principal breadwinner. To add to the low wages he earned as an apprentice coach-builder he busked on London's streets and in 1922 was heard by Jack Hylton, then relief pianist in the band playing at the Queen's Hall Roof. At Hylton's urging Ted was hired and after a spell with Bert Firman's band joined his mentor who had by then formed his own band. In 1927 Ted moved again, this time to join Bert Ambrose's band at the Mayfair Hotel where he remained until the late 1930s when he moved first to Sidney Lipton, then into Geraldo's band.

In 1942 Ted formed his own band with the stated intention of matching the Americans at their own game. Ted still admired the earlier British bands but knew he had to be different. 'We were really the first big modern band in Britain... None of the [earlier] bands... had the accepted big band line-up of eight brass, five saxes and rhythm section; nor did they have an all-out swinging policy. I had the idea there was a big market for this type of music, but the market for it was not my propelling motive. It was just that I liked that kind of music, and I knew literally dozens of great British musicians who also liked it and would give their right arm to play it.'

By the end of 1944 the Ted Heath band was a permanent group and became a national favourite thanks to tours and regular appearances at the London Palladium with its 'Sunday Night Swing Sessions'.

In 1956 the Ted Heath band was part of the first cooperative deal between the British and American musicians' unions. Stan Kenton came to Britain and Ted Heath visited America where he played with June Christy, the Four Freshmen and Nat 'King' Cole, ending the tour with a concert at Carnegie Hall.

The roll call of British musicians who played with the Ted Heath band over the years includes many of the best session players and a number of fine jazz talents. Among them are trumpeters Bobby Pratt and Kenny Baker pianist Stan Tracey, who became a major figure on the contemporary British jazz scene, and drummers Jack Parnell and Ronnie Verrell.

After Ted Heath's death in 1969 the band continued to play intermittently over the years. In the late 1980s the Ted Heath Orchestra, a gathering of top London session men, can still be seen and heard. Under the direction of the highly skilled trombonist Don Lusher, this group recalls the sounds of a band which fulfilled its founder's commitment to match the Americans at the swing game.

Also out to match an American trend in big band music, but of a very different order to that played by Ted Heath, was Vic Lewis.

In the late 1940s Vic's searing big band brought to British concert halls a live version of what fans had been hearing on their Stan Kenton records. Vic's orchestra used charts by Kenton and Pete Rugolo (along with numerous excellent Ken Thorne arrangements along similar lines). The band was an ear-opener for the fans who had seldom heard a British band play with such vigour—or so loud.

Vic gathered several soloists of note, especially trumpeter Johnny Shakespeare, alto saxophonist Ronnie Chamberlain and tenor saxophonists Jimmy Skidmore and Kathy Stobart. A slightly later band brought in trombonist Gordon Langhorne (Don Lang), alto saxophonist Derek Humble, tenor saxophonist Bob Efford and pianist Arthur Greenslade.

In the mid-1950s the masterly tenor saxophonist Tubby Hayes was added to the solo talent but, sadly, the band's days were numbered when the financial problems that trailed all big bands of this period caught up and Vic was obliged to disband.

In the 1980s Vic Lewis returned to the big band scene, recording for his own label a specially assembled big band which included his old sideman Ronnie Chamberlain and featured ex-Stan Kenton soloists Shorty Rogers, Bud Shank and Jiggs Whigham.

Another British bandleader of the 1950s with an all-out jazz policy was Johnny Dankworth. He formed his first big band in 1953 having gained considerable national success with his septet. Against the odds, Dankworth maintained his big band throughout the 1950s, using it to experiment with his advanced ideas in composition and arranging. Instead of the customary saxophone section Dankworth substituted a line-up of tenor saxophone, trombone, trumpet and baritone saxophone. This produced a somewhat brittle but thoroughly identifiable sound.

An ingenious arranger himself, Dankworth also employed the skills of Dave Lindup but perhaps his greatest asset was his singer, Cleo Laine, who later became his wife.

In the early 1960s Dankworth re-formed, using a much more dynamic group of musicians. Driven by the fierce drumming of Ronnie Stephenson the band

National Westminster Bank
PRESENTS
The
TED HEATH
B·A·N·D
DIRECTED BY DON LUSHER
By arrangement with Mrs Moira Heath

1944 1984

40th ANNIVERSARY CONCERT
THE BARBICAN HALL SATURDAY 14th APRIL 1984 7.45 pm
IN AID OF THE MENTAL HEALTH FOUNDATION

Listen to My Music. Ted Heath in the spotlight with his band in its early years. The trumpet section (L & R) features Alan Franks, Harry Latham, Kenny Baker, Stan Roderick; trombones Jimmy Coombs, Joe Cordell, Harry Roche, Jack Bentley; reeds Dave Shaw, Reg Owen, Les Gilbert, Johnny Grey, Ronnie Scott; the rhythm section is Charlie Short, Jack Parnell, Dave Goldberg, Ralph Sharon. (Courtesy: Don Lusher)

featured many fine soloists including trumpeter Kenny Wheeler and tenor saxophonists Danny Moss and Art Ellefson. Ever unconventional, Dankworth also used a tuba played adeptly by Ron Snyder.

One of Dankworth's finest pieces of descriptive writing occurs in his suite, 'What the Dickens', inspired by the works of Charles Dickens.

During his bandleading career Dankworth has regularly drawn upon many of Britain's finest jazz soloists including Tony Coe, Tubby Hayes, Pete King, Dick Morrisey, Ronnie Scott and Bobby Wellins.

The 1950s saw in Britain a brief flourish of excellent jazz-oriented big bands which sank without trace, condemned by the deliberately non-commercial policies of their leaders: Tony Crombie, Malcolm Mitchell, Ronnie Scott and Tommy Whittle.

Bands which adopted musical policies more congenial to the general public's taste enjoyed a consequential measure of success. These included bands led by showman-drummers Jack Parnell and Eric Delaney. On radio, Cyril Stapleton had considerable success with his show band which was made up from top session men; Wally Stott was similarly successful and made an exemplary recording of 'Cat from Coose Bay' which is still recalled with enthusiasm by many big band fans.

Forward-thinking musicians made interesting albums in the 1960s and 1970s, particularly worthwhile being the work of Mike Gibbs and Mike Westbrook. Pianist Stan Tracey, although best known for his small group work, has led occasional big bands. While concentrating on presenting his own forthright musical philosophy, Tracey has also formed a big band especially to pay tribute to Duke Ellington. Featured soloists with Tracey include many top British jazz solo stars, among them Tony Coe and Bobby Wellins.

Unlike Tracey, who made his own statement on the Ellington lode, other British musicians deliberately chose to arrange music in the style of 1920s and 1930s bands. The orchestras they formed, The Midnite Follies and the Pasadena Roof Orchestra, play with great charm and panache.

The British big band scene of the 1980s is very different to that of earlier decades. Most interesting and exciting is the emergence of several bands using new, young and often outstanding musicians who are part of the resurgence of jazz in Britain.

The Jazz Warriors are a 20-piece band of black, London-based young musicians possessed of enormous enthusiasm and potential but still searching for direction and style. The extensive use of Afro-Caribbean percussive patterns, overlaid with powerful blocks of screaming brass inevitably excites even if it sometimes lacks clear form. There is also a marked tendency among the band's soloists to adhere closely to the concepts of John Coltrane. The fact that Coltrane died in 1967, before some of these young men were born, and certainly before they had the faintest notion of becoming musicians, is one that demands thought and attention. If the Jazz Warriors, whose personnel includes such outstanding musicians as Courtney Pine, tenor and soprano saxophones, and Orphy Robinson, vibraphone, can find a new star to guide them, perhaps from within, the band's huge potential augers well for the future of British jazz—and for the new, looser, non-traditional style of big bands.

If the Jazz Warriors deviate more than a little from the traditional concept of big band music then Loose Tubes are somewhere else entirely.

As the band's name implies, there is an engaging informality about Loose Tubes although it is their casual appearance and behaviour which alienate some big band fans. This is an unfortunate loss to the fans concerned because, musically, Loose Tubes has a lot to offer.

In the band's ranks can be found several leading young British musicians whose roots are self-evidently in rock rather than jazz. Among them are Django Bates, who plays keyboards and tenor horn, and Steve Argüelles and Nic France, percussion. There are also a number of outstanding instrumentalists more attuned to the jazz tradition. Notable among these is Iain Ballamy who plays alto saxophone and flute but majors on soprano saxophone where his command and fluency can be breathtaking.

Although the sections rarely play with the precision demanded by some big band fans, the brass has a number of fine players. The trumpets play with aggression and in Dave DeFries and Chris Batchelor have interesting soloists. The trombones, and particularly bass trombonist Ashley Slater, have a command and attack that would have endeared them to Stan Kenton.

In performance Loose Tubes present their music colourfully and with an engagingly light-heartedness that is underpinned by fine musicianship.

The appeal of the band lies elsewhere than among the more traditional ranks of big band fans but the encouragement given to Loose Tubes by a substantial body of young fans bodes well for modern music in Britain.

CHAPTER THIRTEEN

KEEPERS OF THE FLAME

'THE BEAT GOES ON'

'You should hear the band Clem De Rosa has. He's got a jazz band in the sixth grade at South Huntingdon grammar school. And the average age there is 9. You should hear them play Basie.'

Marshall Brown

The last set played by Louie Bellson's Big Band Explosion at Ronnie Scott's had not ended until around 3am but afterwards, at their hotel, several members of the band were in a mood to talk. Their conversation was light-hearted, filled with reminiscences of other nights in other cities with other bands. But, eventually, with a gloomy London dawn easing through the streets outside, the talk turned to serious consideration of the future and the next generation of musicians. Not that there was any absence of young musicians coming out of schools, colleges and universities all over the United States, and, to a lesser extent, in Great Britain, but what could this new generation of musicians expect from life and what kind of musicians would they be?

As Nat Pierce remembered, the educational system had not always been so attuned to the peculiarities of the jazz life as it was now. 'First off, teachers had to have a diploma. Now, none of us guys had diplomas so we were passed over. The men with the college diplomas got the jobs but lately it's turned around the other way. Now, people with experience can teach. That's better because the teachers came right out of school themselves into teaching. They didn't have any idea what a musician's life was all about. That's something they can't teach. You have to learn that all by yourself.'

Where do we go from here?: 'Sometimes I wonder today, with all the young fellas in the country that are studying music, where they're ever going to get a chance to play it, what they're gonna do...'
Stan Kenton

One of the first American universities to take big band music seriously is North Texas State at Denton. In the 1950s the university had a fine 'laboratory band' and in 1959 took third place in a New York contest in which the competition came from commercial dance bands. Since the 1960s the One O'Clock Lab Band of North Texas State University has toured the world, appeared at prestigious international jazz festivals and played the White House. An indication of the high regard in which the profession holds the students at NTSU can be gained from the case of Stan Kenton. Apart from hiring numerous graduates for his own band over the years, in 1962 Stan donated many original scores to the university and on his death it was learned that he had willed almost 100 scores and manuscripts to the university. Apart from Kenton, students have gone on to work with the bands of Don Ellis, Maynard Ferguson, Woody Herman, Thad Jones, Mel Lewis and Toshiko Akiyoshi.

Sonn and Sonny:
In the mid-1950s Larry Sonn led a band on NBC which became very popular with radio audiences. Sonn was a product of the bands of Charlie Barnet, Vincent Lopez, Hal McIntyre and Teddy Powell and his own band could always swing. In 1955 Sonn recorded an album mostly using original charts by Manny Albam and Al Cohn. The band's lightly swinging performances feature such soloists as Jimmy Nottingham, trumpet, Bobby Asher, trombone, Cohn and Frank Socolow, tenors and Hal McKusick, alto. The ensemble is driven along by the mighty rhythm section of Nat Pierce, piano, Milt Hinton, bass, and Gus Johnson, drums. The Manny Albam tracks include such titles as 'Close Cover Before Striking', featuring typical probing trumpet from Nottingham and the broad-toned trombone of Asher, while 'The Sonn Also Rises' includes spots for Pierce's sparse piano and Al Cohn's dry-toned tenor.

In the 1920s Sonny Dunham worked with the bands of Ben Bernie and Paul Tremaine, but in 1931 he started his own band which he named Sonny Lee and his New York Yankees. This band was short-lived and in 1932 he joined Glen Gray's Casa Lomans and stayed until late 1940. Sonny's solo trumpet was one of the highlights of the Gray band and he was featured on 'The Nearness of You', which later became his theme song. On leaving Gray in 1940 Sonny formed a big band featuring arrangements by George Williams, and with Corky Corcoran on tenor and vocalist Ray Kellog. After disbanding in 1951 Sonny worked with various orchestras including Tommy Dorsey's. In 1960 Sonny settled in Florida and was still playing but, due to lip problems, had to give up the trumpet for the trombone.

The example of NTSU and such dedicated educators as Gene Hall and Leon Breeden and their successor Neil Slater is repeated in literally hundreds of other colleges and universities across America.

California State University, Northridge, has several important jazz courses under the direction of Joel Leach and CSUN graduates have found work with the bands of Louie Bellson, Woody Herman, Bill Holman, Harry James, Quincy Jones, Stan Kenton and Gerald Wilson.

Under the direction of Tom Battenberg, Ohio State University's bands have toured extensively, playing festivals and concerts in Europe, including a 1978 appearance at the Montreux Jazz Festival. OSU has provided musicians for the bands of Herman, Kenton and Buddy Rich. The 1967 edition of the Ohio band was led by Ladd McIntosh, later to become a rehearsal band leader of note in Los Angeles.

Good jazz educators are rare but Towson State University in Maryland hired one of the best in Hank Levy, formerly baritone saxophonist with Stan Kenton. Levy is also a gifted arranger and composer, having written extensively for Kenton and Don Ellis. Another top-flight educator is Rayburn Wright at the Eastman School of Music's jazz department which has an enviable record of success nationally and abroad, thanks to rousing performances at such prestigious venues as the 1982 Montreux Jazz Festival.

Among the bandleaders hiring the talents of the graduates of the jazz colleges are several who began leading bands in the 1950s and 1960s and whose own playing experience dates back to the late swing era. In some cases these origins show through their music: hard driving, swinging big band music which gives a nod of acknowledgement towards changing times but is not concerned with breaking too much new ground.

Among these leaders is Buddy Rich, who started his first big band in the 1940s and who, by the 1970s, was attracting the attention of a new generation of big band enthusiasts. In some respects this attention from the younger fans is surprising because, in striking contrast to the experimenters and innovators, Buddy Rich hoed his own row with pugnacious determination. This attitude reflected his character for he was never afraid to assert himself, either on his drums, with his tongue, or, when all else failed, with his fists.

A child prodigy who played drums on stage at the age of six, Buddy's first big band job was in 1938 when he joined Bunny Berigan. Successively with Artie Shaw, Tommy Dorsey and Benny Carter, Rich's reputation was such that in 1946, when he formed his own band, some of the money was put up by Frank Sinatra with whom Buddy had played (and fought) during their time together with Dorsey.

Using charts by Tadd Dameron and Eddie Finckel, and with such young musicians as Al Cohn, Terry Gibbs, Zoot Sims and Earl Swope, the band had a slightly more modern feel than other swing bands of the time although it fell short of being a bebop band. Pressurised by financial contraints, Rich was forced to fold the band and in 1948 to 1951 worked with Norman Granz's Jazz at the Philharmonic.

In 1966, after working with various small groups and spending time in the big bands of Tommy Dorsey, Harry James and Count Basie, Buddy decided to form a new big band. The band's book included work by Bob Florence, Bill Holman, Oliver Nelson and Shorty Rogers but was dominated by standards, just as the band was dominated by Buddy. This was despite the fact that, at first, he employed several sidemen of note, including Don Menza, Art Pepper and Al Porcino.

Later, the average age of the band dropped dramatically with young musicians coming and going with bewildering speed. One result of this high turnover of youngsters in Buddy's 1960s and 1970s bands was the need to use arrangements with character. He acquired writers of considerable skill, including such fine craftsmen as Harry Betts, Bill Holman, Bill Potts and Shorty Rogers whose talents, linked to Buddy's dynamic playing, created extraordinary momentum. The structure of the arrangements and the strength of each section carried the band and the lack of solo originality among otherwise brilliant young musicians was hidden by the band's surging pace.

The band played a number of jazz-rock items, an aspect of the music which helped its appeal to younger fans. Although there was limited scope for ballads, the band concentrated on hard-driving chasers which allowed Buddy to demonstrate his astonishing technique, speed and dexterity.

Until his death in 1987 the band Buddy Rich led was made up largely of young musicians who had learned their often considerable instrumental technique in the leading American universities and in particular Eastman and North Texas.

Another exciting leader who attracted the younger generation, both as fans and as members of his band, is Maynard Ferguson.

Maynard began playing trumpet professionally in Canada when he

A real pro:
'The only good thing about the old days was that before you became successful you played in half a dozen different types of bands, a dixieland band, a society band, a jazz band, a swing band, a marching band and things like that, so you were able to play all these forms... Music is professional. Anything less than professional shouldn't be allowed to be performed... When an audience is coming out and paying money they're not coming to hear you experiment.'

Buddy Rich

•••

'Herb Pomeroy was a great bandleader and teacher.'

Bill Berry

Maynard Ferguson, the high-note trumpet player whom some cool jazz fans once uncooly predicted would "blow his brains out in five years", still performs in the 1980's.

Learning on the road—5:
'Intensive academic schooling is a good idea for those capable of handling the work.'
Duke Ellington

***

'I believe in "legitimate" schooling [but]I want to emphasize that this is second to actually playing on the job.'
Gene Krupa

***

'Thank God for those music schools. That's where a lot of the kids today are coming up.'
Woody Herman

***

'If a band can make you tap your foot without the rhythm section, you'll really get jumping when the rhythm section plays.'
Ed Shaughnessy

was 13 and had his own band at 16. He came to international fame thanks to a stint with Stan Kenton during which he perfected his phenomenal ability in the high register. In addition to Kenton, Maynard played with Charlie Barnet, Jimmy Dorsey and Boyd Raeburn. After leading a series of all-star bands, including the Birdland Dream Band in 1956, he formed his own regular band.

Maynard's band followed the tradition of many swing era big bands in presenting a showcase for the leader's outstanding instrumental gifts. Although this can be limiting to a band's progress, Maynard continued to find work and was always happy to use other young and outstanding instrumentalists. Among sidemen who had early exposure and success with Ferguson bands are trumpeters Bill Chase and Don Ellis, trombonist-arranger Slide Hampton, and saxophonists Joe Farrell and Don Sebesky.

The Maynard Ferguson bands were always very exciting but for his many fans it was the leader's ability to take his trumpet beyond the outer limits that was the main attraction.

Another exciting, hard-swinging instrumentalist who periodically forms excellent big bands is vibraphonist Terry Gibbs.

Before joining Woody Herman in 1948 Terry played briefly with

Buddy Rich and Tommy Dorsey and also had a spell in a Benny Goodman small group in the early 1950s.

From the late 1950s Terry began recording one big band album a year under a contract with Mercury Records. In 1959, he had an opportunity to take a big band into the Seville, a club on Hollywood Place, one night a week—provided he could find musicians who were not too worried about being paid. 'The guys made a rule. Nobody takes off for another job. If a guy did, he was out of the band. And this they did for $15 a night!' Using a band which was substantially that gathered for his 1959 record album, and which included Conte Candoli, Bill Holman, Mel Lewis, Joe Maini and Al Porcino, Gibbs found a highly appreciative audience. The members of the band loved it, too. As Mel Lewis observed, 'This is the greatest swing band I ever played in. It saved my life musically...'

'My band doesn't try to relate to the past at all.'
Buddy Rich

Decades later, and Terry Gibbs is still around, still one of the most exciting vibraphone players in jazz, still assembling a big band for special dates and occasional albums. His bands always have tremendous vitality and effervescence, reflecting the leader's own musical personality.

Another young band which reflected its leader's musical qualities in addition to being one of the most unusual of the early 1960s was Gerry Mulligan's Concert Jazz Band.

Gerry first attracted attention as an arranger for Gene Krupa and Elliot Lawrence where his light, finely articulated scores enhanced the work of these bands. This quality of lightness also pervades Mulligan's playing, no mean feat on the unwieldy baritone saxophone. It is these qualities

Buddy Rich's 1946 band quietly rioting. The band had a second drummer, Stanley Kay here watching the boss in action, for when Buddy was overcome with the urge to sing. The band includes trumpeters Louis Oles and Pinky Savitt and trombonist Earl Swope.

of delicate dexterity that differentiates the sound of the Concert Band from those around it.

Mulligan's own charts for the band were complemented by the work of arrangers John Carisi, Bill Holman, Gary McFarland, Johnny Mandel and Bob Brookmeyer, who was also a featured soloist on his valve trombone. Among the other soloists with the band were trumpeter Clark Terry and tenor saxophonist Zoot Sims.

In some respects the music the band played was an extension of the small group thinking Mulligan has displayed over the years: simple, yet subtle, relying upon colour and dynamics rather than upon the hard-driving brass which was currently in vogue. There was always excitement, however, coming from solos backed by interesting shading exemplified when the trumpet section supports a crackling solo from Clark Terry on 'Little Rock Getaway'. However, although the instruments might be those of Terry, Don Ferrara, Doc Severinson and Nick Travis, the sound they capture is undoubtedly that of Gerry Mulligan.

The band which Louie Bellson brought to Ronnie Scott's in London in 1978 was one of a series he occasionally assembles for short tours and festivals. Like Maynard Ferguson and Buddy Rich, Louie is a remarkable technician with superb swing but, unlike the combative Buddy, a relaxed and unaggressive personality.

Louie first attracted national attention when he won a Gene Krupa drum contest. One of his first jobs was in Gene's old chair in the Benny Goodman band in 1943. He also played in the bands of Tommy Dorsey and Harry James before joining Duke Ellington in 1951. He remained with Duke for two years and helped give the band a new, dynamic, if not strictly Ellingtonian sound. During the next few years Louie worked with various big bands and numerous small groups.

Although Louie's work with small groups is always meticulous, the restraint he applies to his technique sometimes seems a handicap but when seated behind a big band no such restraint is necessary and the awesome power and technical attack of his drumming is one of the most impressive sounds in big band music.

The personnel of the Louie Bellson Big Band Explosion varies but will usually include noted session men with rehearsal band experience and strong solo abilities. Among occasional players are outstanding trumpeters Conte Candoli, Bobby Shew and Frank Szabo and the powerfully inventive tenor saxophonist Pete Christlieb. In the band Louie took to Europe in 1978 was tenor saxophonist Don Menza. Winner of the award as Outstanding Instrumentalist at the 1961 Collegiate Jazz Festival, Menza went on to play with and arrange for numerous name bands including Bill Berry's and Buddy Rich's and to lead his own powerful Los Angeles-based big band. A dynamic and inventive musician, Menza's long and complex solos are often played while the rest of the band lays out. Fellow sideman with Bellson's Explosion, Nat Pierce, remarked, 'When Menza starts, I light up a cigarette; if I don't get to finish it, I know he's off form.'

Unlike Buddy Rich's band, all the soloists with Bellson's band are given a chance to blow because, while Louie's drums are a principal reason for the band's mighty swing, he stays well away from using the band as a showcase thus making the overall content of his programming more interesting than did Buddy Rich. When Louie does solo he displays considerable inventiveness, great visual flair, and, above all, that prodigious technique. Louie's use of twin bass drums, which he pioneered, is

Les Hooper—arranger:
Les Hooper formed a big band in Chicago and was nominated (but pipped by Woody Herman) for Grammy awards in 1974 both for his individual compositions and the album on which they appeared. Using well-schooled musicians, Hooper's band showed off to full advantage his charts which were to become a mainstay of rehearsal and college bands over succeeding years. Hooper, who majored in musical composition at LA State University, also wrote for Don Ellis.

•••

Big Bands 80s:
In 1980 a group of leading Los Angeles musicians headed by Ray Anthony formed an organisation they named 'Big Bands 80s'. Their aim was to stimulate the rising interest in big band music. Apart from Anthony the founder members included Bill Berry, Frank Capp, Pat Longo, Roger Neumann and Nat Pierce. One action of the group was an attempt to interest radio stations in broadcasting from club and dance dates, a return to an old and well-tried formula for bringing big band music to the attention of the mass audience. Sadly, the concept did not survive.

Slurping at Las Vegas. The Billy May band at the Thunderbird Lounge Casino in 1952. Included are vocalist Carol Sims, impeccable lead alto Willie Smith and first trumpet Conrad Gozzo.

far from the tiresome gimmick it became at the feet of less talented musicians; Louie uses them to build a thundering undercurrent of propulsive sound which ignites the whole band.

The musical background of these latterday leaders shows their swing era and progressive big band origins: Buddy Rich came up through the bands of Artie Shaw and Tommy Dorsey; Maynard Ferguson spent time with Stan Kenton and Boyd Raeburn; Terry Gibbs was with Woody Herman; Gerry Mulligan with Gene Krupa; Louie Bellson was with Benny Goodman and Duke Ellington. For all their traditional connections, when they came to lead their own bands they were not stultified but were musically alert to the times in which they lived. Although they did not break new musical ground, they were *live* music bands and steered well clear of the potentially dreary paths followed by some of the Glenn Miller-clone bands which littered the same period.

What the bands of Rich, Ferguson, Bellson and the others demonstrated was the desire of many sidemen to continue playing in a big band, to fill what was otherwise a void in their musical lives. Perhaps it was only for one-off gigs, an album here, a festival appearance there. But it was happening at a time when big band music of the type they wanted to play was not otherwise available. And their efforts were invaluable in providing a place for upcoming young musicians to exercise their college-learned skills.

Of course, there were failings. In that same London hotel room where Nat Pierce reflected on how colleges were providing a musical base for young musicians, another member of the 1978 edition of the Louie Bellson Explosion, Bill Berry, sounded a warning note that many latterday jazz educators would do well to consider.

Bill recalled a conversation he had a few years before with Richie Kamuca. Listening to a particularly fine young band Bill had praised their astonishing technical skill, suggesting that the future was in safe hands. Richie was silent for a moment. Eventually he asked, 'Yes, but what are they going to play *about?*'

LES BROWN AND HIS BAND OF RENOWN

By the time he entered Duke University Les Brown was a skilled musician, having already studied harmony, arranging and composing. At Duke, Les joined the university's dance band, the Duke Blue Devils and under his leadership the band soon built a sound localised reputation. In 1937 Les moved to New York where he wrote arrangements for several bands including Jimmy Dorsey and Isham Jones.

Invited to form a band for the Hotel Edison, an engagement which was linked to a recording deal, Les formed a new band. In 1940 he landed a gig at New York's Arcadia Ballroom also deputising for Charlie Barnet at the Lincoln Hotel. It was during this spell that Les hired a young girl singer currently working with the Bob Crosby band. Doris Day sang with Les's band for a while before leaving the business for the duration of her first marriage.

Unlike many bandleaders of the war years, Les Brown managed to keep on finding men to replace those who were drafted. Fortunately, the resulting rapid turnover of musicians neither destabilised the band's morale nor disturbed its musical qualities. Among the musicians Les used during this period were Butch Stone, Gus Bivona, Hank D'Amico, Ted Nash, Billy Butterfield, Shelly Manne, Alvin Stoller and Dick Shanahan.

The band's future success was enhanced in 1943 when Les persuaded Doris Day to return and in the following year she helped give the band its first hit record, 'Sentimental Journey'. Doris later recalled the first public performance: 'I started to sing the lyrics and by the end of the first eight bars the couples had stopped dancing and were just standing there, arms around, listening to me. It was an overwhelming success. They just stood there, wildly applauding, until we played it again—and again.'

Although Doris soon moved on to even greater acclaim in Hollywood, the band went from strength to strength as it developed a more swinging style, helped by Frank Comstock's distinctive arrangements. It was, however, Skippy Martin's chart of 'I've Got My Love to Keep Me Warm' which gave the band its first post-war hit. From then on, Les Brown's name became synonymous with the best of contemporary dance band music. Yet for all its musical and economic stability, to say nothing of its successful recordings, the band was not a smash. Disappointed with his failure to make it to the very top in terms of popular acclaim, Les disbanded at the end of 1946 but he had forgotten about a date he was contracted to play in March 1947 at the Hollywood Palladium. Obliged to reform, the new Les Brown band was hired as the resident orchestra on Bob Hope's weekly radio show later gaining enviable TV exposure.

More than any other band of its time, for countless post-war fans, Les Brown and his Band of Renown has come to epitomise the big band sound. Crisp section work and a relaxed yet plangent rhythm section, contributed to an impressively swinging band which made a significant contribution to the world of the big bands.

In 1987 Les Brown completed fifty years as a bandleader with highly acclaimed celebratory concerts at many places, among them the Hollywood Bowl and, particularly gratifying for Les, at Duke University, Durham, North Carolina, where it had all begun back in the swing era.

Les Brown happily digging his Band of Renown during a concert at the Strand Theatre in the 1940s.

Texas tenor Harold Land made his name on the West Coast in the 1950s. Land played on many big band studio dates including albums with Red Norvo and Gerald Wilson. (*Courtesy: Bob Charlesworth*)

CHAPTER FOURTEEN

REHEARSING FOR THE FUTURE

'WELCOME TO THE CLUB'

'Wait a minute. This all began with *music*, not with money.'
Bernie Leighton

Walking into the club off Van Nuys the wall of sound hits you, causing you to pause and readjust your hearing while your eyes are adjusting to the dark. Along the left hand wall of the club runs the bar, lined two deep with serious drinkers and other musicians. The room is maybe twenty feet wide, fifty long and against the far wall is the bandstand. Crowded onto it is a band, or most of it because the drums, bass and piano have to sit on the floor out front. The sixteen members of the band are dressed casually, most are smiling when they aren't blowing. Within minutes, seconds even, you know that these guys are having a ball; at the same time you know that they are also serious musicians. This may be a fun band but it is a fun band because everyone in it is a first class musician. The club is Carmelo's and the band this night is Bill Berry's L. A. Band and it is a good example of the rehearsal or workshop band.

From the late 1940s and on through the 1950s the decline in the numbers of permanent big bands left thousands of musicians either out of work or engaged in activities to which they took not at all kindly.

Fortunately, for some of those with the necessary skills there was work to be had in other areas of show business. The 1950s and 1960s saw a boom in TV and there was still radio and the movies; they all needed music, and competent, sight-reading musicians were in great demand.

The main location for studio work of this kind was New York City, still the centre of America's show business. The fact that so many fine big band players were living and working in the city led to the development of one of the most interesting phenomena of the later big band years, the rehearsal band.

The rehearsal or workshop band concept was fuelled by musicians' needs. Pianist Bernie Leighton, who had played with Benny Goodman, was able to use his classically-trained skills to earn a good living in the New York studios. But there was more to being a musician than merely making a living. Leighton expressed this in a 1970 conversation with Voice of America's Willis Conover:

> You spend your early years learning your instrument. Then you feel you should get paid for your work. Producers call musicians who can read and play any music well, for a jingle, a movie soundtrack, a television variety show, or a singer's

'Every chair in the band is equally important.'
Bill Berry

***

Tommy Vig and his Orchestra: Several foreign-born musicians have made a place for themselves in the big bands of America and at least one, Tommy Vig, is now a bandleader in his own right. A Hungarian-born vibraphonist, Vig was originally influenced by hearing swing bands played on radio and records. After coming to live in America in 1957, when he was 18, Tommy moved a little towards the modern end of the jazz spectrum, later forming his own big band in Las Vegas and then in Los Angeles.

Above: Superdrummer—Buddy Rich. (*Photo: Chuck Stewart*)
Below: Moulded for several years by Ray Pitts and Thad Jones, the Danish Radio Big Band toured briefly in Britain in 1987. (*Courtesy: Bob Charlesworth*)

Bill Berry and his LA Band at the Concord Summer Jazz Festival during the recording of their album 'Hello Rev'. (L to R) Berry, Benny Powell, Monty Budwig, Don Menza, Frank Capp, Richie Kamuca, Marshal Royal, Jimmy Cleveland, Lanny Morgan, Britt Woodman, Blue Mitchell, Tricky Lofton, Jack Nimitz, Gene Goe, Cat Anderson, Jack Sheldon. (Courtesy: Bill Berry)

> record date. No mistakes, no arguments, not too many questions—there are more good musicians than good jobs. But you reach a point where you say, 'Wait a minute. This all began with *music*, not with money.' ... A lot of musicians feel the same way, and that's why rehearsal bands are happening.

Happening they certainly were, but it was not something all that new. The previous 20 years had seen several rehearsal bands in different parts of America. Some were formed for fun, others to allow a composer or arranger to pursue his ideas, all allowed musicians outlets for musical inclinations not being met by their regular work.

An early example of a rehearsal band was formed in Washington, D.C. in the 1950s by drummer Joe Timer. The band played in the Woody Herman tradition and featured the driving trumpets of Irving Markowitz and Charlie Walp, the roaring trombones of Earl and Robbie Swope, and had pianist Bill Potts contributing charts as did Timer and Johnny Mandel. The band was helped to a brief period of popularity through being featured on radio by Willis Conover.

'I like everybody to be a soloist'
Bill Berry

In 1957 there were few New York spots large enough to put on a big band. Among them was Birdland which had Count Basie, Duke Ellington, Maynard Ferguson and Woody Herman and the new bands of Oscar Pettiford and Johnny Richards. There was also an appearance by Herb Pomeroy's band from Boston. On the West Coast there were appearances by Ferguson and Les Brown and local rehearsal bands led by Joe Dolney, Gerald Wilson, Ernie Freeman-John Anderson and 'The Jazz Wave', jointly led by Al Porcino and Med Flory.

After 1958 the rehearsal band concept began to settle into a format which is still recognisable three decades on. That was the year in which

A fine example of a West Coast band not afraid to enter the sometimes contentious field of funky jazz-rock is Pat Longo's Super Big Band. Here, Pat direct while Margie Gibson sings. (L to R: John Banister, Longo, Margie, Dave Stone (behind Margie), Gordon Brisker, Jerry McKenzie, Lanny Morgan, Frank Szabo, Dave Wells, Ray Reed, Joe Davis, Lon Norman, Jim Patti, Gary Unwin, Pete Beltran, Jim Germann. (Courtesy: Pat Longo)

pianist Nat Pierce set up a band based largely upon the Herb Pomeroy Boston band (which had, in its turn, evolved out of the Ray Borden band). The policy of this new band was to play easy-swinging charts by Neal Hefti, Bill Holman, Ralph Burns and Nat himself. Some of these charts had been discarded by name band leaders faced with acceding to changing public demand. Nat and his friends, who included trumpeter Doug Mettome, tenor saxophonist Paul Quinichette, trombonist Frank Rehak and drummer Gus Johnson, made a few records, played a few gigs and even had the notable, if sad, honour of playing the closing engagement at the Savoy Ballroom.

Contrasting with the rehearsal bands were a handful of studio bands whose leaders somehow managed to persuade record company executives to part with the cash for big band sessions which allowed musicians to play pretty much as they pleased *and* be paid for doing so. One example of this came in 1956 when Georgie Auld formed a studio band to record for EmArcy. Including Frank Rosolino and Si Zentner among the trombones and the mighty trumpet talents of Maynard Ferguson, Conrad Gozzo, Mannie Klein and Ray Linn, the band's stated policy was to recreate the highly musical and fiercely swinging sound of the old Jimmie Lunceford band.

It was during the 1960s that some rehearsal bands began to take on a more permanent look. By the end of the 1960s the Thad Jones-Mel Lewis band had become a feature of the New York music scene; they made records, played away from their 'home' at the Village Vanguard, and even toured abroad. Clark Terry had his Big Bad Band, there was Chuck Israels's experimental National Jazz Ensemble, Duke Pearson had his band, Bill Watrous was thinking about forming his Manhattan

Hiring and firing—3:
'Stan [Kenton]did me the biggest favour of my life in firing me.'
Frank Capp

Wildlife Refuge band and there was Bill Berry and his New York Band.

By the Spring of 1970 Bill Berry had been a professional musician for 23 years, including stints in the trumpet sections of bands led by Woody Herman, Maynard Ferguson and Duke Ellington. After three years on and off with Ellington, Bill settled in New York in 1963 working as a staff musician for ABC and NBC and in the band on the popular TV show hosted by Merv Griffin. Although he was working steadily, jazz work was a little thin on the ground, apart from occasional appearances with the Thad Jones-Mel Lewis band. Early in 1970 Bill gathered together some like-minded spirits and formed a big band which would rehearse and play primarily for their own musical benefit. Bill was in no doubt why he wanted a band: 'I want to play what *I* think is jazz.'

Bill's concept called for a loose organisation, one which allowed any or all of the musicians to do what they couldn't do in their regular studio work: play solos but within the big band tradition in which they had all paid their dues.

Among the musicians involved in Bill's New York band were John Bunch, Jimmy Giuffre, Jake Hanna, Richie Kamuca, Carmen Leggio, Benny Powell, Bill Watrous, Frank Wess and Britt Woodman. With men like Al Cohn, Dave Frishberg and Zoot Sims eager to play if anyone was forced to drop out, there was clearly no shortage of star names.

The new band was so successful that within two months it was depping for the Thad Jones-Mel Lewis band at the Village Vanguard. Despite this good start, before the end of the year the band folded when the Merv Griffin TV show was relocated in Los Angeles. Among those offered a continuation of their regular work if they moved to LA were Bill Berry and several members of his rehearsal band.

Bill eventually re-formed the band, now renamed, naturally, the LA Band, and it soon became a permanent feature of the West Coast music scene, playing concerts, festivals, clubs and clinics. The roll call over the years since 1971 reads like a who's who of the big band scene of past decades. At one time or another the trumpets have included Cat Anderson, Pete and Conte Candoli, and Snooky Young. In the trombone section have been Jimmy Cleveland, Buster Cooper, Benny Powell and Britt Woodman. The reeds have included Bob Cooper, Bob Efford, Richie Kamuca, Murray McEachern, Jack Nimitz, Marshal Royal and Willie Schwartz, while the rhythm section has seen Dave Frishberg, Mundell Lowe, Monty Budwig, Leroy Vinnegar, Frank Capp and Jake Hanna.

Add in talented musicians from other areas of jazz: Teddy Edwards, Don Menza, Blue Mitchell, Lanny Morgan, Jack Sheldon and it is not hard to imagine the impact this band had on the California scene.

Given the strong influence of his years with Ellington it is not surprising that Bill Berry's book draws heavily on the man he still refers to as 'the Master'. However, there is never any suggestion that the band tries to play Ducal tunes the way Ellington played them. They are a point of inspiration, not something to be slavishly copied.

It is love of the music that has proved to be the cornerstone of the Bill Berry band and is something that is reflected in numerous other rehearsal bands across the world. The music of these bands, however different their sources of inspiration might be, all in their turn mirror a comment Bill once made: 'You can be 100% serious about music and still have a ball!'

How other musicians respond can be discerned from Cat Anderson's view: 'Several times a month I get my kicks with Bill Berry's big, happy

Ray Conniff, his Chorus and Orchestra:
By the time he left junior high school Ray Conniff was an accomplished pianist, a trombone player, and was already writing arrangements. He worked first with society orchestras but then moved on to the bands of Bunny Berigan, Bob Crosby and Artie Shaw. It was during his four-year association with Shaw that Conniff emerged as an arranger of distinction. Among the resulting hits were 'Prelude in C Sharp Minor', "Swonderful' and 'Jumping on the Merry-go-round'. During this same four-year spell Ray worked on radio shows and studied at Juilliard before being drafted. After his army service he was hired by Harry James as staff arranger and scored impressive versions of various songs including a superb 'September Song'. While working for CBS Records, Ray helped on such massive hits as Johnny Ray's 'Walking My Baby Back Home', Guy Mitchell's 'Singing the Blues', and Johnny Mathis's 'Wonderful Wonderful'.

With his own studio band, Ray's most distinctive device is the use of voices with instruments. For example, he doubles female voices with trumpets, higher pitched saxophones and clarinets, while male voices are scored with trombones, trumpets or saxophones in the lower register. This combination results in an intensification of the softer tones, while simultaneously mellowing the harsher sounds. Although very much at the 'easy listening' end of the market, and sometimes in danger of appearing bland, the Conniff sound constantly demonstrates considerable skill in both arranging and performance.

band. We all enjoy each other's playing. It's so full of love. This is where it's at.' A further demonstration of how musicians view the rehearsal band concept comes from Dizzy Gillespie who has been known to sit in with the Bill Berry band, happily playing fourth trumpet all night.

In the early 1980s, Monday night was big band night at Carmelo's in Los Angeles. The four Mondays in July 1980 saw the bands of Don Menza, Tommy Vig, Bill Berry and Joe Roccisano while the five Mondays in September had Louie Bellson, Bill Watrous, Bob Florence, Menza again, and the Capp-Pierce Juggernaut. And if that were not enough for big band fans, there were other odd nights scattered through those months when a big band was on hand: Ed Shaughnessy, Pat Longo, Roger Neumann. Things change and if Carmelo's and Dante's might now have been superseded as the jazz in-place by other clubs, there is still a thriving big band scene in Los Angeles.

Strongly identifying with the Basie band book is the Capp-Pierce Juggernaut. In 1975 drummer Frank Capp organised a date for the Neal Hefti band at King Arthur's Club in the San Fernando Valley, Los Angeles. Before the engagement, however, Hefti folded his band and the club owner asked Frank to hire *any* band to fill the vacant slot. Frank promptly assembled his own band and asked Nat Pierce for the loan of some of his Basie charts and, while he was about it, suggested that Nat might like to co-lead the band. The band's performance was such a success that they were invited back and when Leonard Feather wrote a piece headlined, 'A Juggernaut on Basie Street', the band had a name. The Capp-Pierce Juggernaut became a familiar sight and sound in Los Angeles and their first album held top spot in the British jazz charts for five months.

Juggernaut comes closer to the loosely swinging middle-period Basie band than can most. Apart from his years with Herman, Nat Pierce was first choice to deputise for Basie in the Count's own band when, in later years, illness took its toll. Importantly, too, Nat is a big band arranger of considerable merit and his charts for Juggernaut can simultaneously reflect his personal preference for Basie's style and offer something that is uniquely his own. The Basie influence displayed in the arrangements is aurally demonstrated by the crisp ensemble passages with reeds and brass tirelessly building swinging call-and-response passages.

Among those rehearsal bands which grew out of a desire by a composer to have his own original material played in a manner that was as distinctive as his music, the outstanding example on the West Coast today is the Bob Florence Limited Edition. Bob's compositions display certain striking hallmarks. His use of a six-piece reed section adds greater sonority, especially as there may be two musicians doubling on baritone saxophones, several doubling on flute, clarinet and soprano. The reeds are thus capable of producing an ensemble sound that is darkly warm but which can, when required, flit elegantly through the leader's more reflective compositions. Prominent in the reed section are tenor saxophonists Pete Christlieb, a player of great fluency and inventiveness, and Bob Cooper, a veteran of the Stan Kenton band.

The Florence trumpet section also includes a number of men who double on flugelhorn, allowing greater texture to the writing. Soloists here often include Steve Huffsteter and Warren Luening, a young player from the Los Angeles City College jazz programme, while lead trumpet chores usually rely upon Buddy Childers. The tremendously swinging rhythm section includes Florence himself playing piano (both acoustic

'It's a completey different kind of playing in big bands... you should listen to what's going on around you and build upon that. Because if it has nothing to do with the overall context, what's the sense of playing it.'

Don Menza

***

The lead trumpet's role:
'Playing first trumpet on a band is a lot of pressure. The average listener doesn't even begin to conceive what's involved... you have to realise that the first trumpet is the one that everybody actually hears... you're up on top of the orchestra. So it is demanding. Any mistakes you make, everybody's going to hear it.'

Al Porcino

***

'Our commerciality is mostly the fun and the laughs; we have a lot of humour in this band—which is not contrived.'

Mel Lewis

***

'Whatever kind of music you put your face to, you should play it well, and do everything you can towards achieving that. As many as there are styles of music, there are ways to play well.'

Buddy Childers

Boss Brass:
Big bands thrive in places other than America and Britain. Rob McConnell's Boss Brass, a Toronto-based rehearsal band, was a powerfully swinging example of the genre. The leader's valve trombone playing is exemplary (he was once offered Bob Brookmeyer's place in the Gerry Mulligan Concert Band before Bob changed his mind about leaving). Other fine soloists passed through the band from time to time, some of them Americans resident over the border, notably Phil Woods who has collaborated on a marvellous album, but Rob is the boss man. A string of successful albums has given the band an enviable international reputation for exciting big band music that ranks with the best around. In September 1988 Rob relocated in LA.

***

Multi-track talent:
A 1986 record by Matt Catingub simultaneously demonstrates his extraordinary skills and writes a warning on the recording studio walls of the future. It is a big band record but, thanks to multi-track techniques, Matt plays all the instruments.

Guarding the entrance to the Bunny's warren is the might Juggernaut, the band co-led by Nat Pierce and Frank Capp. (L to R) Pierce, Ray Pohlman, Jim Hughart, Capp, Red Holloway, Herman Riley, Conte Candoli, Garnett Brown, John Audino, Alan Kaplan, Marshal Royal, Snooky Young, Buster Cooper, Jeff Clayton, Bobby Bryant, Jack Nimitz. (Courtesy: Bill Berry)

Bob Florence's Limited Edition. (L to R) Bob Florence, Bob Cooper, Dick Mitchell, Lanny Morgan, Kim Richmond, Joel Di Bartolo, Peter Donald, Rick Culver, Bob Efford, Steve Hufstetter, Charlie Loper, Warren Luening, Herbie Harper, George Graham, John Lowe, Charley Davis, Don Waldrop, Nelson Hatt. (Courtesy: Bob Florence)

and Fender Rhodes), Joel Di Bartolo on bass and, until his untimely death in 1986, the superb Nick Ceroli on drums. Florence was fortunate in being able to replace Ceroli with Pete Donald, another excellent drummer.

Although concentration of studio work in Los Angeles makes this the logical centre for numerous rehearsal and workshop bands, there are many other cities which can boast good bands. Further up the Californian coastline, in San Francisco, can be found the Full Faith and Credit Big Band while Cincinnati, Ohio, is blessed with an excellent jazz club, the Blue Wisp, and a jazz-oriented record producer, Helen Y. Morr of Mopro Records. Thus encouraged, former Stan Kenton drummer John Von Ohlen has built up one of the most formidable bands to be heard in late 1980s America.

The Blue Wisp Big Band's repertoire is rather more eclectic than many rehearsal bands, drawing tunes from the Ellington and Gillespie books, many standards, and a considerable smattering of compositions from bebop which are admirably arranged for the more traditional sound of a big band. The arrangers, who for the most part play in the band, include Al Kiger, trumpet and flugelhorn, and Larry Dickson baritone saxophone. Several good soloists are heard; Tim Hagans in particular is a fine trumpet player with a taut, clipped style and who played in the bands of Stan Kenton, Thad Jones and Ernie Wilkins.

An early rehearsal band in Chicago was led by Dave Remington and today there are the Big Band Machine and the Jazz Members Big Band. JMBB is co-led by trombonist Jeff Lindberg and trumpeter Steve Jensen, both former students at the University of Illinois under music educator John Garvey. Like Blue Wisp, JMBB is eclectic, playing charts by Thad Jones and Don Menza alongside staples from the Ellington and Basie books.

In 1983 Buddy Childers left Los Angeles to return to Chicago, his home town. Buddy had joined Stan Kenton's band during World War II. Then aged 16, Buddy later wryly observed that he passed the audition for Kenton because Stan 'knew I couldn't be drafted for a couple of years. The army couldn't touch me.' There was obviously more to it than that and Buddy's iron lip was well in evidence from his earliest recordings.

Buddy's return to Chicago was quickly followed by the appearance of the Buddy Childers Big Band which called upon the services of mostly younger generation local musicians little known outside the Windy City. The results were superb, the band playing with a propulsive swing thanks to an excellent rhythm section, with a fine bass player and drummer in Larry Gray and Joel Spencer, and strong brass and reed sections which have an enviable looseness.

New York City had seen several excellent rehearsal bands other than those already touched upon. In 1967 pianist-arranger-composer Duke Pearson began preparing a rehearsal band with Donald Byrd. When Byrd decided he was neglecting his small group the band became Duke's own and it quickly built a reputation on the east coast. All fifty charts in the band's first book were arranged by Duke, many of them his own compositions. Although possessing their own distinctive qualities, there are strong resemblances between his work and that of Tadd Dameron. The band included such outstanding soloists as trumpeters Marvin Stamm and Randy Brecker, trombonists Garnett Brown, Benny Powell and Julian Priester, in the reed section were Frank Foster and Lew Tabackin on tenors and Pepper Adams on baritone. With a rhythm

REMO
JUGGERNAUT

section of Pearson, Bob Cranshaw, bass and Mickey Roker, drums, the drive was outstanding. But like so many good things in life that ought to last forever, the Duke Pearson Big Band did not survive.

Trombone virtuoso Bill Watrous's New York band, 'Manhattan Wildlife Refuge', which was founded on an axiom imparted to its leader by Bill Berry, 'Swing and have a ball', impressed fans and musicians in the early 1970s but the two records made for Columbia were inadequately promoted. By 1978, Watrous, whose background includes work with Quincy Jones, Woody Herman and the Thad Jones-Mel Lewis Jazz Orchestra, had formed a new band in Los Angeles but although 'Wildlife West' proved as exciting as the earlier band it failed to interest record companies.

Predictions:
'Anyone wishing to know who will be topping the popularity polls in the years ahead should examine the personnel of NYJO.'
Alun Morgan

New York, the West Coast and the mid-West do not have it all to themselves. The Southwest, too, has its share of the action. The Lou Fischer Rehearsal Band was formed in Dallas, Texas, and several of its members, including its bass-playing leader, were graduates of North Texas State University. Inclining towards a contemporary sound, with a rock-oriented beat, the Fischer band has drive without achieving the lightly swinging impetus of Basie or Les Brown.

The liking for the rock-beat, which is by no means restricted to the Lou Fischer band, is an inevitable occurrence given the ages of the musicians and arrangers working with such bands. The inclusion of rock rhythms in big band scores has raised a few eyebrows but the logic of it is inescapable. Young musicians need the assurance which can come from playing the kind of music they have grown up hearing and it is unrealistic to expect them to fall naturally and easily into playing music from the swing era.

A musician who has assimilated rock and other aspects of contemporary music into the 1980s big band scene is Pat Longo. A typical performance, live or on record by Pat Longo's Super Big Band, brings together elements of the blues, hard rock, bebop and a funky beat. Longo's Los Angeles-based band draws on the experience of men like trumpeters Buddy Childers and Frank Szabo and tenor saxophonist Bob Efford but also finds numerous talents among musicians who are less well-known to big band fans.

Longo's brass ensembles have a bright edge to them as do the reeds which benefit from the use of the soprano saxophone, an instrument not usually associated with big band charts. Early 1980s recordings by Longo had the benefit of Nick Ceroli's dynamic drumming which swung superbly while still retaining a rock beat, a feat of considerable difficulty.

The ubiquitous Buddy Childers turns up again in the Matt Catingub Big Band which is also LA-based. Buddy apart, the musicians Matt has gathered around him are mostly youngsters; drummer Kevin Winard was born in 1964, trombonist Mike Fahn in 1963, trombonist Andy Martin and tenor saxophonist Chris Stewart in 1962 while Matt himself, who plays alto saxophone, was born in 1961. That big band musicians of undeniable skill and technical excellence can be found who were born into the post-Beatles age is a fact which should make older fans rejoice.

But, for every big band like those of Pat Longo and Matt Catingub there are many more which eschew rock influences and base their playing on older but still lively musical elements.

Whether swing era-based or rock-based, Basie- or Ellington-influenced, what is important is that these are *living* bands and that alone is enough to bring reassurance to big band fans.

BRITISH YOUTH BIG BANDS

The American example which brought big band music and jazz into the educational system has been followed in Britian but with noticably less widespread enthusiasm by those in authority. There are exceptions, among them forward-thinking musical educational programmes at Doncaster in South Yorkshire, Walsall in Staffordshire, Wigan in Lancashire, and in Fulham, London.

The Doncaster Youth Jazz Orchestra plays charts by Bob Florence and Sammy Nestico together with many originals, a balance which aids wide acceptance by audiences. The Walsall Youth Jazz Orchestra plays a mixture of originals written for the band, often by members, and charts by Les Hooper, Rob McConnell and Sammy Nestico. Wigan's Youth Jazz Orchestra is similarly eclectic and has also ventured far afield with trips to Europe, America, and the Hong Kong International Youth Festival in 1985. Trombonist Bobby Lamb, whose track record includes stints with Woody Herman, handles the youth band at Fulham, London, where his exhilirating playing style communicates itself to his students and the band regularly attracts enthusiastic audiences in the London area.

Among the targets at which many young British musicians aim is a place in the National Youth Jazz Orchestra. Under the direction of Bill Ashton, NYJO, which was formed in 1965, has built an enviable reputation among musicians and audiences abroad. Ashton's stated musical policy for the orchestra has been to build an identifiable sound and style, something he feels is difficult, if not downright impossible, if the band is shackled to playing charts written originally for someone else. Ashton's oft-quoted response to the cry of 'Why can't you play something we know?' is 'Why can't you know something we play?'.

Today, alumni from early editions of NYJO are coming back to guest with the band having spent the intervening years gaining experience in the wider world of music. Such reinforcement suggests that in one guise or another the National Youth Jazz Orchestra is likely to be a force to reckon with well into the next century.

A welcome annual event is the appearance of a Terry Gibbs big band. This is the 1960 version playing at the Casino Ballroom, Catalina Island. Included are Conte Candoli, Mel Lewis, Bill Perkins, Al Porcino, Herbie Steward

CHAPTER FIFTEEN

THE WAY AHEAD

'NEW HORIZONS'

'It always *feels* good to play the blues.'

Don Ellis

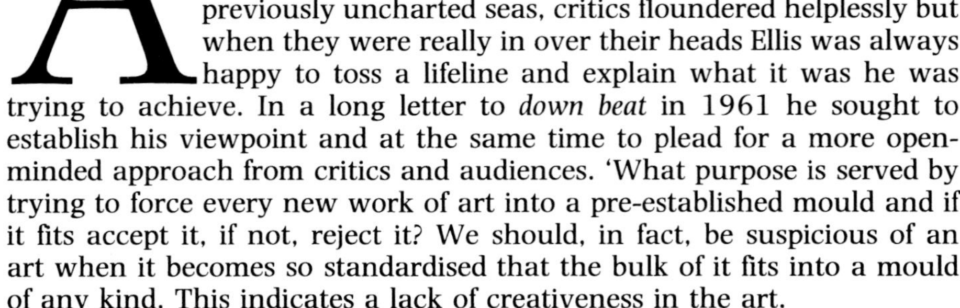

A musician who was determined to forge his own style was Don Ellis. Not content with changing the boundaries of big band music, Ellis redrew the map. Thus plunged into previously uncharted seas, critics floundered helplessly but when they were really in over their heads Ellis was always happy to toss a lifeline and explain what it was he was trying to achieve. In a long letter to *down beat* in 1961 he sought to establish his viewpoint and at the same time to plead for a more open-minded approach from critics and audiences. 'What purpose is served by trying to force every new work of art into a pre-established mould and if it fits accept it, if not, reject it? We should, in fact, be suspicious of an art when it becomes so standardised that the bulk of it fits into a mould of any kind. This indicates a lack of creativeness in the art.

'I am not concerned whether my music is jazz, Third Stream, classical, or anything else, or whether it is even called music. Let it be judged as Don Ellis noise.'

Don Ellis talking:
'Fred Seldon has been an important member of the band for several years now. He first started playing in one of my student rehearsal bands and as our lead sax player has been contributing some of our most intriguing and exciting scores. Hank Levy was one of the first outside writers to contribute scores to our library. He caught on to the unusual meters amazingly fast, and now conducts college stage bands... concentrating on the new rhythm.'

Although many found Ellis's work impossible to grasp and refused to accept his credo, putting his music down as non-jazz, he was much more successful than others who experimented in combining musical styles which outwardly appeared to be incompatible.

One of very few critics to applaud Ellis's work was Leonard Feather who suggested quite early on that Ellis was the logical and likely successor of Stan Kenton's mantle. In a broad sense this was true although in the specifics of their music lie several notable differences. Not least of these is the fact that for all the thunder and lightning of Kenton's band, links with the preceding era of big band music are clearly audible. With Ellis, nothing was ever that easy.

FATHER OF THE TIME REVOLUTION

Don Ellis was born in 1934 and although he worked in high school dance bands, by the time he graduated from Boston University in 1956 the big band scene was hardly one to encourage career-minded musicians.

Ellis found work in the trumpet section of the Glenn Miller band, then under the direction of Ray McKinley, and after a spell in the army played with various surviving big bands. For all this invaluable experience, he found the kind of freedom he wanted only with small groups. Most notably this occurred when he worked with George Russell's sextet in 1961–2 (and appeared on Russell's 'Ezz-thetic' album).

Ellis, a slender young man brimming over with fizzing energy, was eager to experiment with classical form, free form, and the abandonment of preconceptions about time and he was also an articulate spokesman for the involvement of jazzmen in previously unrelated art-forms.

'We take pride in being able to play the shit out of things that no other bands have even attempted.'
Don Ellis

The extraordinarily talented Don Ellis.
(Courtesy: Jazz Journal International)

The early 1960s saw Don forming the first of a series of big bands with which he continued his experimentation. Notable among these experiments was his ardent search for new approaches to group improvisation but the one which caused most problems for the lay audience (and was by no means an easy ride for even the most skilled musicians) was his decision to discard orthodox time signatures.

Whereas most big band music was played at 4 beats to the bar, with most jazz being played at either 4 or 2 beats, Don cheerfully experimented with 5-beat bars, then 9-, 11-, 14-, 17-, 19- and even 27-beat bars. In an interview he indicated that the 'longest metre I have attempted to date is a piece in 85'. Compounding the confusion felt by audiences and musicians alike, he also introduced mixed metres and in order that he could properly instruct his drummers in their difficult task, he learned to play drums. Not surprisingly, he was dubbed the 'Father of the Time Revolution' in jazz.

An important factor in Ellis's work is that much of it is enormous fun, just one of countless cases in jazz and big band music which proves that being serious is not synonymous with being dull. An example of this comes in 'Pussy Wiggle Stomp', a glorious romp in 7/4 time on which Don, in public performance, had the audience happily hand-clapping away as if they'd been familiar with the metre all their lives.

During the 1960s several of his recordings were nominated for Grammy awards. His orchestral performances were dominated by fiery, explosive ensemble passages and the sound of electronic instruments, including experimental electrically amplified wind instruments.

Soloists with Ellis's bands over the years included alto saxophonists Ira Schulman and Frank Strozier and tenors Sam Falzone and the diamond-hard John Klemmer but the major solo voice is always Ellis himself. Although he can be reflective when the mood of a piece so demanded (as, for example, on 'Angel Eyes' and his elegaic album, 'Haiku'), he is at his best on medium and up-tempo numbers when he plays with a searing intensity which ably demonstrates his idolisation of old time jazz trumpet star, Red Allen. In striking contrast to much of what was happening elsewhere in the jazz and big band world, Don Ellis's playing was always hot.

The complexities of the rhythmic drive of Ellis's music demanded enormous skills in the rhythm section, especially the drummer and he was fortunate in finding technically gifted men in Steve Bohannon and, later, Ralph Humphrey, both of whom were comfortably capable of swinging at unlikely tempos and of lifting an often huge band.

As the 1970s began Don Ellis was eager for new challenges and expressed dissatisfaction with the avant-garde, considering it to be a musical dead-end. 'There is no room for development, for new horizons in rhythm and tonality.'

His own horizons broadened and he wrote music for TV and the movies, and books on his musical philosophy. He taught theory, arranging, composition and trumpet. He also performed with symphony orchestras and, of course, performed with his own band for which he did most of the writing.

This huge self-imposed work load had its effect. In 1975 he was diagnosed as having an enlarged heart and was hospitalised. On his discharge he was not allowed to play trumpet and so taught himself to play the special slide-valve trombone that had been designed for Maynard Ferguson.

American Army bands today: World War II saw excellent American service bands led by Glenn Miller, Artie Shaw, Sam Donahue, Ray Anthony and Ralph Marterie, among others, and the tradition of which they were a significant part continues into the nuclear age. The army, air force and, never to be outdone, the navy, have active musical policies which include big bands playing music comparable to that played in the civilian world.

The Army Blues mix innovative sounds of contemporary composers and arrangers with swinging performances of tunes that would be instantly recognised by men who served in World War II. Excellent techinique and an ability to swing has given the Blues a substantial following outside the military community. Another army band is the Jazz Ambassadors which began as a rehearsal band, formed by service musicians who wanted a break from playing concert and military material.

The Airmen of Note were first formed under that name in 1950. Apart from extensive appearances in America, the Airmen have toured most continents and have attracted praise everywhere, especially from musicians. Director of the band in 1950 was Sammy Nestico whose arranging talents have since been employed by countless contemporary rehearsal and university bands. Another air force band is the Falconaires, led by drummer Dave Hardin who has worked with the recreated Glenn Miller band. The Falconaires, which is the band of the United States Air Force Academy, is primarily a dance band, angling its repertoire towards contemporary popular music.

As for the US Navy, they have the Commodores, formed in 1969, who, like their comrades in musical arms, have set out to appeal to the widest possible audience by combining swing era sounds with high-energy rock and pop music of the 1980s.

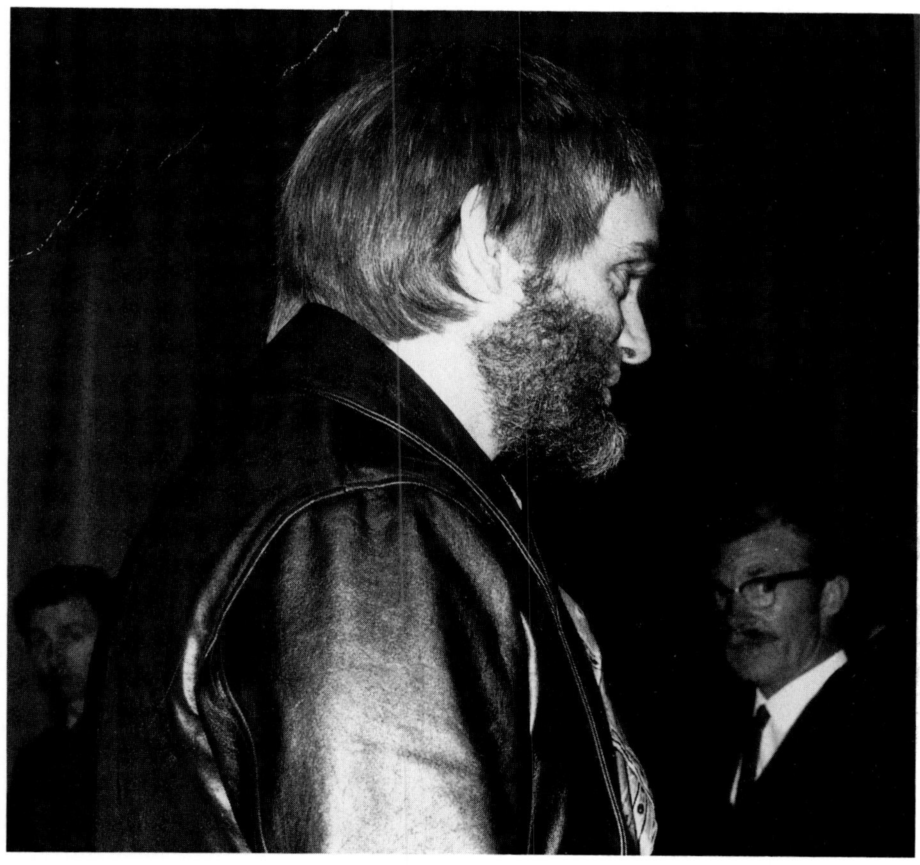

Don Ellis in England in 1969 where he wrote the score for the movie, *Moon Zero Two*. (Courtesy: P.I.C.Photos/Max Jones)

Don also experimented with a Ring Modulator, amplifiers and echo devices which electronically transformed his trumpet into a producer of sounds both strange and disturbingly animal-like. He uses these unusual effects on 'Hey Jude', on his 'Fillmore' album, a reworking of the Beatles song that takes in German bands on its way to a climax of Wagnerian intensity.

In 1976 Don re-formed his big band and was playing trumpet again. Neither the band nor its leader had lost any of their old versatility, fire and zest for new areas of big band music. Leonard Feather, no longer a solitary voice praising Ellis's qualities, wrote of this band that it was 'controversial, talented if not inspired, fielding some ideas that are genuinely progressive and others that are at least novel.' Feather also amended his earlier claims that Ellis would be the Stan Kenton of the 1970s: 'I was wrong; he is much more than that—a new, maturer Ellis for the 1980s.'

The view from Don Ellis's head: 'It's not like a cat who picked his horn up and just learned to blow. That type of musician doesn't fit into this band too well, however brilliantly he might solo. There are so many intricate parts that you have to be a well-rounded musician.'

It was not to be. In April 1978, Ellis announced that following medical advice he was retiring from playing and would henceforth concentrate on writing but in December 1978 Don Ellis died. He was 44.

Don Ellis sought to blend into the jazz idiom and in particular into the world of big bands, ideas and concepts from outside. He used classical music, rock, Japanese poetry, Oriental rhythms and electronics. In so doing it was inevitable that he would alienate many jazz fans and big band enthusiasts. By the more rigid definitions, much of what he did certainly fell outside the parameters of orthodoxy. Nevertheless, for all such reservations, Don Ellis brought drama and vivid life to a period when big band music was going through the commercial doldrums and was at its least adventurous.

It is in 'third stream music' that the elastic boundaries of jazz come into contact with an immovable fence over which only a few have tried to scramble. For the most part those who tried ended up perched in a somewhat undignified manner with their heads in one camp and their rumps exposed to the other. The term 'third stream music' was originated by the New York-born arranger-composer Gunther Schuller who drew equally from jazz and classical traditions in his writing in the late 1950s and onwards. The problem with Schuller's work is that it rarely succeeded in adequately blending the two musical forms even though the concept is by no means impossible.

In 1964 in New York trumpeter Mike Mantler and pianist Carla Bley formed a band they named the Jazz Composer's Guild Orchestra. The band lasted only around six months but was a rare opportunity for the avant-garde of jazz to assemble and play compositions which might otherwise have failed to find anyone to lift them off the page.

It was not only critics and audiences who found third stream music hard to accommodate. Ernie Wilkins was unresponsive to the new wave. Writing to *down beat* in 1961 he observed that 'jazz is an art form complete within itself. It doesn't need alien or outside factors added to improve it. Jazz has and will advance from within. You just can't ... pin on any of the tired devices from classical music that I've found to be happening with the exponents of the so-called Third Stream... everything in the Third Stream that I have heard thus far has failed miserably. It is banal and trite, pretentious, leaves no room for free and uninhibited improvisation, is boring, and most of all does not swing... Thank God, George Russell ... is still a *jazz* composer, and he tells me that that's what he'll always be.'

There are those who might question allocating the place Wilkins gives so readily to George Russell but for all its daunting complexity, Russell's lydian chromatic concept, especially when interpreted by his own specially formed big bands, offers music which is much more integrated than that of many third streamers.

Highly accessible is the late 1970s and 1980s music of Gil Evans. The forward thinking he displayed during his time with Claude Thornhill and his own 1950s bands did not diminish but it changed. Now there was a hard edge to his music, extensive use of electronics and concepts familiar through the concurrent pop music scene.

Of course, only a handful of latterday big bands were treading new paths and even among those that did, few were as completely revolutionary as Ellis, Evans and Russell.

Among those which achieved a hugely successful blend of musical innovation and traditional values were three jointly organised bands: Thad Jones-Mel Lewis, Kenny Clarke-Francy Boland and Toshiko Akiyoshi-Lew Tabackin.

Begun originally as a rehearsal band in New York towards the end of 1964 by Thad Jones and Pepper Adams, The Jazz Orchestra had, by the end of 1965, become the Thad Jones-Mel Lewis band. The band's original name stuck and reflects the strong jazz content of its work and the band's policy which allowed jazz soloists their heads.

Apart from Jones, whose trumpet and flugelhorn playing had enhanced the Count Basie band of the late 1950s and early 1960s, The Jazz

Bandstand broadside—5:
'I can't take an arrangement seriously that shows little or no understanding of Ellington, any more than a solo that doesn't in some way utilise the wisdom of Armstrong. Such work, in my estimation, will always show a lack of culture.'
Ruby Braff

***

Outposts of big band music:
Big bands can be found in some of the least expected corners of the world. In Malaga, Spain, there is the 17-piece 'Los Angeles Band', a group of young musicians gathered together by Artie Graham. Across the world in Japan is the Tokyo Union Orchestra, formed in 1964 and which, in 1978 and 1980, played respectively at the Montreux and Monterey jazz festivals under the direction of Tatsuya Takahashi. There is also Toshiyuki Miyama's New Herd, formed in 1951 and which has built both a reputation and a following in North and South America, in Europe and in India.

Thad Jones-Mel Lewis Orchestra at Ronnie Scott's in 1973. Co-leader Lewis on drums with trombonist Cliff Heather and trumpets Jim Bossy, Jon Faddis, Danny Moore, Steve Furtado. (Courtesy: *Crescendo International*)

Orchestra in its earliest form included trumpeters Bill Berry, Jimmy Nottingham, Marvin Stamm, Danny Stiles and Snooky Young, trombonists Bob Brookmeyer, Garnett Brown and Jimmy Cleveland, and such reed players as Pepper Adams, Seldon Powell and Jerome Richardson. But a big band has to be more than just a string of soloists, however good these might be, and in his writing for The Jazz Orchestra Thad Jones developed a style which retained a light, flowing, yet richly textured pattern of sound which gave the section players music of interest to play when they were not soloing.

Resident soon after its formation at New York's Village Vanguard, the band quickly established a reputation not only for its live club and concert performances but also for records which brought its blend of creative jazz solos and powerhouse ensembles to an international audience.

The gutsy swing of the Jones-Lewis boys is particularly well illustrated on live recordings the band made at the Village Vanguard. On 'Don't Get

'Our commerciality is mostly the fun and the laughs; we have a lot of humour in this band—which is not contrived.'

Mel Lewis

***

'Very few people understand improvisation and are attuned to the changes in jazz. They want to hear a little melody.'

Buddy Rich

***

'Everything [Francy Boland]writes seems so simple, so normal, but just try to dissect his colours and you end up pretty badly; all the secrets lie between the lines.'

Benny Bailey

Above: The National Youth Jazz Orchestra of Great Britain under the direction of Bill Ashton in 1984. Rhythm section: Dave Arch, Dave Hage, Chris Watson, Mike Bradley, Mike Smith. Trumpets: Richard Sidwell, John Hinch, Russell Cooke, Andrew Mitchell, Paul Higgs. Trombones: Colin Hill, Mark Nightingale, Fazzay Virji, Adrian Lane, Nigel Barr. Horn: Liz Price. Saxophones: David O'Higgins, Clive Hitchcock, Clifford Tracy, Simon Currie, Julie Davis. (*Photo: NYJO*)
Below: Perhaps the best known British Armed Forces band was the Royal Air Force Dance Orchestra, the Squadronaires, which came into existence long before the Battle of Britain.

In 1987 a group of musicians led by Harry Bence decided to renew the old tradition and soon the New Squadronaires were in business, bringing back a heady mixture of good swinging big band music and nostalgia for the days when, war torn or not, life seemed so much better. (*Harry Bence*)

Sassy' the tremendous solo strength of the trumpet section is exemplified by the preaching horn of Jimmy Nottingham and there is also fine, stomping piano by Sir Roland Hanna. Wonderfully swirling sounds emanate from the reed section driven along relentlessly by Lewis's drumming and Richard Davis on bass and leading towards an extrovert Joe Farrell tenor outing. 'Little Pixie' features staccato section work by reeds and brass which bite joyfully into a Jones arrangement with Lewis once again swinging the whole thing in dynamic fashion.

The exhilarating sound of the Jones-Lewis ensemble features many charts from the pens of Jones and Bob Brookmeyer with occasional arrangements from Manny Albam, Garnett Brown and Tom McIntosh. Typical of the band's output is the tongue-in-cheek excitement of the mock-gospel arrangement, 'Mornin' Reverend'. The remarkable rhythm section yet again propels excellent solos with Eddie Daniels outstanding on an extended tenor excursion. Another Jones arrangement, 'The Waltz You "Swang" For Me', again relies heavily on the rhythm section with the soprano of Jerome Richardson adding a delightful lustre.

The Thad Jones-Mel Lewis Jazz Orchestra was without doubt one of the most exciting bands of the late 1960s and early 1970s. Eventually, in 1978, Jones quit—not only the band but America too—and went to live in Denmark where he formed a big band made up from Scandinavians and fellow Americans-in-exile and he worked extensively with the Danish Radio Big Band. After Count Basie's death Jones led the Count Basie band for a while but then, in 1986, he died.

Meanwhile, back at the Village Vanguard, drummer Mel Lewis continued to drive The Jazz Orchestra into the late 1980s with the enthusiastic zeal he has displayed since the band's formation twenty years before.

Around the same time as the Jones-Lewis partnership was getting under way in America, over in Europe another pair of skilled musicians were putting their heads and their talents together.

They were the black American drummer Kenny Clarke and white Belgian pianist-arranger Francy Boland. The band mixed races and nationalities, musical styles and personalities, with apparent abandon and yet contrived to produce polished music which never lacked fire.

The band was equipped with an imaginative book, much of which was original material by Boland. The use of two drummers, Clarke and Englishman Kenny Clare, did not make the rhythm section too heavy but gave the band an often exhilarating lift and helped provide inspiration for its wealth of solo talent. With the crackling lead trumpet of Benny Bailey and the warm, accurate lead alto of Derek Humble the band swung ferociously through many fine Boland arrangements. Typically brilliant playing can be heard on 'The Wildman', which appears on the 'All Blues' album. Solos by trumpeters Dusko Goykovich and Benny Bailey add brilliance while Sahib Shihab, flute, and Tony Coe, tenor, are not easily outshone. On the strolling 'The Jamfs Are Coming' Shihab takes up soprano in telling fashion, eventually stepping aside to allow Johnny Griffin a notable tenor outing. Ake Persson finally blows a sublimely-toned trombone solo against driving section work by brass and reeds.

Although not in continuous existence, the Clarke-Boland Big Band lasted more than a decade and was certainly a major force in big band jazz and was always marvellous to hear.

Japanese pianist Toshiko Akiyoshi (she was actually born in Manchuria)

first attracted attention in the late 1950s but it was not until 1967 that Toshiko formed a big band in New York for a concert to play some of her own compositions. Later, in 1973, she and her husband, tenor saxophonist Lew Tabackin, settled in North Hollywood and formed the Akiyoshi-Tabackin Big Band. This band had all the qualities expected of a latterday big band: powerful ensemble work, strong jazz soloists, a workmanlike rhythm section. What made the band very different from most others was its book and the reasons for these differences lay in Toshiko's background. In an interview with Leonard Feather in *down beat* she stated: 'I had the belief that I should try to create something from my heritage, something unique enough that I could maybe ... return something *into* jazz, in my own way, not just reap the benefits of American jazz.' This she certainly succeeded in doing and the band's repertoire, built almost entirely from her compositions, contains subtle hints of a different musical form yet never moves too far from the central jazz core. As Toshiko herself observed, 'there's a certain essence about

The Clarke-Boland Big Band takes a break during a recording session. Featured in this version of the multi-national CBBB are (L to R) Francy Boland, Sal Nistico, Benny Bailey, Derek Humble, Jimmy Woode, Fats Sadi, Dusko Goykovich, Carl Drevo, Kenny Clarke, Shake Keane, entrepreneur Gigi Campi, Jimmy Deuchar, Nat Peck, Sahib Shihab, Ake Persson. (Courtesy: *Crescendo International*)

The Way Ahead? Loose Tubes (*Photo: Jazz News*)

Toshiko Akiyoshi directing the powerful big band she co-led throughout the 1980s with her husband tenor saxophonist Lew Tabackin (left) here concentrating on reading her superbly original charts.

jazz music which is important not to lose when infusing jazz with other ethnic music.'

Early in his career Lew Tabackin played with commercial bands in New York City, among them those led by Cab Calloway, Les and Larry Elgart and Maynard Ferguson. He later worked with a number of workshop bands in the city: Clark Terry, Duke Pearson, Chuck Israels, and the Thad Jones-Mel Lewis Jazz Orchestra. Tabackin enjoyed the experience and has commented how much he learned from playing alongside leading players of an earlier generation. 'The older I get, the more empathy I have towards that kind of playing... There's a certain kind of musical integrity there that maybe some contemporary players don't have—an emphasis on sound and warmth which is something that's kind of leaving the scene.'

Enthusing over his wife's writing, Lew observed that she was never afraid to experiment, 'to try devices that haven't been used before. The woodwind aspect is very noteworthy, her saxophone voicings have a heavier sound than most reed sections, she uses five-part harmony rather than let two instruments double the same note.'

Soloists with the Akiyoshi-Tabackin big band have included trumpeters Steve Hufstetter and Bobby Shew, trombonists Jimmy Knepper and Bill Reichenbach, and saxophonists Dick Spencer and Bill Byrne, all of whom have benefitted from Toshiko's practice of writing with specific musicians in mind. However, Tabackin is the principal soloist with the band. He doubles on flute for some of the more reflective numbers, 'Elusive Dream', 'Since Perry/Yet Another Tear', 'Transcience', which adds to the ethereal quality of this area of Toshiko's writing. On tenor, Tabackin plays with a hard-edged tone, driving headlong through solos and elaborate cadenzas with great panache: 'Roadtime', 'Strive for Jive', 'Tuning Up'.

After several years in Los Angeles, the mid-1980s found Toshiko and Lew returning to New York where they re-formed with a slightly different billing. Now it is Toshiko Akiyoshi and Her Orchestra featuring Lew Tabackin. The name may be different but the quality keeps them in the front rank of contemporary big bands.

Acknowledging Duke Ellington as her main influence, Toshiko's reasons for her admiration and respect are enlightening: '... his music was deeply rooted in his race and he was proud of his race. That encouraged me to draw some heritage from *my* roots.'

Toshiko's view of her role in music is unequivocal. 'My main job is to write, create, keep creating some music that will be a little different from the mainstream of the American tradition.'

The success with which Toshiko is accomplishing her aims, and the similarly interesting work produced earlier by Don Ellis, leads to a suspicion that those who strove to find a correlation between jazz and other musical forms might have done better turning not to Europe and the nineteenth- and twentieth-century classicists, nor even to the Caribbean and South America, but to the East and an extensive musical heritage which is as yet largely untapped by western musicians.

Another problem for the present-day big band scene lies not so much in musical directions but in the need for new movers and shapers. Those young musicians coming out of universities are comfortably capable of playing complex Stan Kenton charts, or of riffing through Basie with elan. The youth band scene is heavy with the work of brilliant arrangers like Bob Florence, Bill Holman, Les Hooper, Sammy Nestico, Sal Nistico and Hank Levy, all of which is superb, and which the young musicians interpret with consummate skills.

But where is the music going next? Where is the new Duke Ellington? Or the new Don Ellis?

Those two names are not chosen at random. They are two men who sought to change perceptions of big band music; Ellington to great public acclaim, Ellis to near-total disregard.

It may not be entirely coincidental that these two men are both much less than highly rated by big band enthusiasts, and both occupy a curiously unintegrated part of the jazz fan's world. Could it be that this is because they were both unique talents who owed little to popular conceptions and chose to follow paths they themselves signposted in ways which sometimes only they could read and understand?

Today, almost everything that Ellington did, and some of Ellis's work, is readily accessible on record, yet the rehearsal bands and university bands play only a tiny fraction of Ellington's more than 2,000 compositions and almost never touch his major works. And is anyone, anywhere playing Ellis?

As to the form the inspiration of today's young musicians should take, perhaps what is needed is the tonal colourings and melodic perceptions of Ellington, the experimental spirit of Ellis, and the earthy, plangent swing of the blues. Curiously enough, despite the significant part played in the development of big band music by the Kansas City style, the blues, too, has become something of a no-go area for latterday big bands. It is an error of omission neither Ellington nor Ellis ever made.

Wherever and whenever the inspiration arrives, some things are certain: many fine musicians will be available to take notice and play on with zest and determination; and there are sure to be more than enough fans around to provide the enthusiastic following that has always been a hallmark of the big band years.

THE ARRANGER'S TOUCH—4

The so-called 'progressive' bands all had their entourages of arrangers eagerly seeking new expression. Boyd Raeburn used the intricate talents of George Handy and Ed Finckel. Writing about Handy, Arthur Jackson noted that he 'invariably endeavoured to cram all his musical knowledge into one three-minute score.' Yet, at times, Hardy wrote some extremely skilful arrangements, notably 'Yerxa', a vehicle for alto saxophonist Hal McKusick. Handy's arrangements of 'There's No You', 'Tonsillectomy' and 'Dalvatore Sally' caused a minor sensation at the time. Less extrovert than Handy, Finckel produced a number of fine arrangements for Raeburn, in particular 'Boyd Meets Stravinsky', which captures delightful solos by Dodo Marmarosa, piano, and Lucky Thompson, tenor saxophone.

The Four Brothers sound, the line up of alto, three tenors and baritone, originated with arranger Gene Roland. Apart from working with the Herman band Roland worked with Stan Kenton alongside other arrangers of considerable talent including Johnny Richards and Bill Russo. These two, with Kenton's *alter ego* Pete Rugulo, strayed far from the jazz path but they were concerned not simply with jazz but with composition and arranging for the modern orchestra. Russo's work on Kenton's 'Sketches on Standards' is one of his finest achievements, and similarly successful is Richards' respectful reworking of Leonard Bernstein's 'West Side Story'. Pete Rugulo, an uncommunicative man, let his music speak for him. Musically open-minded, he always sought new regions to explore but acknowledged 'Stan was *my* influence.'

The innovations with which Stan Kenton is associated were concerned not with soloists but with concepts of writing; it is the arrangers who are the real stars of the Kenton orchestra and it is their work which largely decided the success of Kenton's music.

Among several sound arrangers who developed personal styles in the late 1940s was Tiny Kahn who provided some excellent swinging arrangements for the bands of Georgie Auld, Chubby Jackson, Elliot Lawrence and Boyd Raeburn. Kahn, who died in 1953, was an influence upon other young arrangers of the period including Al Cohn and Johnny Mandel. Another efficient arranger, Bill Holman, has the distinction of having provided the Stan Kenton orchestra with its most swinging charts. Manny Albam provided one of the best adaptations of the music of 'West Side Story' on his album of the same name, while Marty Paich's arrangements for the Art Pepper Eleven album provided the alto saxophonist with a simple framework which allowed him free rein to develop imaginative emotion-filled solos.

In contrast to other, sometimes discordant, progressive orchestras there was the relaxed pastel-toned textures of the Claude Thornhill band. Like Kenton, Thornhill originated his own sound but arrangers Bill Borden and, later, Gil Evans continued his ideas. Thornhill seemed to be concerned with sound for its own sake. Gil Evans recalled how 'the sound hung like a cloud, I think he would have had the band hold a chord for a hundred bars if it had been possible.' Thornhill's requirements became too static for Evans who felt there should have been more movement in the melody and harmony, 'more dynamics, more syncopation'.

Evans may have been disenchanted with Thornhill's preoccupation with sound but he remained sold on the general principals of Thornhill's multi-coloured impressionism in the evolution of which he had played no small part. While Evans was with Thornhill young Gerry Mulligan had joined the band and later both men became involved in creating the influential Miles Davis 'Birth of the Cool' album under the studio direction of Pete Rugulo. Evans's association with Miles Davis continued long afterwards and a series of albums resulted. 'Miles Ahead', while not in the mainstream of big band music, represents a rationalisation of the Thornhill sound with the saxophone section broken up and replaced by a combination of woodwinds and alto. Extending the brass section with bass trombone and tuba enabled Evans to write melodic parts in a lower than usual register. Overall, he was able to increase the range of colours and textures and extend the limits of orchestration.

Among many excellent record albums made by Evans under his own name, all of which offer eloquent testimony to his advanced musical thinking, are 'Big Stuff' and 'Great Jazz Standards'.

As the 1960s segued into the 1970s Gil Evans increasingly moved away from conventional big band sound. He was not alone. Many free thinkers were investigating fresh boundaries. George Russell re-examined traditional harmonies, discovering fresh resources; Sun Ra investigated orchestral disciplines and all the time the experimenters moved further from the middle ground than most enthusiasts of big band music cared to follow. Despite extreme use of time signatures, Don Ellis carried his audience with him, using arrangers, like Hank Levy and Les Hooper, who have since continued in the big band format, encouraging and becoming involved in the upsurge of interest in college and university bands.

SELECTED RECORDS

Countless thousands of records have been made by the big bands and more are being added every month. Sometimes the new releases are by present day bands, other times reissues of old favourites, occasionally even a newly discovered gem by a long forgotten band. Keeping up with these new arrivals on record store shelves is a full time occupation and so too is keeping track of reappearances under different titles on other labels, frequently with inadequate identification of exactly what is on record. And then there is the swiftness with which record albums are deleted. All this makes compiling a meaningful list of recommended records a frustrating and often misleading task.

Wherever possible record albums listed are the most recently issued but as experienced collectors of big band music and jazz will already know, many will be found only from specialist record shops and even then, possibly only in the second-hand rack. LP records only are listed although several companies offer the alternative of cassettes while compact discs are rapidly gaining in popularity and are beginning to extensively cover big band music and jazz.

Good hunting!

Toshiko Akiyoshi-Lew Tabackin:
'Road Time' RCA Victor CPL2-2242 (dbl)
'Live at Newport' RCA Victor PL 40821
'Tanuki's Night Out' Jam JAM 006
'European Memories' Ascent ASC 1003

Bert Ambrose:
'Tribute to Cole Porter' Jasmine JASM 2017

Cat Anderson:
'Cat On a Hot Tin Horn' Mercury MMB 12006/Trip TLP-5577

Ray Anthony:
'Jam Session at the Tower' Capitol T 749

Louis Armstrong:
'Swing That Music' (1935–44) Coral CP 1

Harry Arnold:
'Big Band Classics 1957–58' Dragon DRLP 139/140

Walter Barnes (rev. George E. Lee):
'Ruff Scufflin'' Retrieval FJ 125

Charlie Barnet:
'The Indispensable CB' Vol 1/2, 3/4 RCA Jazz Tribune NL 89743, 89483 (dbl)

Count Basie:
'The Complete CB' Vol 1–10, Vol 11–20 CBS 66101, 66102 (2 sets of 10)
'Complete Recorded Works 1937–1939' MCA 510.167–510.170 (Set of 4)
'The Atomic Mr Chairman' Vogue VJD 517 (dble)
'Kansas City Suite' Roulette R 52056
'On My Way and Shouting Again' Verve MGV 8511

Louie Bellson:
'150 MPH' Concord CJ 36
'The LB Explosion' Pablo 2310 755 Super

Tex Beneke:
'Loose Like' Hep 29

Bunny Berigan:
'BB' RCA Victor LSA 3108

Bill Berry and the LA Band:
'Hello Rev' Concord CJ 27

The Big 18:
'The Swing Collection' RCA International PJM-2-8003

Blue Wisp Big Band:
'Rollin' With Von Ohlen' Mopro M 112

Will Bradley:
'1939-1941, 1941-1942' Bandstand BS-7101, 7110

Tiny Bradshaw (rev: Teddy Hill):
'1934' Harlequin HQ 2053KK

Les Brown:
'Concert at the Hollywood Palladium' Vol 1, 2 Jasmine JASM 1001, 1002
'The Sound of Renown' Jasmine JASM 1012
'Swing Song Book' Jasmine JAS 1503

Billy Butterfield:
'1946' Hindsight HSR-173

California Ramblers:
'1920s Flapper Party' Halcyon HAL 8

Cab Calloway:
'Kicking the Gong Around' Living Era AJA 5013
'16 Classics' CBS 62950

Capp-Pierce Juggernaut:
'Juggernaut' Concord CJ 40
'Live at the Alley Cat' Concord CJ 336

Benny Carter:
'Swingin' at Maida Vale' Jasmine JASM 2010
'Further Definitions' World Records ST 864/Impulse AS 12 & IMPL 8037
'Additions to Further Definitions' Jasmine JAS 57

Casa Loma Orchestra:
'CL' Hep 1010
'Shall We Swing?' Creative World 1055

Matt Catingub:
'My Mommy and Me' Sea Breeze SB 2013
'Hi-Tech Big Band' Sea Breeze SB 2025

Buddy Childers:
'Just Buddy's's Trend TR 539

The Chocolate Dandies:
'1928-33' Parlophone PMC 7038

The Clarke-Boland Big Band:
'All Blues' MPS BMP 29747-0
'At Her Majesty's Pleasure' Polydor 2460 131/'Doing Time' Black Lion 65119
'Change of Scenes' Verve 2304 034 Super

The Coon-Sanders Nighthawks:
'Radio's Aces' RCA Victor LSA 3068

Al Cooper's Savoy Sultans:
'Jump Steady' Affinity AFS 1009

The Cotton Club Orchestra:
'Harry Cooper, R. Q. Dickerson and the CCO' Collectors Items 006

Bob Crosby and his Orchestra:
'South Rampart Street Parade' MCA MCFM 2578
'Mournin' Blues' Affinity AFS 1014

Bob Crosby's Bob Cats:
'Big Noise From Winnetka' MCA MCFM 2695

The Danish Radio Big Band:
'Crackdown' Hep 2041

Sam Donahue:
'Hollywood Hop' Hep 25

The Dorsey Brothers:
'Mood Hollywood' Hep 1005

Jimmy Dorsey:
Vol 1, 2, 3, 4, 5 Hindsight HSR-101, 153, 165, 1178, HUK 203

Tommy Dorsey:
'The Indispensable TD' Vol 1/2, 3/4, 5/6 RCA Jazz Tribune NL 89752, 89163, 89589 (dbl)
'Making Big Band History' First Heard FH 1003

Billy Eckstine:
'Mr B and the Band' Savoy SJL-2214 (dbl)
Duke Ellington:
'The Indispensable DE' Vol 1/2, 3/4, 5/6, 7/8, 9/10, 11/12 RCA Jazz Tribune NL 89749, 89762, 89750, 89582, 89972
'The Blanton-Webster Band' RCA Bluebird 5659 1 RB (Box of 4)
'... at Newport' CBS S 63531
'Such Sweet Thunder' Philips BBL 7203
'Second Sacred Concert' America AM 006/007
'The English Concert' (inc. 'Toga Brava Suite') United Artists UAD 60032/33
'Eastbourne Performance' TCA SF 8447
Don Ellis:
'At Fillmore' CBS CG 30423 (dbl)
'Electric Bath' CBS 63230
'Autumn' CBS 63503
'Live at Monterey' Pacific Jazz PJ 10112
'Soaring' MPS MB 25123/JS 041/ BAP 5066
'Haiku' MPS 68.050
Seger Ellis:
'Choirs of Brass 1937' Alamac QSR 2048
Gil Evans:
'Out of the Cool' Jasmine JAS 52
'Into the Hot' Impulse A 9
'At the Royal Festival Hall' RCA PL 25209
'Live at the Royal Festival Hall' Mole Jazz MOLE 3
Maynard Ferguson:
'Newport Suite' Roulette Birdland R 52047/Saga Eros 8133
'Trumpets Out Front' (rev. Herb Pomeroy) Vogue VJD 567 (dbl)
Bob Florence:
'Concerts By the Sea' Trend TR 523
'Trash Can City' Trend TR 545
'Westlake' Discovery DS 832
Roy Fox:
'Strictly Instrumental' Halycon HAL 1
Terry Gibbs:
'Launching a New Band' Trip TLP 5545
'The Exciting TG Big Band Recorded Live at The Summit in Hollywood' Verve 2304 441
Dizzy Gillespie:
'1946-1949' RCA Jazz Tribune NL 89763 (dbl)
'Live at the Shrine Auditorium 1949' Queen-Disc Q-003
'The New Continent' Emarcy 6641.647/Trip TLP-5584
Jean Goldkette:
Bix Beiderbecke 'Bixology' Vol 2, 3 Joker SM 3558, 3559
Benny Goodman:
'Carnegie Hall Concert—Digitally Remastered' CBS 450983-1 (dbl)
'The Indispensable BG' Vol 1/2, 3/4, 5/6 RCA Jazz Tribune NL 89755, 89756, 89587 (dbl)
Benny Goodman Small Groups:
Trio and Quartet: 'The Complete Small Combinations' Vol 1/2, 3/4 RCA Jazz Tribune NL 89753, 89754 (dbl)
Jerry Gray:
'Big Dance Tonight' Jasmine JASM 1039
Lionel Hampton:
'Leapin' with Lionel' Affinity AFS 1000
'Jam Band' First Heard FH 54
'Newport Uproar!' RCA Victor SF-7933
'All Star Band at Newport '78' Timeless SJP 142
Erskine Hawkins:
'The Complete EH Vol 1/2, 3/4 RCA Jazz Tribune NL 89603, 89482 (dbl)
Tubby Hayes:
'Tubb's Tours' Mole Jazz MOLE 4
Ted Heath:
'All Time Top 12' Memoir MOIR 126
'Spotlight on Sidemen' Jasmine JASM 2026
'Swing Session' Jasmine JASM 2205
Neal Hefti:
'The Band with Young Ideas' Jasmine JASM 1021
Fletcher Henderson:
'A Study in Frustration' CBS BPG 62001 (Box of 4)
'1931' VJM VLP 63
'Wild Party' Hep 1009
'Yeah Man!' Hep 1016
Fletcher Henderson All Stars:
'Big Reunion' Jazz Greats JG 264/Session LP-126/Jazztone J-1285
Woody Herman:
'The Band That Plays the Blues' Affinity AFS 1008
'The First Herd at Carnegie Hall, 1946' Verve 2317 031
'The V Disc Years' Vol 1, 2 Hep 34, 35
'Blowin' Up a Storm' Affinity AFS 1043
'The Best of WH' CBS 52551
'40th Anniversary Concert at Carnegie Hall' RCA PL 02203
'Gold Star' Concord CJ 330
Teddy Hill (rev: Tiny Bradshaw):
'1935-1936' Harlequin HQ 2053
Earl Hines:
'The Complete EH' Vol 1/2, 3/4, 5/6 RCA Jazz Tribune NL 89764, 89605, 89618
'Deep Forest' Hep 1003
Bill Holman:
'The Fabulous' Jasmine JASM 1009
Les Hooper:
'Look What They've Done' Creative World 3002
Spike Hughes:
'SH and his All American Orchestra' Jasmine JASM 2012
Jack Hylton:
'JH' Jasmine JASM 2018
The International Sweethearts of Rhythm:
'The IS of R' Rosetta RR 1312
Harry James:
'Big John Special' Hep 24
'King Porter Stomp' Hep 31
'HJ' Vol 1, 2, 3, 4, 5, 6 Hindsight HSR-102, 123, 135, 141, 142, HUK-150
Jazz Members Big Band:
'May Day' Sea Breeze SB 2014
Jazz Warriors:
'Out Of Many, One Peoples' Antilles New Directions AN 8712
Buddy Johnson:
'1944-1952' MCA Coral 6.22417 AK
Isham Jones:
'1929-30' Sunbeam MFC 8
'1936 featuring Woody Herman' Sunbeam HB 306
Quincy Jones:
'This Is How I Feel About Jazz' Jasmine JASM 1035
'Go West Man!' Jasmine JASM 1048
'Live at Newport, 1961' Trip TLP-5554
Thad Jones-Mel Lewis:
'Presenting TJ-ML' United Artists SULP 1169
'Live at the Villge Vanguard' United Artists USS 7008
'Consummation' Blue Note BST 84346
'Potpourris' CBS PIR 80411
Stan Kenton:
'Greatest Hits' Capitol CAPS 1002
'New Concepts in Artistry in Rhythm' Creative World 1002
'The City of Glass'/'This Modern World' Creative World 1006
'The Kenton Era' Creative World 1030 (Box of 4)
'Live at Butler University' Creative World 1058 (dbl)
Andy Kirk:
'All Our For Hicksville' Hep 1007
'Walkin' and Swingin'' Affinity AFS 1011
Gene Krupa:
'Drummin' Man CBS BPG 62289/62290
'Drummer Man' Affinity AFS 1042
'What's This? Hep 26
Elliot Lawrence:
'Elevation' First Heard FH 38
'Plays Kahn and Mandel' Fantasy 0902 109

George E. Lee (rev. Walter Barnes):
'Ruff Scufflin'' Retrieval FJ 125
Harlan Leonard:
'HL' RCA Victor LPV-531
Mel Lewis:
'20th Anniversary' Atlantic 781 655
Vic Lewis:
'In Concert—1954' Hep 20
'Plays Stan Kenton' Harlequin HQ 3014
'Mulligan's Music' Mole Jazz MOLE 9
'Back Again' Concept VL 1
Guy Lombardo:
'The Best of GL' Capitol T 1461
Pat Longo:
'Crocodile Tears' Town Hall S 30
Loose Tubes:
'Loose Tubes' Loose Tubes LTLP 001
'Delightful Precipice' Loose Tubes LTLP 003
'Open Letter' Editions EGED 55
Jimmie Lunceford:
'The Complete JL' 1939-40 CBS 66241 (Box of 4)
'Rhythm Business' Hep 1013
'Ohy Boy' Hep 1017
'Runnin' a Temperature' Affinity AFS 1033
'JL' Jasmine JASM 1023
Don Lusher:
'Pays Tribute to the Great Bands' Horatio Nelson SIV 110
Rob McConnell:
'Atras Da Porta' Innovation JC 0010
'Boss Brass and Woods' Innovation JC 0011
Ray McKinley:
'Blue Skies' First Heard FH 32
'Featuring the Arrangements of Eddie Sauter' Golden Era Ge-15030
McKinney's Cotton Pickers:
'The Complete McKP' Vol 1/2, 3/4 RCA Jazz Tribune NL 89766, 89738
Jay McShann:
'Hootie's K. C. Blues' Affinity AFS 1006
'Confessin' the Blues' Affinity AFF 66
Billy May:
'Sorta May' Creative World 1051
Glenn Miller:
'On the Air Volumes 1-3' RCA Jazz Tribune NL 89714
'The GM Story Vols 1-4' RCA Jazz Tribune NL 89005/89221-3
'The GM Legend Vols 1-3' RCA PD 89713
'The Very Best of GM' RCA PL 89009
Glenn Miller and His Army Air Force Band:
'Uncle Sam Presents' Hep 32
Lucky Millinder:
'Apollo Jump' Affinity AFS 1004
Mills Blue Rhythm Band:
'Savage Rhythm' Hep 1015
Bennie Moten:
'The Indispensable BM' Vol 1/2, 3/4, 5/6 RCA Jazz Tribune NL 89881, 89616, 89617
'Count Basie in Kansas City 1930-1932' RCA LPM-514
Gerry Mulligan:
''63 the Concert Jazz Band' Verve SVLP 9037
National Jazz Ensemble:
'Volumes 1 and 2' Chiaroscuro CR-140 and CRD 151 (dbl)
National Youth Jazz Orchestra:
'With An Open Mind' NYJO NYY 007
'To Russia with Jazz' NYJO DNYJ 501 (dble)
'Playing Turkey' NYJO NYJ 003
Sammy Nestico:
'Night Flight' Sea Breeze SBD 103
Red Norvo:
'Featuring Mildred Bailey' Sounds of Swing LP-112
King Oliver:
'Volumes 1–5' Joker SM 3808-12
Sy Oliver:
'Sentimental Sy' Jasmine JAS 1513
Marty Paich:
'What's New?' Discovery DS 857
Nat Pierce:
'Ballad of Jazz Street' Hep 2009
Ben Pollack:
'BP and his Park Central Orchestra' RCA Black & White FXM 1 7283
Herb Pomeroy:
'Pramlatta's Hips' Shiah HP 1
'Trumpets Out Front' (rev. Maynard Ferguson) Vogue VJD 567 (dbl)
Boyd Raeburn:
'The Eagle Rules' Hep 1
'Where You At' Hep 3
'Memphis in June' Hep 22
'Hep Boyds' Golden Era GE 15104
Don Redman:
'Shakin' the African' Hep 1001
'Doin' the New Low Down' Hep 1004
Luis Russell:
'The LR Story' Parlophone PMC 7025
'Henry "Red" Allen and his New York Orchestra' RCA FXM 1 7060/LPV 556
Buddy Rich:
"47–'48' Hep 12
'Rich Riot' First Heard FH 27
'The Big Band Sound of BR' Verve 2317 058 Select
'Mercy, Mercy' Liberty LBL 83168E
Johnny Richards:
'Wide Range' Creative World 1052
'Aijalon' Discovery DS 895
Shorty Rogers:
'Blues Express' RCA Master FXL 1 7234/RCA Jazzline NL 89502
'Courts the Count' RCA Masters PM 42359
Pete Rugolo:
'Introducing PR' Fresh Sounds (Columbia CL-635) FSR-520
'Rugulomania' Fresh Sounds (Columbia CL-689) FSR-519
George Russell:
'So What' Blue Note BT 85132
Edgar Sampson:
'Swing Softly Sweet Sampson' Jasmine JASM 1020
The Savoy Bearcats (rev: Arthur Gibbs):
'The Savoy Bands' RCA PM 42044
Artie Shaw:
'The Indispensable AS' Vol 1/2, 3/4, 5/6 RCA Jazz Tribune NL 89820, 89774, 89914 (dbl)
'At the Hollywood Palladium' Hep 19
Larry Sonn:
'The Sound of Sonn' Jasmine JASM 1007
Charlie Spivak:
'1934–46' Hindsight HSR-105
Lew Stone:
'The Echo of a Song' Halycon HAL 12
Jack Teagarden:
'Masters of Jazz' Vol 10 Storyville SLP 4110
'JT' Halycon HDL 104
Clark Terry:
'Big Band Live at 57th Street' Big Bear BEAR 13
Claude Thornhill:
'The Song Is You' Hep 17
'The Memorable CT' Columbia PG 32906 (dbl)
'1947' Hindsight HSR-108
Joe Timer:
'Willis Conover Presents...' Jasmine JASM 1016
Skeets Tolbert:
'ST and his Gentlemen of Swing 1939–1942' Everybody's 3001
Stan Tracey:
'Genesis' Steam SJ 114

Joe Venuti:
'The Big Bands' Vol , 2 JSP 1111, 1112
Including Geraldo, Roy Fox: 'Dance Band Years—the 1940s' Saville SVL 145
Including Sam Lanin: 'Jazz from the Golden Era' VJM VLP 52

Tommy Vig:
'Encounter with Time' Discovery DS 780
G01**Walsall Youth Jazz Orchestra:**
'Head Over Heels' Zella Zel LPS 411

Bill Watrous:
'Manhattan Wildlife Refuge' CBS KC 33090

Chick Webb:
'King of the Savoy' 1937–1939 MCA 510 020
'In the Groove' Affinity AFS 1007

Paul Whiteman:
Bix Beiderbecke 'Bixology' Vol 7, 8, 9, 10 Joker SM 3563, 3564, 3565, 3566
'Shaking the Blues Away' Halycon HAL 21;

Wigan Youth Jazz Orchestra:
'Steaming Jazz' Gateway 001

Ernie Wilkins:
'EW and the Almost Big Band' Storyville SLP 4051

Gerald Wilson:
'Lomelin' Discovery DS 833
'The Golden Sword' Discovery DS 901

Sam Wooding:
'Bicentennial' Jazz Vista Twin Saga TS 1000

University Bands (America):
California State University, Northridge: 'Giant Steps'
Mark MCJS 20758
Eastman Jazz Ensemble: 'Montreux' Mark MJS 57605 (dbl)
North Texas State University One O'Clock Lab Band: 'Lap '86' NTSU LA 8602-NS

Compilations:
Including Jim Europe's Society Orchestra, Ford Dabney:
'JAZZ Some Beginnings' Folkways RF-31
Including Jim Europe's Society Orchestra, Lt. Jim
Europe's 369th Infantry 'Hellfighters' Band, Arthur
Pryor: 'Too Much Mustard' Saydisc SDL-221
Including Erskine Tate, Carroll Dickerson, Charlie Johnson, Leo Reisman: 'Sweet and Low Blues' New World NW 256
Including Zack Whyte, Alphonso Trent: 'Territory Bands 1929–1933' Historical ASC 5829-24
Including Baron Lee and the Blue Rhythm Band, Don Redman, Claude Hopkins, Teddy Hill, Erskine Hawkins and his 'Bama State Collegians, Benny Carter, Coleman Hawkins: 'the World of Swing' CBS 88134 (dbl)
Including Elgar's Creole Orchestra, Charlie Straight: 'Chicago in the Twenties Vol 1, 2' Arcadia 2011, 2012
Including Troy Floyd, Fess Williams: 'Hot Town' BBC REB 647
Including Chick Webb: 'Big Bands on Film 1928–1935' Harlequin HQ 2038

CHRONOLOGY

1899 Duke Ellington born; Jean Goldkette born; John Philip Sousa plays in Kansas City; Boer War sieges at Mafeking, Kimberley and Ladysmith.

1900 Don Redman born; race riots in New York; Boxer Rebellion in China; relief of Mafeking, Kimberley and Ladysmith.

1901 Death of Queen Victoria; assassination of President McKinley.

1902 Chick Webb born; Jimmie Lunceford born; all-black show 'In Dahomey' opens in New York; first recordings made of 'authentic American Negro music' by the Dinwiddy Quartet; Boer War ends.

1903 Bix Beiderbecke born; Wilbur Sweatman and 6-piece Negro band make cylinder records; Claude Hopkins born; Mrs Pankhurst forms Suffragette movement; 'In Dahomey' performed at Buckingham Palace.

1904 Count Basie born; Glenn Miller born; Jimmy Dorsey born; Coleman Hawkins born; New York subway opens; Russian-Japanese War.

1905 Tommy Dorsey born; Harlan Leonard born; Earl Hines born; Jack Teagarden born; Russian troops fire on workers in St Petersburg; race riots in New York.

1906 Original Creole Band first organised in New Orleans; San Francisco earthquake; Dreyfuss declared innocent at retrial; British Independent Labour Party formed.

1907 Benny Carter born; Cab Calloway born; Mildred Bailey born; Buddy Bolden confined in mental institution.

1908 Bunny Berigan born; Henry 'Red' Allen Jr born; Jack Johnson beats Tommy Burns for heavyweight boxing title; Butch Cassidy and the Sundance Kid reported killed in Bolivia; William H. Taft elected President.

1909 Benny Goodman born; Lionel Hampton born; Gene Krupa born; Claude Thornhill born; W. C. Handy publishes 'Memphis Blues'; Louis Bleriot flies English Channel; first Harlem theatre, the Lincoln, opens; Henry Ford's first assembly line.

1910 Clef Club founded in New York; Jack Johnson's defeat of James J. Jeffries followed by race riots; Charlie Chaplin and Stan Laurel tour America with Fred Karno; Dr Crippen hanged; King George V ascends throne.

1911 Speed Webb born; Roy Eldridge born; Irving Berlin's 'Alexander's Ragtime Band' published; Jim Pendergast dies in Kansas City, brother Tom takes over; Amundsen reaches South Pole.

1912 Stan Kenton born; Jelly Roll Morton produces his first written arrangements; Lafayette Theatre opens in Harlem; Woodrow Wilson elected president; 'Titanic' sinks.

1913 Woody Herman born; Louis Armstrong sent to Waif's Home in New Orleans.

1914 James Reese Europe forms Tempo Club; Apollo Theatre opens in Harlem; World War I begins in Europe.

1915 Barron Wilkins opens club in Harlem; Billie Holiday born; Gallipoli campaign; 'Lusitania' sunk by U-boat.

1916 Harry James born; Rasputin assassinated; Easter rising in Ireland; battle of the Somme.

1917 Buddy Rich born; Dizzy Gillespie born; US Navy closes Storyville; Joe Oliver arrives in Chicago; ODJB makes first jazz records; Jim Europe and Jim Brymn form army bands; Buffalo Bill Cody dies; United States enters war.

1918 Will Marion Cook takes orchestra to London; World War I ends; votes for women over 30 in Britain; Tsar Nicholas and family murdered.

1919 James Reese Europe murdered; Luis Russell arrives in New Orleans from Panama; League of Nations founded; Mussolini forms fascist party in Italy; Amritsar massacre.

1920 Charlie Parker born; Paul Whiteman opens in New York; Mamie Smith makes first blues record; Prohibition begins; civil war in Ireland, Home Rule Act; Palestine state established.

1921 Connie's Inn opens in Harlem; all-black musical 'Shuffle Along' opens in New York; Harry Pace forms first Negro-owned record company; Russian naval mutiny.
1922 Will Vodery's 67-piece regimental band plays at Manhattan Casino; Duke Ellington joines Wilbur Sweatman band; Cotton Club opens with 'whites only' policy; King Oliver sends for Louis Armstrong; fascists march on Rome.
1923 Thad Jones born; King Oliver and Bennie Moten make first records; Paul Whiteman plays in London; Fletcher Henderson opens at Club Alabam; Adolf Hitler imprisoned.
1924 Louis Bellson born; Sonny Berman born; Paul Whiteman concert at Aeolian Hall; Louis Armstrong joins Fletcher Henderson at Roseland; the Missourians arrive in New York; first Labour government in Britain; death of Lenin.
1925 Sam Wooding begins tour of Europe; Duke Ellington plays first Harlem engagement; Benny Goodman joines Ben Pollack band; Marcus Garvey convicted of fraud.
1926 Savoy Ballroom opens in Harlem; LeRoy Smith at Connie's Inn; Jean Goldkette at Roseland; Barron Wilkins murdered; General Strike in Britain.
1927 Duke Ellington hired for Cotton Club; Don Redman joins McKinney's Cotton Pickers; King Oliver big band records million copy hit; Al Jolson's 'The Jazz Singer' opens; Lindbergh flies Atlantic; Russian revolution.
1928 Ben Pollack opens at Park Central Hotel; Cab Calloway joins Missourians; Earl Hines opens at Grand Terrace; Bennie Moten tours upstate New York; Alexander Fleming discovers penicillin.
1929 Toshiko Akiyoshi born; Glen Gray elected leader of Casa Lomans; St Valentine's Day massacre; Martin Luther King Jr born; US stock market collapses.
1930 Hal Kemp tours Europe; Empire State Building erected.
1931 Bix Beiderbecke dies; Duke Ellington leaves Cotton Club, succeeded by Cab Calloway; Dorsey Brothers on tour with own band; Al Capone imprisoned.
1932 Louis Armstrong's first European tour; Franklin D. Roosevelt elected president; Lindbergh kidnapping.
1933 Red Norvo marries Mildred Bailey; gangster Owney Madden retires; Adolf Hitler becomes Chancellor of Germany; Stalin purges communist party; Prohibition ends.
1934 Don Ellis born; Chick Webb signs Ella Fitzgerald; Benny Goodman forms band; Bennie Moten dies; John Dillinger killed by G-Men; Hitler becomes Führer; Mao Tse-Tung begins 'Long March'.
1935 Benny Goodman breakthrough at Palomar Ballroom; Bob Crosby elected front man for band; Benny Carter goes to Europe; British Musicians Union bans Americans; Italy invades Ethiopia.
1936 Artie Shaw and Woody Herman form bands; Count Basie comes to New York; Harlem Cotton Club moves downtown; Jesse Owens wins three Olympic gold medals; abdication of Edward VIII; Spanish Civil War.
1937 Count Basie opens at Roseland and Apollo; airship Hindenburg destroyed; Bessie Smith dies; Japan invades China.
1938 Benny Goodman Carnegie Hall concert; Count Basie broadcasts from Famous Door; Benny Carter and Eddie South return from Europe; Germany annexes Austria.
1939 Chick Webb dies; Sy Oliver leaves Lunceford for Dorsey; Benny Goodman hires Fletcher Henderson; Artie Shaw quits in mid-performance; Spanish Civil War ends; World War II begins.
1940 Benny Goodman hospitalised, band folds; Cotton Club closes; Japan joins Axis powers; Italy declares war; evacuation from Dunkirk; Battle of Britain.
1941 Lionel Hampton forms band; Jelly Roll Morotn dies; Rudolf Hess parachutes into Scotland; Japan bombs Pearl Harbor, US enters war.
1942 Bunny Berigan dies; AF of M recording ban; Singapore falls to Japanese; battles of Stalingrad and El Alamein.
1943 Charlie Parker joins Earl Hines; Woody Herman's First Herd; Italy surrenders.
1944 Glenn Miller disappears; Billy Eckstine forms band, joined by Charlie Parker; first Norman Granz JATP concert; Harlan Leonard band folds; invasion of Normandy; Paris liberated.
1945 Boyd Raeburn at Apollo Theatre; Jay McShann at Down Beat Club; Roosevelt dies; Mussolini assassinated; Hitler commits suicide; Germany surrenders; atom bombs dropped on Hiroshima and Nagasaki, World World II ends.
1946 Don Redman tours Europe; Woody Herman Carnegie Hall concert; civil war begins in Indo-China (Vietnam); United Nations formed; Nuremburg trials.
1947 Jimmie Lunceford dies; Sonny Berman dies; Woody Herman forms Four Brothers band; Al Capone dies; Dizzy Gillespie Carnegie Hall concert; India gains independent; partition of Palestine.
1948 First Nice Jazz Festival; Dave Tough dies; state of Israel declared; Berlin blockade and air-lift; Ghandi assassinated.
1949 Miles Davis records 'Birth of the Cool' album; apartheid policy adopted by South Africa; Mao Tse-Tung forms communist state in China.
1950 Stan Kenton 'Innovations' tour; Korean War begins; McCarthy hearings begin.
1951 Sid Catlett dies; Mildred Bailey dies; British troops occupy Suez Canal zone.
1952 Fletcher Henderson dies; Elizabeth II becomes Queen; Mau-Mau terrorists in Kenya.
1953 Benny Goodman forms band for abortive tour with Louis Armstrong; Everest conquered; Stalin dies; Korean War ends.
1954 Woody Herman's Third Herd tops *Metronome* poll; French defeated in Vietnam, country divided; first 4-minute mile.
1955 Charlie Parker dies; James P. Johnson dies; Warsaw and Baghdad Pacts; Eoka terrorism in Cyprus.
1956 Tommy Dorsey dies; Stan Kenton tours Britain; Ted Heath tours America; Toshiko Akiyoshi moves to US; Hungarian uprising crushed.
1957 Jimmy Dorsey dies; Count Basie tours Britain; Suez Canal reopened; Russia launches first Sputnik.
1958 US launches Explorer I; De Gaulle elected President of France.
1959 Alphonso Trent dies; Billie Holiday dies; Sidney Bechet dies; Lester Young dies; Fidel Castro becomes President of Cuba.
1960 John F. Kennedy elected president.
1961 Yuri Gagarin first man in space; Berlin Wall built.
1962 Jean Goldkette dies; Cuban missile crisis; Telstar communications satellite launched.
1963 Military coup in South Vietnam; Kennedy assassinated; first woman in space.
1964 Jack Teagerden dies; US involvement in Vietnam stepped up; Khrushchev ousted.
1965 Claude Thornhill dies; India-Pakistan war; Winston Churchill dies.
1966 Boyd Raeburn dies.
1967 Paul Whiteman dies; Henry 'Red' Allen dies; 6-Day War in Middle East.
1968 Martin Luther King assassinated; Robert F. Kennedy assassinated; Russian troops in Czechoslovakia.
1969 First man on moon; Richard M. Nixon becomes president.
1970 US invades Cambodia.
1971 Louis Armstrong dies; Ben Pollack dies; China joins UN.
1972 Jimmy Rushing dies; Britain takes over direct rule in Northern Ireland.
1973 Gene Krupa dies; Britain joins EEC; US troops withdrawn from Vietnam.
1974 Duke Ellington dies; Nixon resigns after Watergate.
1975 Akiyoshi-Tabackin record 'Kogun' album; Lee Wiley dies; Vietnam war ends.
1976 Connee Boswell dies; Mao Tse-Tung dies; Jimmy Carter elected president.
1977 Ethel Waters dies; Bing Crosby dies.
1978 Don Ellis dies; UN forces enter Lebanon.
1979 Stan Kenton dies; Israel-Egypt peace treaty; Shah of Iran ousted; Russian troops in Afghanistan.

1980 Barney Bigard dies.
1981 Toshiko Akiyoshi forms New York band.
1982 Gene Roland dies.
1983 First Duke Ellington Convention; Harry James dies.
1984 Count Basie dies; Trummy Young dies.
1985 Joe Turner dies; Dicky Wells dies; Jo Jones dies.
1986 Thad Jones dies; first Stan Kenton Convention.
1987 Benny Goodman dies; Woody Herman dies; Buddy Rich dies.
1988 Ray Bauduc dies; Al Cohn dies; Gil Evans dies; Billy Butterfield dies; Sy Oliver dies

BIBLIOGRAPHY

Baker, William J., *Jesse Owens: An American Life* (New York: The Free Press [Macmillan],1986)

Basie, Count, Jack Teagarden, Maynard Ferguson, 'Three in the Afternoon', *down beat* 4 July 1963

Bigard, Barney, *With Louis and the Duke: the Autobiography of a Jazz Clarinetist* (London: Macmillan, 1985)

Blandford, Edmund L., *Artie Shaw: a Bio-Discography* (Hastings, Sussex: Castle, 1973)

Burns, Jim, 'Benny Carter', *Jazz Monthly* November 1968

Burns, Jim, 'Stan Getz: the Early Years', *Jazz Journal* Vol. 18, No. 8, August 1965

Carr, Ian, Digby Fairweather, Brian Priestly, *Jazz: the Essential Companion* (London: Grafton, 1987)

Charters, Samuel B., and Leonard Kunstadt, *Jazz: a History of the New York Scene* (New York: Doubleday, 1962)

Chilton, John, *Who's Who of Jazz* (Philadelphia: Chilton, 1972)

Clatworthy, Paul, 'Brass Boss', *Jazz Journal International* Vol. 38, No. 1, January 1985

Clayton, Buck, *Buck Clayton's Jazz World* (London: Macmillan, 1986)

Conover, Willis, 'Don't Get Around Much Anymore', *Saturday Review* 14 March 1970

Cook, Eddie, 'Doc Cheatham: "Life Has Been Very Good to Me, I Can't Complain" ', *Jazz Journal International* Vol. 37, No. 6, June 1984

Crowther, Bruce and Mike Pinfold, 'Edges of Ellington: an Interview with David Sternberg', *Jazz Circle News* No 8, September 1978

Crowther, Bruce, 'The Bill Berry Story', *Jazz Journal International* Vol. 33, No. 2, February 1980

Crowther, Bruce, *Gene Krupa: His Life and Times* (Tunbridge Wells, Kent: Spellmount, 1987/New York: Universe, 1987)

Crowther, Bruce, *Benny Goodman* (London: Apollo, 1988)

Dahl, Linda, *Stormy Weather: the Music and Lives of a Century of Jazz Women* (London: Quartet, 1984)

Dance, Stanley, ed., *Jazz Era: the 'Forties* (London: MacGibbon & Kee, 1961)

Dance, Stanley, *The World of Duke Ellington* (London: Macmillan, 1971)

Dance, Stanley, 'J. C. Heard', *Jazz Journal International* Vol. 39, No. 11, November 1986

Driggs, Franklin S., 'The Buddy Tate Story', *Jazz Monthly* April 1959

Driggs, Franklin S., 'Don Albert', *Jazz Monthly* July 1959

Easton, Carol, *Straight Ahead: the Story of Stan Kenton* (New York: Da Capo, 1973)

Esposito, Bill, 'Eddie Miller', *Jazz Journal International* Vol. 26, No. 4, April 1973

Esposito, Bill, 'Jazz Lightning: Woody Herman's "First Herd" ', *Jazz Journal* Vol. 29, No. 1, January 1976

Feather, Leonard, 'East Meets West, or Never the Twain Shall Cease', *down beat* 3 June 1976

Feather, Leonard, *The Jazz Years: Earwitness to an Era* (London: Quartet, 1986)

Fernett, Gene, *A Thousand Golden Horns* (Midland, Michigan: Pendell, 1966)

Fox, Ted, *Showtime at the Apollo* (London: Quartet, 1985)

Gardner, Barbara J., 'Portrait of a Band: Count Basie', *down beat* 28 April 1960

Gleason, Ralph, ed., *Jam Session: an Anthology of Jazz* (London: Peter Davis/The Jazz Book Club, 1961)

Goodman, Benny, and Irving Kolodin, *The Kingdom of Swing* (New York: Frederick Ungar, 1939)

Gridley, Mark C., *Jazz Styles* (Englewood Cliffs, NJ: Prentice-Hall, 1978)

Haskins, Jim, *The Cotton Club (New York: Random House, 1977/ London: Robson, 1985)*

Hentoff, Nat, *Jazz Country* (London: Rupert Hart-Davis, 1966)

Hentoff, Nat and Albert McCarthy, *Jazz* (London: Quartet, 1977)

Hoefer, George, 'Luis Russell', *down beat* 8 November 1962

Hoefer, George, 'Fess Williams', *down beat* 3 January 1963

Hotchner, A.E., *Doris Day: Her Own Story* (London: Star, 1977)

Jackson, Arthur, *The World of Big Bands: the Sweet and Swinging Years* (Newton Abbot, Devon: David and Charles, 1977)

Jewell, Derek, *Duke Ellington* (London: Pavilion, 1986)

Jones, Max, *Talking Jazz* (London: Macmillan, 1987)

Kaminsky, Max, with V. E. Hughes, *My Life in Jazz* (New York: Harper and Row, 1963)

Kenton, Stan, 'Big Band Jazz: Look to the Colleges', *down beat*, 27 September 1967

Lambert, Constant, *Music Ho!: a Study of Music in Decline* (London: Faber & Faber, 1966)

Lee, William F., *Stan Kenton: Artistry in Rhythm* (Los Angeles: Creative Press of Los Angeles, 1980)

McCarthy, Albert, 'Life & Death of Walter Barnes', *Jazz Monthly* January 1970

McCarthy, Albert, *The Dance Band Era* (London: Spring, 1971)

McCarthy, Albert, *Big Band Jazz (London: Barrie & Jenkins, 1974)*

Malcolm X, with Alex Haley, *The Autobiography of Malcolm X* (London: Penguin, 1980)

Morgan, Alun, 'Terry Gibbs', *Jazz Monthly* July 1965

Morgan, Alun, *Count Basie* (Tunbridge Wells, Kent: Spellmount, 1984)

Morgenstern, Dan, and Ole Brask, *Jazz People* (New York: Harry N. Abrams, 1976)

O'Day, Anita, with George Eells, *High Times Hard Times* (London: Corgi, 1983)

Ostransky, Leroy, *Understanding Jazz* (Englewood Cliffs, New Jersey: Prentice-Hall, 1977)

Ostransky, Leroy, *Jazz City* (Englewood Cliffs, New Jersey: Prentice-Hall, 1978)

Page, Drew, *Drew's Blues* (Baton Rouge: Louisiana State University Press, 1980)

Palmer, Richard, 'Woody's Winners', *Jazz Journal International* Vol. 31, No. 10, October 1978

Palmer, Richard, 'NYJO', *Jazz Journal International* Vol. 38, No. 5, May 1985

Parry, Betty, 'Bobby Rosengarden: "Having a Good Time" ', *Drums Unlimited*, Vol II, No. II, 1978

Pinfold, Mike, *Louis Armstrong: His Life and Times* (Tunbridge Wells, Kent: Spellmount, 1987/New York: Universe, 1987)

Placksin, Sally, *American Women in Jazz: 1900 to the Present* (New York: Wideview, 1982)

Russell, Ross, *Jazz Style in Kansas City and the Southwest* (Los Angeles: University of California Press, 1971)

Rust, Brian, *The Dance Bands* (London: Ian Allan, 1972)

Sandford, Herb, *Tommy and Jimmy: the Dorsey Years* (New York: Da Capo, 1972)

Schiedt, Duncan, 'Speed Webb', *Jazz Monthly* November 1968

Simon, George T., *Simon Says: the Sights and Sounds of the Swing Era 1935–1955* (New York: Galahad, 1971)

Simon, George T., *The Big Bands* (New York: Collier, 1974)

Simon, George T., *Glenn Miller and His Orchestra* (London: W. H. Allen, 1974)

Southern, Eileen, *The Music of Black Americans: a History* (New York: W. W. Norton, 1971)

Stewart, Rex, *Jazz Masters of the 30s'*, (New York: Macmillan, 1972)

Tomkins, Les, 'Benny Bailey Interviewed', *Crescendo International* May 1968

Tomkins, Les, 'Don Menza Interviewed', *Crescendo International* June 1968

Tomkins, Les, 'Al Porcino Interviewed', *Crescendo International* February 1969

Tomkins, Les, 'Mel Lewis Interviewed', *Crescendo International* October 1973

Tomkins, Les, 'Buddy Childers Interviewed', *Crescendo International* February 1982

Traill, Sinclair, 'Teo Macero', *Jazz Journal* Vol. 18, No. 6, June 1965

Tynan, John, 'Vamp Till Ready: Terry Gibbs' Big Band', *down beat*, 8 November 1962

Vacher, Peter, 'Benny Waters', *Jazz Monthly* March 1969

Voce, Steve, 'The Herds on Record, Part 1', *Jazz Journal* Vol. 19, No. 3, March 1966

Voce, Steve, 'The Herds on Record, Part 2', *Jazz Journal* Vol. 19, No. 4, April 1966

Voce, Steve, 'The Herds on Record, Part 3', *Jazz Journal* Vol. 19, No. 5, May 1966

Voce, Steve, 'Phil Wilson', *Jazz Journal International* Vol. 37, No. 10, October 1984

Voce, Steve, '... Talking of Tommy', *Jazz Journal International* Vol. 38, No. 2, February 1985

Voce, Steve, *Woody Herman* (London: Apollo, 1986)

Walker, Leo, *The Big Band Almanac* (Pasadena, California: Ward Ritchie, 1978)

Waters, Ethel, with Charles Samuels, *His Eye Is On the Sparrow* (London: W. H. Allen, 1951/The Jazz Book Club, 1958)

Wells, Dicky, with Stanley Dance, *The Night People* (London: Robert Hale, 1971)

Wilmer, Valerie, 'Musicians Talking: Lawrence Brown', *Jazz Monthly* April 1965

Wilmer, Valerie, *Jazz People* (New York: Bobbs-Merrill, 1971)

Woolley, Stan, 'Latin Kenton' *Jazz Journal* Vol. 27, No. 4, April 1974

Woolley, Stan, 'Farewell Kenton: an Historical Tribute', *Jazz Journal International* Vol. 32, No. 10, October 1979

Woolley, Stan, 'Kenton in Retrospect', *Jazz Journal International* Vol. 38, No. 6, June 1985

ACKNOWLEDGEMENTS

In preparing this book we have been greatly helped by the pioneering work of certain writers who had the opportunity to interview past giants of big band music. The interviews given to these writers by musicians, together with the published reminiscences of some musicians, have provided fascinating insight into life during the earlier big band years. In some cases mention is made of these musicians and writers in the text while details of articles and books appear in the Bibliography. However, special acknowledgement must be made of the work in preserving invaluable source material carried out by Peter Clayton, Bill Coss, Stanley Dance, Leonard Feather, William Gottlieb, Max Jones, Eddie Lambert, Albert McCarthy, Rosetta Reitz, George T. Simon, Steve Voce, Valerie Wilmer and John S. Wilson whose work has appeared sometimes in book form and also in certain specialist magazines including *The Big Bands, Crescendo International, down beat, Jazz Journal International, Jazz Monthly, Melody Maker* and *Metronome*.

We have also talked with a number of musicians and big band enthusiasts during the period over which this book was researched and also in earlier years when interviews were conducted either for publication in magazine articles or for radio broadcasts, or simply for reference as general background information. Additionally, we have been greatly assisted by others who have either directed us to or loaned us valuable archive material and rare recordings.

We are extremely grateful for the courtesy and patience of all these individuals, named below or not, and we unhesitatingly acknowledge that without their contributions this book would be much less than it is: Eddie Anderson, Kenny Baker, Bill Berry, Ruby Braff, Monty Budwig, Conte Candoli, Pete Candoli, Frank Capp, Benny Carter, the late Nick Ceroli, Arnie Chadwick, Bob Charlesworth, Buddy Childers, George Chisholm, Bob Crosby, Ian Darrington, Eddie 'Lockjaw' Davis, Barrett Deems, Eileen Dunsford, Harry Edison, Teddy Edwards, Dave Frishberg, Edric Gee, Dexter Gordon, Al Gray, the late Johnny Guarnieri, Bob Haggart, Adelaide Hall, Lionel Hampton, Sir Roland Hanna, John Hughes, George Kelly, John Killoch, Irving Kluger, George Lambelle, Yank Lawson, Mike Lovell, Eddie Miller, Johnny Mince, Jack Nimitz, Johnny Pearson, Nat Pierce, Spike Robinson, Red Rodney, Lou Stein, David Sternberg, Buddy Tate, Clark Terry, Ronnie Verrall, Cyril Vicars, Eddie Vinson, Jack Walrath, Jiggs Whigham and the late Teddy Wilson.

In addition to individuals and organisations acknowledged elsewhere we wish to express our gratitude to the following:

For use of record sleeves as illustrations: Concord: Harlequin/Interstate Music; Hep; Jazztone; Rosetta Reitz; Retrieval Recordings.

For permission to reprint extracts from books:

Barney Bigard, *With Louis and the Duke: the Autobiography of a Jazz Clarinetist*, Macmillan, 1985
(c) Barney Bigard

Benny Goodman (with Irving Kolodin) *Kingdom of Swing*, Frederick Ungar, 1939
(c) Benny Goodman and Irving Kolodin, 1939

A. E. Hotchner, *Doris Day: Her Own Story*, W. H. Allen/Star, 1977
(c) Doris Day, 1975

Constant Lambert, *Music Ho! A Study of Music in Decline*, Faber & Faber, 1966, The Hogarth Press, 1985, Chatto and Windus, 1987
(c) Constant Lambert, 1934

Malcolm X (with Alex Haley), *The Autobiography of Malcolm X*, Penguin/Century Hutchinson, 1980
(c) Alex Haley and Malcolm X, 1964; (c) Alex Haley and Betty Shabazz, 1965

Anita O'Day (with George Eells) *High Times Hard Times*, Corgi/Transworld, 1983
(c) Anita O'Day and George Eells, 1981

Drew Page, *Drew' Blues: A Sideman's Life with the Big Bands*, Louisiana State University Press, 1980
(c) 1980 by Louisiana State University Press

Herb Sandford, *Tommy and Jimmy: the Dorsey Years*, Da Capo Press, 1972
(c) Arlington House, 1972

Rex Stewart, *Jazz Masters of the 30s*, Macmillan, 1972
(c) Estate of Rex W. Stewart, 1972

Steve Voce, *Woody Herman*, Apollo, 1986
(c) Steve Voce, 1986

Ethel Waters, *His Eye is on the Sparrow*, W. H. Allen, 1951

For permission to reprint extracts from magazine articles: Eddie Cook, *Jazz Journal International*, 35 Great Russell Street, London WC1B 3PP; Leonard Feather; Max Jones; Les Tompkins and Dennis H. Matthews, *Crescendo International*: Steve Voce; Stan Woolley

For additional photographs and other illustrative material: Bill Ashton, NYJO; Pete & Conte Candoli; Bill Berry; Bob Charlesworth; Eddie Cook, *Jazz Journal International*; Bob Florence; Max Jones; Pat Longo; Don Lusher; Dennis H. Matthews, *Crescendo International*, 230 Vauxhall Bridge Road, London SW1V 1AL; Dara O'Lochlainn, *Jazznews*, 28 Lansdowne Road, Dublin 4; Harry Bence; Chuck Stewart

INDEX